Don't Sweat It...

Hire It!

An A to Z Guide to Finding, Hiring & Managing Home Improvement Pros

By

Philip Schmidt

Creative Publishing international

CHANHASSEN, MINNESOTA
www.creativepub.com

**Creative Publishing
international**

Copyright © 2007
Creative Publishing international, Inc.
18705 Lake Drive East
Chanhassen, Minnesota 55317
1-800-328-3895
www.creativepub.com

Printed by R.R. Donnelley

10 9 8 7 6 5 4 3 2 1

Library of Congress Cataloging-in-Publication Data

Schmidt, Philip.
  Don't sweat it, hire it : an A to Z guide to finding, hiring &
managing home improvement pros / Philip Schmidt.
      p. cm.
  Summary: "Easy-to-understand guide to hiring professionals to
do your home repairs and improvements"--Provided by publisher.
  Includes index.
  ISBN-13: 978-1-58923-310-2 (soft cover)
  ISBN-10: 1-58923-310-7 (soft cover)
  1. Dwellings--Remodeling. 2. Contractors--Selection and
appointment.
  I. Title.

  TH4816.S276 2007
  643.7--dc22

2007007258

President/CEO: Ken Fund
VP for Sales & Marketing: Peter Ackroyd

Home Improvement Group

Publisher: Bryan Trandem
Managing Editor: Tracy Stanley
Senior Acquisition Editor: Mark Johanson
Production Editor: Jennifer Gehlhar

Creative Director: Michele Lanci-Altomare
Senior Design Manager: Brad Springer
Design Managers: Jon Simpson, Mary Rohl

Director of Photography: Tim Himsel
Lead Photographer: Steve Galvin
Shop Manager: Bryan Mclain

Production Managers: Linda Halls, Laura Hokkanen

Page Layout Artist: Kari Johnston
Author: Philip Schmidt

Contents

Introduction

BACK IN MY DAYS WORKING AS A CARPENTER, people I met socially often asked me to work on some project at their own houses. A new deck, drywall, a kitchen remodel...it didn't matter what type of job it was or whether I was qualified—they just needed help. They were desperate for it.

Now that I'm a full-time writer of home reference books, people still want to hire me to do the hands-on work for them. That's a little like asking a pharmacist to handle your surgery, but if I happened to have written about ceramic tile or whatever project they're currently struggling with, the next question is "Can I hire you?"

Don't Sweat It...Hire It! is my tenth book, and I can say unequivocally that I've never seen such universal enthusiasm for a subject. Whenever someone learns what I've been working on, I hear responses like, "I could have used that six months ago when I hired that loser to do my bathroom" or "I *need* that book. When does it come out?"

The point I'm making is that people *need* hired help almost as much as they hate the process of finding that help. How else can you explain people so desperate for a professional that they'll offer the job to a writer?

The fact is, there's no easy answer to the question of how to find a good, honest, reliable contractor. There is, however, a tried-and-true process that works regardless of the size of the job or the number of pros needed to complete it.

This book teaches you that process. It also teaches you about virtually every type of professional you're likely to hire for work on your home—from architects to window cleaners, gardeners to basement remodelers. The Ps alone include painters, plasterers, plumbers, pest control operators, and pressure washers (yes, there is such a job as professional pressure washer).

Learning about the pros themselves will help you focus on contractors who specialize in your type of project. For example, if you need an electrician for a remodel, you want someone who's good at snaking wires through walls and tying into existing systems, not someone who primarily does new commercial work. And although you're hiring out the labor, you'll be reminded time and again to do some project planning, shop around for materials, and decide what you want before starting your contractor search. This knowledge will guide you when looking for a pro and make you a shrewd negotiator when hiring one.

Surrounding this book's A to Z list of professionals are four chapters that together cover the basics of finding and interviewing contractors, making sure your job contract and other matters of fine print are in order, and preparing for and managing the crew of workers who'll be invading your home. Chapters 1 through 3 are intended for anyone hiring out any type of project or repair work. Chapter 4 offers additional help for those recklessly brave souls contemplating a major home improvement—the kind big enough to warrant using a general contractor.

So you see? There's really nothing to fear. If you follow the process and do your homework, you'll soon be the proud owner of a newly enhanced or repaired home. And you'll stop wondering how you can ask your mail carrier to build you a new garage.

—PHILIP SCHMIDT

CHAPTER ONE

Getting Started

Before we address the big question of where to look for home improvement contractors, let's preview the basics. Just as there are 10 Commandments, 10 points in a perfect score, and 10 fingers on your hands for conveniently counting off 10-item lists, there are also *10 Rules for Hiring and Working With Professionals*. In different numbers and different combinations, these rules can help you no matter where you happen to look for professional help and will apply to almost any type of project (no matter how small) and any type of contractor (no matter how pricey).

You'll also reencounter the rules in various forms throughout this book, usually when a particular item is especially important. In general, however, you should assume that all 10 rules apply. So without further ado...

10 RULES FOR HIRING & WORKING WITH PROFESSIONALS

1.   Know your project and get involved.
This is first on the list because, in many hiring situations, it helps to know exactly what you want or need before you cast about for a contractor. For example, let's say you're planning to replace your old deck. Do you want traditional redwood decking, or are you ready to try one of those low-maintenance composites everyone is talking about? For railings, you could go with steel cable, vinyl, iron, or basic wood. Making these decisions requires researching the various products available and considering your options and needs. (Here's a tip: asking contractors for recommendations isn't always a good idea, because many will simply steer you toward the products they like to use.) Once you know what you want, you've already narrowed down your contractor search to those who specialize in your chosen material (see Rule #7).

The other critical aspect of understanding your project comes later, after you've hired a pro. Before any work starts, make sure your contractor knows exactly what you expect. Check his work at the end of each day, and most importantly, make sure you're reachable at all times. See Chapter 3 for a complete discussion of how to keep the job going smoothly.

2.   Seek referrals.
A personal referral from someone you know (or an industry professional whom you trust) is the best way to learn about a contractor. And there are many other legitimate ways to learn about good local pros, as you'll see below. It's usually wise to avoid door-to-door solicitors; door-to-door marketing and aggressive mail or flyer campaigns are still favorite avenues for shysters.

3. **Ask for proof of insurance and a license (if required in your area).**

Anyone you hire for work on your property should be insured (see Chapter 2). If not, you can be held responsible for their mistakes or injuries. Don't be shy about asking for proof of insurance–it's the uninsured contractor who should be embarrassed. Contractors' licenses mean different things for different professions and in different states and municipalities (see Chapter 2). At the very least, licensure is an indication that a contractor isn't trying to avoid having his name on the books.

4. **Get three estimates.**

By conventional definition, the three-bid rule states that you should get price bids from three contractors and choose the one in the middle. However, this is too simplistic. While it's true that obtaining three bids provides you with a small sample of market pricing (and thus an "average" or, technically, a median price), the more important benefit of the three-bid rule is to get each pro's take on your project–just like talking to three surgeons before having a procedure done. Pricing is only one aspect, and it should be considered relative to the proposed services; the pro's expertise, reputation, and guarantees; and the quality of the materials used.

To get the most accurate bids, provide each contractor with as much information as possible (products you intend to use, what you expect in the finished product, a complete list of tasks you're requesting from the contractor, etc.). Make sure that all contractors receive the same information, so you'll be comparing apples to apples when evaluating the different bids. See Chapter 4 for more tips on obtaining accurate bids for a large project.

5. **Check references and past work.**

As with any successful business, good contractors have a long list of satisfied customers. These pros are proud to pass on a few names of former clients; if a contractor balks at the idea, don't use him. Here are some questions to ask your fellow consumers:

- Were you happy with the work?
- Did the contractor stay on the job until it was finished?
- Did the contractor communicate well and listen to your wishes and ideas?
- Were the contractor and his employees respectful of your property?
- Was all work completed according to the job contract or agreement?
- Were the specified materials used (were any cheap substitutes made)?
- Were there any surprise charges?
- Would you use this contractor again?

For many projects, checking references is not enough; you need to see the contractor's work firsthand. This can be tricky to set up with past clients ("When will your family be done showering for the day so I can come over to see your tile work?"), but sometimes this is the only way. A better option is to visit a home or a major remodel under construction. Also, you can ask whether the contractor has done some commercial work on publicly accessible buildings or if he has a shop where you can see a work in progress.

6. Shop for value rather than price alone.

The old adage, "You get what you pay for," applies to most contracted services, albeit in a limited way. Automatically choosing the lowest bidder to save money often isn't the best investment. But at the same time, going with the highest bidder is no guarantee you'll get the best product or service. As discussed in Rule #4, price is only one consideration in selecting a contractor. The bottom line is this: If you want quality work, you must be willing to pay the fair market price for it (see: Higher Price Consciousness, on page 14).

7. Hire a specialist.

No pro is equally good at all things within her trade. That's why it's important to look for contractors with direct professional experience with your type of project, product, or material. In other words, don't hire a faux-finisher to paint the outside of your house, and don't hire a framing carpenter to install fine cabinetry. As a general rule, limit your search to full-time professionals, and avoid hiring someone who takes on your type of project only as a side job. When you like a contractor, you're tempted to hire her for all sorts of projects around your house, rationalizing that her skills are translatable. But just because a wallpaper hanger is good at wallpaper doesn't necessarily mean she's good at wall tile or wall texturing.

8. Run a background check.

Contact the local Better Business Bureau or government regulatory agency to look for a history of consumer complaints filed against your contractor (see Checking a Contractor's Background, on page 12). While this can help protect you from repeat offenders, it doesn't necessarily give a complete picture. What's important to note is not the number of complaints but, rather, the nature of the complaints and whether they were resolved. Problems and miscommunication occur on all types of jobs, but the best contractors try their best to resolve legitimate complaints and make their customers happy.

9. Get everything in writing.

Written contracts are customary—and essential—for large projects, but they are just as important on small jobs. Always obtain a signed work order or other type of official receipt that describes the work that was done, lists the materials and equipment installed, and shows how much you paid for the entire job. All

guarantees must be documented and include contact information for the party responsible for honoring the guarantee. (Sometimes products are warranted by the contractor; other times the homeowner must contact the product's manufacturer directly.) A warranty that's not in writing is but a kiss in the wind when it comes to legal action.

10. Make payments following approved work.

Never pay in full before the job is complete. On large projects, it's customary to establish a payment schedule in which incremental payments coincide with completed stages of work. This gives you control over the payments and also motivates your contractor to complete each phase. Another important rule is to avoid substantial down payments. Pay only what is standard for the industry. For example, if two of your three contractor bids include a 5% down payment and a third bid requires 30% up front, chances are the 30% guy is a crook or that he hasn't established a good line of credit with local suppliers. And that's not your problem. Contractors who custom-fabricate goods, such as cabinetmakers, may ask for a large down payment, but that's because they're creating products to your specifications and may not be able to resell the stuff if you back out.

RESOURCES FOR FINDING CONTRACTORS

As Rule #2 states, the best way to find good contractors is through people who have used the pros for projects on their own homes. Other good word-of-mouth sources include trade professionals related to the type of contractor you seek. For example, if you know a good interior designer, she can probably refer you to good upholsterers, painters, and wallpaper hangers with whom she contracts. Best of all, people you know (friends, relatives, neighbors, and coworkers) will give you unbiased, firsthand accounts of their experiences with contractors and can show you their contractors' work. This is why many good contractors get most or all of their business through word-of-mouth referrals.

But personal referrals aren't always easy to come by, no matter how many people you ask ("Say, Bill, I noticed your front stoop is nice and level. Have you ever had it mud jacked?"). And even if a friend has used a contractor, the project in question must be similar to yours to make the referral meaningful. Just because a contractor did a great job on your friend's kitchen remodel doesn't mean he's the best choice for finishing your basement.

So, where do you look for contractors when you're starting at zero? There's always the trusty, old phone book, and the Internet is an increasingly helpful resource. Both sources will lead you not only to contractors but also to professional associations, which often provide a list of member contractors and certified practitioners in your area, as well as loads of consumer-friendly information.

The Internet & the Phone Book

The fact is, even in the age of computerized households, the phone directory is still a good place to start looking for contractors. It gives you a sense of professional markets at a glance. Large ads are especially informative because they often feature product logos, available services, trade associations, and guarantees—all points that you can research to learn more about a given industry. Better still, the phone numbers of dozens (or sometimes hundreds) of local contractors are right there. Spending an hour calling around can teach you a great deal about different contractors and companies. From there, you can turn to the Internet for more information, or head right into battle by setting up a few free consultations with contractors you liked on the phone.

It's important to note that many qualified professionals don't advertise in the phone book. But if for nothing else, it's a good place to get a feel for what's out there.

The Internet, being the vast commercial pool that it is, not surprisingly offers an abundance of home improvement products and information. Virtually every home-related website has some kind of link connecting you to local contractors and services: "Find Pre-screened Contractors!" "Free Home Improvement Quotes!" Should you trust these teasers? It's hard to say; it depends on the source and how up-front they are about their contractor selection process. You should never assume a contractor is good simply because his name is on a website. And keep in mind that the Internet today is a lot like advertising in the old days: there's little or no accountability, so why would everybody tell the truth?

A handful of websites are devoted to helping homeowners find contractors. When these sites say that their contractors are pre-screened, it usually means the contractors are licensed to work in a given area and have met minimum insurance requirements—at least at the time they were initiated to the site. If a contractor lets his insurance lapse, the website folks probably won't know about it. Of course, it would be impossible for a website to vouch for thousands of contractors. So what good are these sites? They can give you a list of contractors in your area that match the criteria you've entered to describe your project. From there, you can call the contractors and discuss your job (pretty much like the phone book process).

Some contractor-locator websites are informed by consumers who have submitted ratings of local contractors they've hired. This lets you compare many local contractors based on ratings received for things like quality of work, price, and professionalism. You also can get a profile of the contractors, including the types of services they provide or their specialties. The rating information may come from local consumers, and contractors cannot pay to be on the sites. One such website is Angie's List (www.angieslist.com), which is supported by consumer subscription fees. You can go to the site to see how it works, but you have to subscribe to access the listings of local contractors.

Above all, the Internet is great for information. Too much information, for sure, but it's always there if you need it. If you're shopping for any new product for your home–from siding to flooring to wallpaper patterns–the Internet is a good place to start. See Researching Your Project, on page 15.

Professional Associations

Virtually every industry, trade, and group of professionals of any kind has at least one association. You've probably heard of the National Association of the Remodeling Industry (NARI) and the National Kitchen and Bath Association (NKBA). But what about the PWNA? That would be the Power Washers of North America. Or the IWCA–the International Window Cleaning Association? Chimney sweeps, lawn care workers, wallpaper hangers, basement waterproofers, and septic tank cleaners–all have professional associations. The funny thing is, the smaller organizations (the ones you've never heard of) often have better websites and offer more help for consumers than many of the large trade groups.

In your search for a quality contractor and, ultimately, a successful home improvement or repair project, professional associations can assist you in two ways. First, their websites and printed literature can teach you about their given industry or trade. For example, the International Society of Arboriculture (tree care) offers loads of information on buying and maintaining trees, dealing with common tree problems, and selecting a professional tree care service. As you'll hear again and again throughout this book, having a little background information can help you enormously, both in finding and negotiating with contractors and in making sure the work is done properly.

One of the primary functions of professional associations is to train and educate their members in order to raise the standards of practice in their industry. Most do this through certification programs and continuing education. And therein lies the second benefit to the consumer: Certification or association membership (if membership requires a minimum level of experience and/or expertise) is one indication that a contractor has demonstrated a reasonable level of proficiency in her craft. Unfortunately, that's all it means. Of course, certification has little to do with how skilled or dedicated a contractor is, or how honestly she conducts business. Most associations require enrolling members to comply with a "code of ethics," but you can't expect the association to hold them to it.

The value of certification and association membership depends on the industry and the association. Decide for yourself what you think they're worth in each case. For the most part, the general information is of high quality and reflects the industry's accepted standards. Helpful association websites and related resources are indicated throughout this book.

CHECKING A CONTRACTOR'S BACKGROUND

Running a basic background check usually means looking for a history of customer complaints filed against your contractor. In most areas, you can do this by contacting the local Better Business Bureau, licensing board, or other source. Checking for a complaint history is a good rule of thumb when hiring contractors for most situations, but it should be considered with several caveats, which are discussed below. If your project is extensive, you may choose to look into a contractor's financial history as well. Keep in mind that the most important things to check for before hiring any contractor are insurance and a license (when applicable). These are covered in Chapter 2.

Checking for Customer Complaints

The easiest place to find a record of complaints on a contractor is the Better Business Bureau. The BBB is a national, non-profit organization aimed at promoting quality business commerce through reviews of businesses, consumer education, and dispute resolution. At the local level, businesses voluntarily join the BBB (and their fees help support the organization), but the Bureau does not endorse or recommend any business or individual. The BBB provides their Reliability Report on both member and non-member businesses.

Start your search by finding your local BBB chapter through the national website at www.bbb.org. At your local chapter's site, simply enter the name of the contractor or business to bring up their Reliability Report. If there is no report, it may be that the contractor's business is too new (or new to the area) or the local Bureau does not have enough information to develop a report. If a contractor has recently moved to your area, you may be able to check his history through the national BBB website. You also can run a general search for local BBB-member contractors by selecting the appropriate service category.

Another place to check for customer complaints is your state's licensing board. Many boards or agencies offer consumer complaint services in addition to reporting the status of a contractor's license. You also may learn whether the board has taken any disciplinary action against a contractor. Keep in mind that these reports are available only on licensed or registered professionals. Each state or local government has its own terms and titles for licensing departments; if you're having trouble locating the appropriate source, try searching with terms like labor, licensing, regulatory, consumer affairs, and professional or occupational regulation.

Finally, some Chambers of Commerce offer information on local businesses. It might be worth a quick scan of your local chapter's website to see what consumer help is available. However, the role of the Chamber of Commerce is to promote business activity in a given area and is less involved with consumer issues than the Better Business Bureau.

Now, about those caveats....When looking at a consumer complaint record, take into account the volume of the contractor's work. With a large business, five or six complaints may represent only a tiny fraction of their total number of customers for the given time period. Also consider the nature of the complaints. The BBB and other services typically offer a limited description of each type of complaint for this reason. A high number of complaints in the same category indicates a pattern of problems in that area of the contractor's business. Finally, check whether the complaints were resolved. Reputable contractors make an effort to rectify problems, sometimes even when the customer is truly at fault. A contractor who ignores complaints is one you should avoid.

It's important to note that a clean or nearly clean complaint record doesn't mean a contractor is perfect. Most consumers don't report problems they've had with contractors, or they report them to the wrong sources. That's why talking to previous customers provides a more meaningful evaluation of a contractor's professionalism than a complaint record.

Does This Contractor Pay His Bills?

If you feel compelled to look into a contractor's financial history, you can start at the places where he does business. Find out where he buys bulk materials, and check with those suppliers. Many building and installation contractors have lines of credit with one or more supply houses. Another option is to pull a credit report on the contractor or business. This can be done through a number of sources, including bankers and websites such as www.ussearch.com. Of course, you'll have to pay for the report, starting at about $70 a pop.

If all of this sleuthing feels a bit sneaky to you (although it's perfectly legal), you might simply ask a contractor for a financial statement. Larger companies may be required by law to create annual reports, so they won't take your request personally.

"KNOW YOUR PROJECT AND GET INVOLVED"

HIGHER PRICE CONSCIOUSNESS

When it comes to hiring professional services, many people are funny about the money. They think nothing of paying a premium for everyday items like coffee and cable TV, but when it comes to a contractor's hourly rate, they insist on finding the lowest bidder.

This is simply bad economics. Here's why: Hiring a pro for most services involves a one-time cost, not a fixed cost (like that monthly cable bill), yet the return on the investment is long-term. Spending a little more for quality work means you'll enjoy better results over a long period.

On the other hand, hiring an unqualified or uninsured contractor could cost you more in the long run—on several levels. There's the intangible cost of having to live with ugly results, for one. And work that's faulty may have to be redone, at added expense, of course.

This is not to suggest that you unthinkingly choose the highest bidder, either. Indeed, a pro's pricing should be competitive. Unless you're dealing in a highly skilled or obscure trade, such as fine art restoration, there's usually no reason a pro should charge considerably more than his competitors with similar qualifications.

It comes down to this: When a contractor is good, he knows it and usually charges accordingly. Sometimes prices are high because the contractor works for a big company that must cover a lot of overhead. It's up to you to figure out whether you're paying for above-average skill or hefty operating expenses.

Ideally, you'll find a dedicated, experienced professional who keeps her overhead down, does a great job, and charges fairly. These are the gems who get the most word-of-mouth promotion and are worth the investment.

RESEARCHING YOUR PROJECT

Most major household projects require some initial research—or you can call it shopping, if you'd like. As Rule #1 makes clear, knowing your project often is the first step to finding the right contractor. Whether you're looking for products, technical information, or design ideas, the Internet can be a candy store of knowledge (but beware: like candy, too much Internet can make you feel a little queasy).

Here are some good sources for online browsing and research:

- Major manufacturers of products and materials for around the home spend a lot of money creating a flashy online presence, which makes for fun window shopping. Most won't give prices on their sites but can direct you to local dealers who sell their products.
- Home improvement magazines, construction magazines, and home-related TV shows usually have a companion website offering a range of homeowner information. Better sites give you access to in-depth articles and reviews of the latest products and professional services.
- Professional associations, discussed previously, often have consumer-oriented web pages with links to additional resources.
- Design and decorating ideas can literally come from anywhere (such is the nature of creative inspiration). Good places to look are the websites of home and design magazines. Most publishers' sites feature an article archive with limited offerings for free reading and a complete list of articles that have appeared in past issues, for purchase.
- Government sources, including city, state, and federal offices, have a surprising amount of helpful online information (time to reap the rewards of your tax dollars). Federal sources include the U.S. Environmental Protection Agency at www.epa.gov (for anything remotely health-related) and the U.S. Department of Energy at www.eere.energy.gov (for energy-efficiency information on windows, appliances, etc.).
- Consumer Reports, the popular non-profit product-testing group, has an extensive website at www.consumerreports.com. You must become a subscriber to access most of their information, but when it comes to comparing products based on price and detailed performance data, they can't be beat. Their site also features articles with background information and buying tips on specific product categories.

After a few hours of Internet surfing, when your head is reeling from all the pop-up ads and bad grammar, you'll probably decide it's time to see the real thing. Local showrooms and materials suppliers are the places to go to view products and building materials, compare prices, and possibly pick up some names of local contractors to check out. In turn, contractors know the good places to shop around town and can steer you toward the better retailers and suppliers.

CHAPTER TWO

Protecting Yourself

The modern retail business world is full of safeguards for protecting the consumer. If you buy something at a store and it turns out to be faulty, you can march right back with your sales receipt and promptly get a refund. You can even get your money back if you decide you bought the wrong color, or the wrong size, or simply change your mind and decide you don't need an item. As nice as they are, these implicit guarantees have made us complacent when it comes to protecting ourselves. That's why so many homeowners run into trouble when hiring contracted labor.

Doing your own hiring comes with the responsibility of making sure you're protected. What protections are available vary by state (and sometimes by city or county), as do the requirements for establishing those protections. You must never assume the government or legal system will help you simply because you've been wronged by a contractor's illegal or unethical behavior. The following are the main points of protection for typical home improvement projects. If you do your homework and follow the recommendations of local experts and officials, you'll be in good shape. You should even be able to change a color without too much hassle...but it had better be in your contract.

PROFESSIONAL LICENSES

Many states and municipalities require contractors to carry a license (or be officially registered). Not all contractors, just some. And while certain contractors must be licensed in some areas, they could be completely unregulated in others. Not surprisingly, standards of licensure from one region to the next are anything but standard. Sound confusing? It is. Fortunately, you don't have to make sense of it. All you have to do is find out if your contractor—whether a plumber, carpenter, animal control operator, or anything else—is required to have a license to work in your area. If so, don't hire a contractor who isn't licensed.

Here's why:

- If the law says a contractor must be licensed, you probably won't get into trouble for using an unlicensed professional, but you may find that City Hall is unable (or at least unmotivated) to help you resolve a problem with the contractor.
- Many states and licensing boards use licensing as a regulatory tool and keep records of complaints or disciplinary actions made against contractors. Authorities often use the threat of fines or license suspension to get licensed contractors to cooperate.
- Unlicensed pros may bypass requirements such as insurance coverage, work experience, and competency testing. This may not be a big concern when hiring a painter or window washer, but it's of critical importance when it comes to highly technical pros like electricians or architects. (Note: Licensure in many trades and in many jurisdictions indicates little or nothing about a pro's competency or expertise.)

- An unlicensed contractor may be hiding something. Granted, there's no direct correlation between failure to get a license and intent to defraud, but if you were a crook, would you register your business with the local government?
- Some states have a general "recovery" fund that licensees must contribute to. Money in the fund is available to consumers who get ripped off by contractors. If your contractor isn't licensed, you can't get a refund.

It's important to verify a contractor's license. Printing a business card with a fake or invalid license number is as easy as stretching the truth on a resume. Most state licensing agencies offer free licensing verification. All you need is the contractor's name, and you can confirm whether a license is valid and pick up any other information the agency provides. Some agencies and boards maintain detailed profiles of licensees, including insurance information, reports of contract disputes, and records of disciplinary actions filed within the past several years. To learn about licensing requirements and verification in your immediate area, contact your city's office or building department.

WHY ALL CONTRACTORS MUST BE INSURED

For better or worse, insurance is the way of the world. Handshakes and promises are nice, but those agreements quickly dissolve in the face of difficult financial issues. And it usually doesn't matter whose fault it is.

So while we're on the serious subject of liability, here's an example of why your contractor should be covered: Let's say you hire a tree service to prune your trees. You don't check for insurance, and one of the workers gets hurt on the job. Turns out the company has no insurance, and not much money either, judging by the 20-year-old truck they drive. You, however, appear to have plenty of money, judging by your 20-acre lot full of old trees. Such is the perception of a certain type of lawyer. And which one do you think the lawyer is going after—the acreage or the old truck?

In many cases, homeowners' insurance doesn't cover accidents that occur on your property. Therefore, protecting yourself means you have only one option: asking contractors about their insurance coverage and verifying that their policies are adequate and active. It's a perfectly legitimate request—simply ask the contractor for a copy of her insurance certificate. All she has to do is call her insurer, and they will mail a certificate to you. Or you can get the insurer's information and call them to verify the contractor's policies and status. Always check for the type of insurance, the amounts, and the effective dates of coverage.

The two most critical types of insurance you're looking for are liability and workers' compensation. Most contractors carry general liability insurance. This covers them and their customers for property damage and bodily injury resulting from the contractor's work. Liability insurance won't compensate you for faulty or incomplete work done by the contractor—bonds do, but compensation is usually quite limited (see What About Bonding?, below). Typical liability policy amounts range from $100,000 to $500,000.

Workers' compensation insurance is necessary when contractors will have employees working on your project. Workers' comp covers medical expenses, death benefits, and lost wages for work-related injuries. In our example of the tree-care worker, it's the company's failure to carry workers' comp that can get you into trouble. Regulation of, and requirements for, workers' comp for employers is generally handled at the state level of government. For more information specific to your area, contact your state's division of workers' compensation or the U.S. Department of Labor at www.dol.gov.

Other types of insurance contractors may carry include:

- Professional liability (for damages resulting from misrepresentation)
- Product liability (for damages resulting from materials or equipment supplied by the contractor)
- "Tail" liability (for damages occurring after a project is completed but resulting from the project work).

Keep in mind that insurance coverage varies among contractors, policies, and insurers. You'll have to decide for yourself whether a contractor's coverage seems adequate for your project. In any case, it's a good idea to consult with your own insurance provider to get his recommendations and to learn about what additional coverage you may have through your homeowners' insurance.

What About Bonding?

While bonds are often mentioned along with insurance (Licensed & Bonded, say the ads), bonding is not a form of insurance. Rather, it's a guarantee for a fixed amount of money payable to property owners, suppliers, and subcontractors who have been ripped off by a contractor. A basic *performance bond*, or *surety bond*, is payable if the contractor fails to fulfill the requirements of a contract, with limitations and stipulations, of course.

Many states require licensed contractors to purchase a surety bond, while some contractors and companies do so voluntarily. The face values of bonds are typically in the neighborhood of $5,000 to $15,000. Now, if you're putting on an addition to the tune of $150,000, a bond may cover only 10% of your investment (and probably not even that much, because suppliers and subs may make claims on the same bond). But some money is better than none.

If your contractor claims to be bonded, or if it's mandated by law, be sure to obtain a bond certificate clearly showing the bond number before signing your job contract.

PERMITS & PERMISSIONS

Building codes and the permit process may seem like just another way for the government to check up on you, and in some ways they are, but they do serve an important purpose: They protect homeowners by ensuring that contractors' work meets minimum safety and health standards. All codes are established and enforced at the local level and are designed around the local climate. This ensures that structures are built to withstand the prevailing weather conditions.

Without local codes, builders and contractors would be held only to regional or national standards, but methods that work in Arizona may be completely inappropriate for North Dakota. Because codes make accommodations for the climate and other conditions specific to your area, you don't have to worry about it. What you do have to do is apply for all required permits for your project. Or better yet, have your contractor do this for you.

Permits are obtained by filling out a form and paying a fee at the city's building department. Fees vary by township and project. Having your permit on the books means the city is aware of your project plans and will send out an inspector at specified intervals to check your contractor's work. Typically, your contractor (or you) calls to set up each inspection. Unless you're acting as general contractor on a large project, it's usually best to have your contractor obtain the permits in his own name. That way, he's technically responsible for passing all inspections. One of the main reasons for hiring a local contractor as opposed to one from another area is that pros who do a lot of work in your town will know the local codes best and will be familiar with the permit and inspection process.

As you'll be reminded throughout this book, it's a good idea for you to contact the local building department early in your planning process, regardless of the size of your project. Building officials can tell you whether you'll need a permit and inform you of any restrictions that may apply. If your plans run afoul of codes or ordinances, you may be able to apply for a variance. Usually, it's easier to apply for a variance in your own name instead of your contractor's.

Other laws that may have an impact on your plans are zoning restrictions, which control things like the size and height of structures, setbacks from property lines, and no-build zones such as easements. Zoning laws typically apply only when you're putting on an addition or otherwise expanding the existing height or footprint of your home, or when you're changing the use of the property—such as converting your basement into an artisan cheese factory.

HOA or DOA

Homeowners' associations have been known to wield more power than the British navy, so you'd be well advised to consult your association board before making any serious plans for a home improvement. Paint color, windows, doors, roofing, siding, landscaping, fences … all must conform to the board's covenants. And don't even think about putting up those house numbers written in fancy longhand. Better to get approval first.

If your project will need permission from an architectural review board, save yourself the headaches and find out what the board's parameters are first. Don't start by joining forces with an architect in the hopes of dazzling the review committee with a nice but rule-breaking design. It's a common and understandable mistake. Asking an architect to design a project according to a committee's specifications can be a little like asking an artist to paint a picture that matches your upholstery. But don't be discouraged—creating within limits is what architecture is all about. A good architect will be happy to work with the board's rules, although you may have to be insistent. If their ego gets in the way and they refuse to comply, it will only end up costing you more money as you pay to have the plans re-drawn time and again.

CONTRACTS & JOB SPECIFICATIONS

There is a clear consensus among consumer affairs departments that homeowners having work done tend to run into the most trouble in the area of contracts. More specifically, consumers fail to use contracts, or they rely on inadequate contracts that leave too many decisions up to their contractor. The result is often an ugly dispute which must be settled in arbitration (or court), all because no one had the foresight or assertiveness to demand a written agreement. There's a Latin phrase that describes this situation—*caveat emptor*, which means, roughly: If you buy something without a guarantee, you'd better pray there aren't any problems.

Contracts for Everyday Jobs

Contracts aren't reserved for large projects, nor are they always complex documents written in legalese (in fact, even full-scale construction contracts are generally readable and light on confusing jargon). For ordinary jobs, such as a service call on your garage door, a contract will most likely be a work order written on the company's or contractor's standard form. It should include:

- The company's or contractor's name, address, and phone number.
- A work order number.
- The date of service.
- Your name and address.
- A description of the problem or work requested by you.
- All services performed.
- The technician's name (if different than that on the letterhead).
- All charges—itemized—and total payment received by the contractor.
- Any additional notes about the job.

The work order may also include a list of general conditions and any warranty or guarantee information, usually printed on the back of the form. By signing the form, as is typically required, you're agreeing to all conditions therein (even though you probably didn't read the fine print) and accepting the work as complete and satisfactory.

In essence, a work order is a brief contract that serves as an official record of what transpired on the service call. It protects both you and the contractor in the event of a problem related to the work performed, parts installed, etc. It can also be a handy reference for you the next time your garage door is on the fritz—you can pull out the work order and see exactly what was done the last time.

Contracts for Big Projects

As you move up the scale in project size and expense, contracts change accordingly. For a large kitchen remodel or home addition, a contract may be a dozen or more pages long and include statements for every aspect of the work and clauses for all probable and improbable complications. Medium-size projects, such as for window or siding replacement, may have somewhat simpler contracts but still should include many of the clauses and conditions of a large-scale document and must have detailed warranty information for all new products and materials. Contracts of almost every size also should include a set of job specifications, or design specifications, detailing precisely what products and materials are to be used and exactly how they will be installed and by whom (see Job Specifications, on page 24).

Whatever type of contract you use, there are two important things to remember:

1. All contracts and contract contents are negotiable. With the exception of clauses and wording that are required by law, you can challenge any statement in a contract. Your contractor might not go for it without a fight or compromise, but it's your right to request changes.

2. A contract can never be too detailed. Scant or vague information in contracts is one of the leading sources of contractor-client disputes. Think of it this way: If any item presents the possibility of more than one interpretation, there's not enough detail.

Should you hire a lawyer to write or review your contract? It depends on the size of the project and your confidence in any existing written agreement. The larger the project, the more valuable a lawyer's input may prove to be. New homes, additions, and even extensive remodels often involve enough money to warrant hiring a lawyer. If you know a good lawyer, get her opinion on the matter. She may refer you to a colleague who specializes in remodeling or construction contracts (including real estate attorneys and others who work with construction law). Using a specialist is particularly important if you're having the lawyer draft the contract.

Discuss contracts with prospective contractors during the interview process—before you hire anyone. Find out about their standard procedure and whether they'll work under an owner-supplied document, if that's your desire. Not all pros accept owner's contracts. Unless you have a strong reason for supplying your own contract, it usually makes sense to let the contractor prepare the paperwork. Of course, anything he provides has to meet your (and perhaps your attorney's) approval before you sign it.

FYI

In most cases, the contractor supplies the contract. You may have the option of providing your own written contract (typically drafted by an attorney), or you may ask that the contractor use one of the standard contracts of the American Institute of Architects or other source. AIA contracts are highly detailed documents that are commonly used in agreements between homeowners and contractors, as well as between architects and clients. Many contractors use one or more of the AIA A Series forms and make changes to suit their business and customers as needed. For more information about AIA contracts or to order copies, visit the AIA website at www.aia.org.

Contract Items to Consider

Following are some of the major elements you might want to include in your contract. This is by no means a complete list of necessary items for all types of jobs. For professional contract assistance, consult an attorney who specializes in construction law. Your state's Attorney General's office may provide additional information regarding construction documents. Depending on the contract you use, some terms and conditions may appear in the job specifications, which should be part of the contract document.

Owner's and contractor's information.

All contracts must have the name, address, and phone numbers of the owner (you), the contractor (and contractor's company), and the job (if the address is different than your primary residence).

Contractor's license and insurance information.

Contracts should include documents verifying all applicable licenses held by the contractor, insurance coverage, and bond information, plus a copy of the contractor's driver's license. The contract should also stipulate that all subcontractors will carry (and verify) adequate insurance coverage and required professional licenses.

Project specifications.

Perhaps more than anything else, a contract is a communication tool. Clear and accurate description of all project materials and installation methods is the best way to protect yourself and prevent misunderstandings. See Job Specifications, on page 24.

Start and completion dates.

These may be approximate or set in stone, depending on your needs, the contractor's policy, and the project in question. Some contracts set a completion deadline and assess a fine for the contractor for each day beyond the target date. If a deadline is important to you, you might also consider offering the contractor a bonus for finishing early. Hard deadlines must be accompanied by a clause for exceptions, such as weather-related setbacks.

Payment terms and schedule.

Payment amounts and terms must appear in any contract. For most large jobs, payments occur at several specified intervals, starting with a down payment of perhaps 5% to 10% of the total job cost (Note: Some states restrict down payment amounts by law). As an example, a full-scale kitchen remodel may include payments at the following stages:

- Signing of contract (down payment)
- Day the job starts
- Completion of rough-ins and drywall
- Installation of cabinets and countertops
- Job completion
- Final payment

The final payment should be a minimum of 10% to 20% of the total job cost, thereby serving as a retainer to protect you against problems with equipment or incomplete work. See Chapter 4 (page 188) for more tips on making final payments on large projects.

Avoid making payments in cash or in checks made out to "Cash," as these payments are not traceable. Contractors who request cash are either evading taxes or have something to hide. Always make payments to the owner of the business rather than any contractor personally (unless the contractor is the owner).

Change orders.

Even the best laid plans require modification sometimes. Your contract should outline the procedure for making changes to the original job specifications once the job is underway. The standard method is to have the contractor write up a *change order*, a written description of the proposed changes and their cost. Change orders should be signed be all parties and serve as official addenda to the job contract. Failure to document change requests is a major source of customer–and contractor–complaints.

Arbitration.

Contracts involving sizeable sums should include a statement describing how disputes will be resolved. In most cases, arbitration is preferable to going to court. You and your contractor will have to choose an arbitration service and agree to make the arbiter's word final. The Better Business Bureau, the American Arbitration Association, and some county bar associations offer arbitration services (some of which are free). It's a good idea to get a lawyer's opinion before selecting a service.

Protection against liens.

Jobs involving a general contractor or third party should include lien protection in the contract. See Mechanics' Liens: Avoiding a Nasty Surprise, on page 26.

Permits and code compliance.

The contract should state that the contractor is responsible for obtaining all building permits required by the local building department. As for permit fees, it's usually easiest to include them in the total contract price. The contractor is also responsible for arranging and passing all required inspections. Some contracts include a clause, or performance statement, specifying that all work and supplies meet local code requirements.

Verbal agreements.

Any promises or offers you or your contractor have made verbally must be put in writing. If it's not in writing, there's no guarantee. Also, if you're planning to do some work, such as cleanup, demolition, painting, etc., it must be described in detail in the contract. Miscommunication over who's doing what is a common pitfall in home projects.

Warranties and guarantees.

The contractor's guarantees for labor, workmanship, materials, and other elements must be in writing. All guarantees should include a description of what's covered and for how long. You should obtain a copy of all manufacturer's warranties for new materials and equipment installed.

Various clauses.

Substitutions

stipulating that the contractor must have the owner's written approval for all materials substitutions to the original job specifications.

Cleanup

who is responsible for job site cleanup and how often (daily, weekly, upon job completion, etc.)? Also, who is responsible for refuse collection and disposal, including related fees?

Liability

stating that the contractor is responsible for all damages, injuries, and related costs associated with the project. Liability clauses must be worded carefully and usually warrant the help of an attorney.

Unforeseeable extras

a contingency plan for ugly surprises. For example, if your contractor opens up a wall and finds major termite damage, how should you proceed?

Services and amenities

toilets, drinking water, telephone, etc.–if the contractor is supplying these services for his crew, it should be in the contract.

Right to cancel.

Some states mandate a period (such as three days) in which homeowners can rescind their contract agreement after signing. Other states allow no such grace period. Learn about the local laws through your state's Attorney General's office. Acknowledgement of your right to cancel may need to be in the contract. Also be aware that many right to cancel laws are effective only when contracts are signed outside of the contractor's place of business (in other words, sign the contract at your home or you'll lose the right to cancel).

Signatures and general notes.

All contracts must be signed and dated by both the owners and the contractor. Job specifications and any addenda should also be signed and attached to the contract document. Contract pages should be numbered (as in "1 of 4," "2 of 4," etc.). Blank areas and wording that does not apply to your project should be crossed out. Be sure to obtain an original version of the contract for your records.

Job Specifications

Job specifications serve as the shopping list and installation instructions for your entire project. By describing each item in detail, your specifications leave nothing open to interpretation. All contracts must include specifications; without them, there's no written record of what the project entails.

Note how the revised example on page 25 covers not only the surface finish (tile) but the grout, the underlayment, and transition materials. The same thoroughness should be applied to all elements of a project. For example, a specification for painted walls should include the brand, color, and type of paint and primer, and the number of coats desired. Specs for carpeting must include all of the manufacturer's information for the carpet and also the type and thickness of carpet pad. Descriptions of appliances and fixtures must include *all* options and features that you want. Think of it this way: Your specs should be detailed enough so that a salesperson or store clerk could pull everything without having to ask questions.

In the first example below, the person responsible for installing the tile (the contractor) is implied. This is acceptable only if the specifications include a statement such as "Contractor is responsible for labor and materials described in all specifications, except where noted otherwise." Another option is to state who is responsible for the work and materials in each item description. Always make sure there is no ambiguity regarding who is doing what.

Given the level of detail required for drafting a good set of job specs, most homeowners get professional help for large or complex projects. Architects and interior designers often create job specifications as part of their design packages. You might also get help and advice from an experienced remodeling contractor, who can offer an additional level of practical knowledge.

Job specs are an integral part of any contract, but they also make it easy to obtain accurate bids from prospective contractors. With each contractor bidding on the same thing, you can readily compare the different estimates. Specifications for remodels, additions, and new construction should include a set of drawings for the project. Drawings ensure that everyone is working from the same blueprint, as it were, and they help enormously to clarify details.

Finally, job specifications may direct the order of things. For example, if you want to have your wood floor refinished before the walls are painted, you can make note of that in the specifications.

EXAMPLE

Here's an example of a basic specification item as seen in many (poorly executed) contracts:

"Install white tile in hallway."

With this limited description, the contractor is free to purchase any brand, color, type, and style of tile he sees fit, and he can install it any way he likes. Even if he tries his best to please the customer, there's a good chance something will be misinterpreted.

Here's a better way to write the same specification:

"Install 12 × 12" white ceramic floor tile (brand: FloorEssence; item #12ES01) with sanded floor grout (brand: TEC; color: Silverado) in hallway per plan drawings, using manufacturer's recommended thinset adhesive; underlayment shall be ½"-thick Flatrock cementboard secured to existing subfloor with adhesive and corrosion-resistant screws. All threshold material at flooring transitions shall be approved by owner prior to installation."

Protecting Yourself Checklist

✔ Know that protecting yourself when working with contractors often is your responsibility.

✔ Check a contractor's license (if required in your area) and confirm insurance coverage. These are the first steps to protecting yourself.

✔ Discuss your project with the local building department. Even if you don't need a permit, you may pick up some valuable tips for getting the job done.

✔ Have your contractor obtain all required permits.

✔ Gain approval from your homeowners' association and other governing bodies before investing in a project.

MECHANICS' LIENS: AVOIDING A NASTY SURPRISE

The mechanics' lien law allows a contractor to place a legal hold on your home if you fail to pay him. Fair enough, right? But get this: Even if you pay the contractor the agreed amount, and instead of paying his subcontractors or materials suppliers he takes the money to the horse track, any of those subs or suppliers can slap a lien on you. Unfair? Yes, but true (feel free to write your congressperson at any time).

A lien is almost like having a second—but evil—mortgage placed on your home. If you fail to pay a lien claimant, or if you can't afford to do so, it's possible that your home can be sold in foreclosure to pay off the lien. In many cases, homeowners end up biting the bullet and paying off claimants, which means they pay twice for the same work or products. Once a lien is filed against your property it stays on your record with the county; even if the lien turns out to be invalid (each state has its own requirements and time limits for filing liens), its presence can make it difficult to qualify for loans or sell your property.

You may have to hire a lawyer to help you get the lien removed from your record.

So, how do protect yourself from this hideously misguided law? Start by hiring a contractor with a proven track record and no history of litigation. Ask your contractor for a complete list of all subcontractors who will work on your job (including confirmation of their licenses, as required) and all suppliers he will use. This allows you to identify all potential lien claimants, which will help you keep track of who has been paid at each stage of the project. Before work gets underway, file a Notice of Commencement with your county court or county recorder's office. This gets your project on the books and may be a legal requirement for processing any lien litigation.

In many states, subcontractors and materials suppliers are required to send you a Notice to Owner, which essentially states that they will be supplying labor or materials for your project and that they are potential lien claimants. If your state

- ✔ Don't allow any work to begin without a written and signed contract.
- ✔ Make sure the level of detail in your contract is commensurate with the complexity of the project. For large jobs, explicit design specifications are the best way to avoid problems.
- ✔ Establish a payment schedule that reflects the work progress. Never make a final payment until the work is 100% complete.
- ✔ Protect yourself against mechanics' liens by requiring lien release forms or other methods appropriate for your area.

does not require a Notice to Owner, it's up to you to keep track of all potential claimants.

Depending on your state's laws, you may be able to use one of the following means to protect your property against liens:

1. Joint checks. You can include the names of both your contractor and the appropriate sub or supplier on payment checks. Both parties have to endorse the check to get the dough, so your contractor can't just take the money and run.

2. Lien release clause. You can stipulate in your job contract that each sub and supplier must sign a lien release with each payment. In the typical process, the lien claimant first signs a conditional (or partial) release form before he is paid. After he is paid, the claimant signs an unconditional (or final) release of lien. You can withhold any subsequent payments until you receive the unconditional release. Before making the final job payment to your contractor, be sure you have an unconditional release form from each lien claimant. You also can state in your contract that the contractor is responsible for obtaining—and delivering to you— all release forms.

When the work on your home has concluded, file a Notice of Completion with the county court or recorder. This starts the clock ticking on the time limit in which lien claimants can file a lien. It also may reduce the time allowed for filing.

For detailed information about mechanics' liens in your area, check with your state's licensing agency or consumer affairs department. Better yet, consult a lawyer who specializes in construction contracts. If you are financing your project through a lender, the lender will likely have their own rules and safeguards for preventing liens and can advise you accordingly.

CHAPTER THREE

Ensuring a Smooth Job

After you've hired a contractor and sorted out the finer details, it's time to prepare for the actual work. This may be as simple as moving boxes out of the way so the plumber can access your water heater or as involved as setting up a temporary kitchen in your family room (see Take-out Trauma, on page 123). While paving the way for workers is a necessary step, what's more important to the success of the overall project is your ongoing involvement.

Your input and regular communication are the keys to preventing costly misunderstandings, helping to keep the work moving efficiently, and making sure you get the most for your money. Of course, sometimes, despite your best efforts, a disagreement leads to deadlock. How you respond to a problem can significantly affect its outcome.

THE PROBLEM WITH CONTRACTORS (& THEIR CLIENTS)

By definition, trade professionals are skilled craftspeople, not (necessarily) good businesspeople. They're better at laying brick or setting tile than they are at managing money, balancing multiple jobs, and returning phone calls. The upshot is that you shouldn't necessarily view irregularities in scheduling and paperwork as a sign a contractor is inferior. Many contractors who do excellent work can be maddeningly irregular in staying on schedule. Is this your problem? It shouldn't be, but in most cases it is.

First of all, it's no secret that contractors juggle jobs. Whether they plan to or not, they often end up working on multiple projects simultaneously, which means your house may be put off in favor of someone else's. Part of the problem lies in the nature of construction work, where unpredictable delays are common and often unavoidable. Supplies arrive late, changes are made, inspections get derailed, or other contractors on the same job fail to finish on time, holding up everyone down the line. Having multiple jobs going is one way to minimize downtime for contractors.

When juggling jobs, most pros operate on the "squeaky wheel" principle— that is, the customer who squeaks the most gets the oil that day or soon thereafter. If your contractor doesn't show up one day or is likely to miss a deadline, call her. Don't wait for her to get in touch with you, because chances are she's on another job and could just as easily be on yours. Blowing off the clients who are more patient and understanding (or at least quiet about their frustration) is the essence of job juggling. This is not to say you should call your contractor at 3:00 a.m. or scream epithets on her voice mail. Be reasonable but persistent, and you'll get results.

As a side note, there are times when you should show zero tolerance: If you've arranged an appointment to meet with a prospective contractor and he is very late or doesn't show up at all, scratch his name off your list. This is a clear indication that he doesn't really want your business or he is too disorganized to complete a job effectively.

Contractors of all kinds are notorious for making lame excuses for not being on the job or for having trouble finishing a project. Good contractors may even be more susceptible to this, since they are in such high demand that standing customers up once in a while is almost inevitable. How much bull you're willing to accept is up to you.

After all, you hired the contractor, and that makes you the boss. But many people are uncomfortable in this role, especially when they don't know much about construction. The best solution is to let the original plans or design specifications do the talking. For example, if you come home to find a new window installed 3" to the left of where it was supposed to go, and the contractor didn't mention any problem before the window was put in, there's a 99% chance that the offset was due to the contractor's error. After the fact, he might claim there was a pipe or wiring interfering with the original placement. This is almost certainly a feeble fib to save his rear end, because he surely would have discussed this with you when the problem became evident. At this point you can simply assert that you want the job done according to the plans, period. No arguments. If that's what's in the contract, that's what he has to do.

Now, when it comes to customers, they aren't always perfect either. Many are indecisive, or they get in the workers' way or aren't available when a question arises. A homeowner dragging his feet when choosing materials or appliances can hold up a job as surely as a subcontractor who doesn't show. As the customer, it's important to know your role in the project as well as you know the contractor's. After all, it's your house, and you'll have plenty to say about how things are done and when. And as you'll see below, being a good customer means more than writing the checks on time.

BE A GOOD CUSTOMER & OTHER TIPS FOR A SUCCESSFUL PROJECT

While your mother would automatically expect you to be polite to any hired helper, this kind of good behavior is also in your best interest to help the job run smoothly: The more you can do to facilitate the work and keep your contractor informed, the better your chances for quality, accurate, and timely results. Of course, politeness never hurts (as Mom might say, "You catch more bees with honey than vinegar").

Own your project.

If this tip starts to sound familiar, it's because it's basically the same idea as Rule #1 on page 6. And that is, don't take a completely passive role in the process. Decide what you want and convey that to your contractor. Don't just point toward the backyard and say you want some bushes out there as you're heading out the door to the office. Develop a plan and define your goals before the professionals show up. They can offer suggestions and advice, but they're not there to make decisions for you.

Prepare the work site.

Designate an entry for all workers to use, and lay down tarps or plastic as needed (painters have their own tarps, but most other tradespeople don't). Clear the way for the work—your plumber should not have to spend time carefully removing your candle collection from the top of the toilet tank. Also, be realistic about the mess: work is messy, workers are messy. They're not going to walk around with a wet paper towel and clean up every spill. If you don't want drywall mud on your Tiffany lamp, remove it from the work area.

Put away valuables and breakables.

You're not accusing anyone by doing so; you're just eliminating the potential for problems. And your contractors will appreciate not having to work around your crystal centerpiece.

Keep pets, children, and yourself out of the way.

Asking workers not to "let the dog out of the house" is a bad idea and an inappropriate request. Keep pets sequestered during the work or board them if necessary. Kids (and spacey adults) should also stay well clear of the job site, for safety reasons. Construction workers as a group aren't exactly cautious people. They often assume personal risk in order to work more efficiently, but they aren't thinking about children being nearby.

As for yourself, don't hover over the pros while they work. This drives most people crazy and may have them wishing a stray nail would ricochet in your direction, just to send you the message.

Set boundaries, as needed.

For example, if you don't want the painters cleaning their tools in your kitchen sink, direct them to the mop sink in the basement. In general, be aware that not everyone has the same rules as you do. Some people think it's okay to jam the toe of a shoe under a door to prop it open (no matter that it's one of your handmade Italian loafers) simply because that's what they would do in their own houses. It's best to just keep an eye out and speak up before something gets damaged.

Establish a dust plan.

Good remodelers and some other pros are keenly aware of dust in the home; most others are not. If you don't have plans for dust containment written into your job contract, discuss the issue with your contractor before work begins. A dust plan may include covering floors with plastic (and possibly a protective layer of hardboard or plywood), sealing doorways and other passages with draped plastic, requiring workers to cut outside whenever possible, and requiring vacuum systems on sanders (such as drywall sanders and wood-floor sanding machines). If you have a forced-air heating and air-conditioning system, carefully seal all registers and vents in the work area, close supply-duct dampers to the work area, and replace the furnace filter at least once a week during construction.

Communicate, communicate, communicate.

When your pros arrive, take the time to discuss the situation. For a repair, tell them exactly what the problem is—or what it sounds, feels, or smells like. For other projects, tell them exactly what you want done. Even if you prefer a hands-off approach and don't care *how* they do the job, you at least must tell them what you expect in the finished product: "I want it to look like this when it's done." Always communicate in person, or on the phone, if necessary; leaving notes for contractors is an invitation to trouble. And while it's helpful to acknowledge all employees on a job (see the next tip), make sure to discuss all important matters directly with the on-site supervisor.

Be friendly and respectful.

Unless you have good reason to do so, don't assume your contractor is trying to rip you off. If you did your homework before selecting a pro, you should be able to trust him for the most part, and things will go much more smoothly if you're on the level with one another. An air of suspicion is a bad environment to work in.

When it comes to employees of contractors (especially young, less experienced helpers), homeowners tend to avoid contact with them. A better approach is to learn the names of all helpers (not just the boss's) and to talk with them (not just through the boss). Helpers are more likely to take pride in their jobs and go the extra mile if they feel that you're noticing the quality of the work they're doing.

Allowing workers to use your bathroom is a basic courtesy and will be appreciated. However, this won't be an issue if the job is big enough to warrant temporary facilities provided by the contractor.

"OWN YOUR PROJECT"

Be reachable.

Cell phones have made this critical rule easier than ever. If you don't have a cell phone, make sure your pros know your work number and any other means of contacting you. Also expect to be home more often than usual. Whenever possible, don't schedule a repair or an important project phase on a day when you have meetings and can't run home if something goes wrong.

Inspect the work.

You may not be a construction or design expert, but you are the owner and you know what you want. Besides, it never hurts to have another set of eyes on a project. Carefully inspect the job at the end of each day (or perhaps each hour on small jobs) and make note of anything that looks wrong or appears to be headed in the wrong direction. Don't be afraid to pull out a level and check walls, countertops, and floors, or to shine a bright light on a paint or texture job. If anything, your contractor will quickly get the idea that you mean business. Discuss any concerns with the contractor as soon as possible, lest continued work compounds the problem or renders it unfixable.

Learn from the pros.

There are times to be firm about what you want, and there are times to ask and learn from the experts. For example, let's say that you'd like to have a dogwood tree planted in your yard. If you tell your landscaper to include a dogwood on his order, he might do so without asking questions, just to respect your wishes. However, if you ask the landscaper his opinion, he might tell you that he has five clients with dogwoods, all of which are struggling in the local climate. It's this kind of practical knowledge that makes experienced contractors such a valuable resource.

Another way to get your money's worth from a contractor relationship is to inquire about your home. You'd be surprised at how forthcoming most pros are with tips and advice that can save you money. Many will readily tell you how to

"DISCUSS ANY CONCERNS WITH YOUR CONTRACTOR ASAP"

avoid having to call them back or will tell you how to fix a problem yourself if it recurs. Of course, you should respect the contractor's time (which may cost you money), but how often do you have an experienced professional around to ask specific questions about your house?

Don't hold up the job.

If you're the type who agonizes over choosing a paint color, make your decisions before the job begins. When supplying anything for the job, such as appliances or materials, make sure it's there when the pros need it. Homeowner delays give contractors an excellent excuse to leave your job and work on another instead.

Deliver on promises.

For example, if you say you'll clean up each night (to save yourself a little money) be sure to do it. If you don't fulfill your end of the bargain, why should the contractor fulfill his?

Demand a journeyman or supervisor at all times.

Some contracting outfits run jobs by dropping off a crew of laborers, giving them minimal instructions, then taking off to make an appearance at the next job. Meanwhile, if a problem arises on the first project, no one is there to make an executive decision. Don't let this happen to you. Firmly request that there be at least one experienced worker (journeyman) or supervisor on your job at all times.

Non-English-speaking workers are increasingly common in the construction and home repair industries. This is not a problem in itself, as their work may be excellent, but it can create a huge communication gap. Workers who nod or say "Yes, yes" to your requests probably aren't getting the real picture and are just placating you. Insisting on an English-speaking supervisor is the only way to avoid problems due to miscommunication.

Make changes judiciously.

Midstream changes cost money. They also slow down a job and put a crimp in contractors' schedules. Just be aware of this, and avoid requesting changes on a whim. Even if you don't care about the cost, extensive or frequent changes put a strain on contractor-client relationships and often delay projects dramatically. All proposed changes must be written up in a detailed change order (including extra costs) that is signed by you and the contractor.

Money talks.

Don't make incremental payments until the specified work is done. And absolutely don't make a final payment until every aspect of the job meets your satisfaction. Withholding money is the only leverage you have against a recalcitrant contractor. On the other hand, when the project is shipshape and a payment is due, prompt payment is expected and will be appreciated.

RESOLVING DISPUTES

The first rule in settling disagreements with contractors is to always try to solve the problem on your own. Start by calmly explaining the problem as you see it and asking the contractor what he's willing to do about it. If you feel the problem represents a breach of any written agreement or contract, refer to the specific wording that supports your case. This just might work; you'd be surprised at how many contractor-client disputes are resolved after a few minutes of frank discussion. (In a great many cases, the problem originates with poor communication.)

So, you've shared your grievances, but your contractor isn't ready to make nice. Now it's time to write a letter. Include everything you discussed in step 1, plus a detailed request for repairs or corrections as appropriate, or a dollar amount that you feel is owed to you. Send the letter by certified or registered mail so the contractor has to sign for it, thus proving it was received. Since the contractor is already digging in his heels, the letter may get you nowhere, but your having sent it could strengthen your case if the dispute ends up in arbitration or court.

The letter didn't work? Time to consider your options for outside help. Here are some sources for advice and information on consumer complaints and dispute resolution:

- State Attorney General's office
- State department of consumer affairs
- Local district attorney
- The Better Business Bureau
- Community mediation programs
- Local bar association
- State or local regulatory agency, such as a contractor licensing board
- Local court (or county court)

Any of these sources is likely to recommend seeking mediation or arbitration services as the next step in solving your problem. In addition to offering both of these services, the Better Business Bureau accepts complaints from consumers about BBB-member and non-member businesses. Once a complaint is filed, the BBB (typically your local chapter) contacts the contractor or business and requests a response. Businesses have incentive to respond, since complaints end up on their BBB Reliability Report.

Mediation

In a mediation session, you and your contractor voluntarily sit down with a trained mediator and thoroughly discuss the disagreement at hand. The mediator's role is to clarify the issue and facilitate communication so that you and the contractor can (hopefully) resolve the problem on your own. Mediators do not make judgments or have any legal bearing on a case. Some mediation services will contact a contractor for you and try to persuade him to agree to having a session.

Mediation services are available through the Better Business Bureau, many local bar associations, and some community mediation programs. You also can find professional mediation services in the phone book, under Mediation Service.

Arbitration

Arbitration is a step up from mediation and a step down from civil court. In an arbitration hearing, both parties present their case to a certified arbiter. Each side may present witnesses, photographs, documents, and other material evidence to help plead their case. Lawyers are allowed in some instances. Under *binding* arbitration, the arbiter's decision is final, and both parties must agree to abide by the decision. Failure to do so may kick the case up into the court system. There is also *non-binding* arbitration, which is essentially mediation, because neither party is held to an arbiter's judgment.

Many, many unresolved contractor-client disputes are put to rest in arbitration. Considering the relative costs and time involved, settlement in arbitration is far preferable to a full-blown civil court case. That's why it's usually advisable to include an arbitration clause in home improvement contracts—if you and your contractor can't find a solution on your own or through mediation, the next course of action is already set down in writing, and there's no need to argue about what lies ahead.

If your dispute is headed toward arbitration, it's important to prepare yourself for the hearing. Don't assume your contractor—your opponent—will act as dopey or confused as he did the day when you first brought up the problem. Find out what will be allowed in the hearing, and prepare your case accordingly. You might want to consult a professional (a lawyer, for instance) for expert advice on how to present your case.

Arbitration services are available through the Better Business Bureau, the American Arbitration Association, some local bar associations, and independent professional arbitration businesses. As mentioned in Chapter 2, it's a good idea to talk with a lawyer before choosing an arbitration service, if you haven't chosen one already.

Small Claims Court

Small claims court is often used as an alternative to arbitration, but only when cases fall within the claim limits of the local court—typically $5,000 or less—and only when the contract doesn't require arbitration. Most people have seen some version of small claims court on TV and more or less know the drill: The plaintiff (you) and the defendant (the contractor) briskly plead their cases in front of a judge. Many courts do not permit attorneys, particularly for plaintiffs. The judge may make a decision on the spot, and you're done. If the plaintiff loses, he cannot appeal to a higher court, in most jurisdictions.

Small claims court is a good option if your claim is small (and meets the court's requirements) and you seek a cash award for damages. Claims for pain and suffering and other intangible losses often are not successful in the world of small claims. For information on how to file a small claims action and details on court requirements, contact the clerk or advisor of the small claims court in your jurisdiction. Also be aware that there are time limits for filing claims.

Civil Court

Legal trials may be entertaining to watch on TV, but they're no fun in real life, especially when you consider the long, drawn-out process of filing a lawsuit, preparing for trial, and dealing with counter motions and pleadings that cause further delays. And it's expensive, sometimes very expensive. That's why filing a lawsuit should be thought of only as a last resort.

The basic process starts with a careful examination of the facts in order to: 1) determine who is at fault, and 2) decide whether the case warrants litigation. This is as far as you can go without hiring an attorney. If an attorney supports your case and takes the job, she will probably send a demand letter to the culprit (soon to be defendant) you've identified. The demand letter explains your complaint, why the culprit is at fault, and how much you seek in damages. The culprit may decide to settle at this point, and the case is closed.

No settlement? There usually isn't one. On to the next step—filing a complaint. Your lawyer conducts a thorough review of the job contract (if you have one) and drafts a formal complaint based on specific areas where the law has been broken or the contract has been breached. Filing a complaint will likely be subject to time limits. For example, if your claim is against a product manufacturer, you may have only two years from the time the problem occurred—not since the problem was discovered. Claims for contract disputes or real property damages usually have longer time limits, but you should find out what the laws are in your area.

The complaint makes your lawsuit official. It is followed by motions on both sides, hearings, a deposition (in which those involved in the lawsuit are asked questions by the opposing attorneys), and possibly a mediation session that may lead to a settlement. There usually is one. No settlement means the case goes to trial, typically with a jury. As simple as it may sound here, this process can be convoluted and very slow. Often it takes many months and even years to settle a civil court case.

As a final note, the whole idea behind this stepped approach to dispute resolution is simple practicality: The sooner you resolve the problem and the less outside help you need to do it, the sooner you can get back to your life or get your project rolling again. Each successive stage of escalation costs more money and takes more time. So, no matter how much you hate your contractor or how many times you've imagined him getting run over by a concrete truck, it's in your best interest to remain calm and diplomatic (yet assertive) and try to come to an agreement without escalating to the next stage. Good contractors have a reputation to maintain and are motivated to resolve disputes with customers. Crooks and hacks, on the other hand, don't care about bad references, and you may have to do whatever you can to bring the law to bear on them without spending a fortune in the process. In any case, good luck.

Ensuring a Smooth Job Checklist

✔ Be assertive about getting a contractor to finish your project. If he's not there when he's supposed to be, don't hesitate to call.

✔ Refer to the original project description, plans, or design specifications when directing the work or demanding necessary changes.

✔ Get involved and stay involved in your project. This will help you make decisions with confidence and will prevent delays caused by poor communication or indecision.

✔ Stay in close contact with your professionals during work hours, and always be reachable by phone.

✔ Don't let kids, pets, household clutter, or your curiosity interfere with the work progress.

✔ Make payments only after the related work is completed to your satisfaction.

✔ Try to resolve all disagreements and disputes with reason and clear communication with your contractor.

✔ When a dispute can't be resolved through discussion, send a letter to your contractor detailing your complaint and what you would like him to do about it.

✔ Consider mediation services if verbal and written communication have failed. This requires voluntary participation by all parties but can be the simplest and cheapest solution at this stage.

✔ Failing mediation, turn to arbitration to resolve your dispute. Small claims court is another option for cases involving less than $5,000 (typically).

✔ Resort to filing a lawsuit only after all other attempts at resolution have failed.

AIR-CONDITIONING CONTRACTOR

SEE: HEATING, VENTILATION & AIR-CONDITIONING CONTRACTOR

AIR DUCT CLEANER

For Help With Cleaning:

- Metal & fiberglass ductwork
- Furnaces & furnace flues
- Air-conditioning coils
- Dryer vents
- Exhaust systems

Duct cleaning services have become more common in recent years, due to concerns that home air duct systems may spread contaminants such as dust, mold, and allergens throughout the home. Professional cleaners use a variety of methods to remove dust and debris from the inside surfaces of ductwork. They also clean the interiors of furnaces, air-conditioning units, and any equipment directly related to a home's air-handling system.

Cleaning Methods

To clean inside ductwork, professionals may use hand-operated vacuum brushes, pressurized air, or a rotary brush that is snaked down through the ducting. All removed debris is collected by a portable or truck-mounted vacuum. Vacuums used in the home should include a HEPA (high-efficiency particle air) filter, so dust doesn't go from your duct to your dining room. Steam cleaning is another method you might encounter. However, this is not recommended because it introduces moisture that could become trapped in the system, potentially leading to mold growth.

Snake Oil or Sound Science?

The benefits of duct cleaning remain debatable. Certainly there are plenty of hucksters out there who exaggerate the health risks of dirty ducts and claim that their cleaning services will reduce allergies and promote good health for you and your family. According to the U.S. Environmental Protection Agency (EPA), there currently is no substantial evidence that duct cleaning reduces airborne contaminants or has any measurable effect on indoor air quality. That said, the EPA does recommend duct cleaning in the following cases:

- Substantial mold growth is visible on the insides of bare sheet metal ductwork or on other system equipment.
- Rodents, insects, or other vermin (not just dust mites) are living in your ducts.
- Excessive deposits of dust and debris are inhibiting airflow in the ducts, or you can see dust coming out of supply registers.

Of course, if you have severe allergies and your doctor or specialist recommends cleaning your ducts, it's probably worth a try. In addition, common sense tells you that regular cleaning of heating and air-conditioning equipment (including replacing filters, removing dust and dirt from cooling coils and fins, and cleaning dust from air registers) will make your system run more efficiently. If you hire a pro to shine up your ductwork, make sure they clean everything related to the heating and cooling system, and particularly any parts that deal with air movement. Also make sure that all access panels and other openings are properly closed and/or sealed when the cleaning is completed.

Despite what some cleaning pros will tell you, regular or annual duct cleaning is not necessary or beneficial under normal home conditions.

Things to Watch Out For

Your air duct cleaner may recommend extra treatments to improve the efficiency or healthfulness of your system. Don't agree to any of these before checking it out. Common treatments include "sanitizing" ducts with a biocide or other chemical solution and sealing ducts with an airborne sealant, to prevent dust intrusion.

The EPA warns against using any biocide (commonly applied as a mold and bacteria inhibitor) or other treatment that is not registered by the EPA specifically for use in HVAC (heating, ventilation, and air-conditioning) systems. Also, the EPA asserts that even registered products have not been thoroughly tested; in other words, use them at your own risk. Mold problems in ductwork usually indicate excessive moisture, which must be eliminated to prevent future mold growth. Biocide treatment won't cure the problem.

If the insides of your ducts are lined with fiberglass that has become wet and moldy (or is smelly), consult an HVAC professional (see page 109) about having the lining or ductwork replaced. Currently, no biocides are registered by the EPA for use on fiberglass-lined ducts or fiberglass duct board.

Sealants, particularly non-localized types, ring some alarms with the EPA, as well as with the North American Insulation Manufacturers Association (NAIMA). The latter warns that, on fiberglass lining or duct board, sealant should be used only locally and in small areas, and that the sealant should comply with the insulation manufacturer's specifications, as well as the local building code.

As a rule, don't hire any company that claims to be certified by the EPA. The EPA does not certify or endorse any duct cleaning company or personnel. Some companies offer fireplace flue cleaning among their services. While this may be perfectly legit, be aware that an important aspect of chimney sweep service (see page 65) is a visual inspection of the flue and chimney; ask your duct cleaner whether he's qualified to do this before proceeding.

Licenses & Insurance?

Duct cleaners should be insured. Some states require duct cleaners to be licensed. All cleaners should follow the guidelines set by the NADCA (National Air Duct Cleaners Association).

☎ In the Phone Book

Air Duct Cleaning, Duct Cleaning.

ANIMAL CONTROL

SEE ALSO: PEST CONTROL

For Help With:

- Removing nuisance wildlife from the home

Animal control operators are the people to call when there's a raccoon living rent-free in your chimney, a skunk family squatting under your porch, or squirrels partying in your attic at all hours of the night. Animal control, or wildlife control, deals with evacuating or removing wild animals from inside or around your home. If you have a problem with insects or small rodent pests, such as mice or rats, seek the help of a Pest Control specialist (page 141). Some services handle both animals and pests. For problems with domestic pets (dogs, cats) or to report mistreatment of domestic animals, contact your city's animal control agency or local animal shelter or humane society chapter.

Animal control pros use a variety of techniques to do their job. Live trapping is a very common method for capturing the offending critter. Once caught, the animal may be taken to a rehabilitation facility, it may be relocated some miles away, or it may be killed. It all depends on the operator's policy. There are also traps that kill the animal upon capture, using a lethal mechanism or poison. As an alternative to trapping, some pros employ an "eviction" technique, plugging up the entry holes used by the animal, and installing a temporary one-way door over one of the holes.

Many animal control operators also repair the damage caused by the animals, as well as clean up the mess they've made with all that late-night partying. A good operator will advise you on prevention techniques, and many can install chimney caps, vent screens, and other equipment to discourage the animals from coming back. If the operator offers a guarantee, make sure you know the terms in detail and what's required of you to keep the guarantee valid.

"Humane" Is a Relative Term

If you're concerned about the welfare of your uninvited guest, it's important to ask about the animal control operator's methods. Every one will tell you their approach is humane (and who can resist the cute photos of animals in their phone book ads?), but that doesn't guarantee your personal criteria of fair treatment will be met. One important question to ask is whether the operator's approach is lethal or non-lethal. If you're not opposed to killing the animal, you might prefer some trap types or extermination methods over others, so you should ask about the equipment used.

"Relocation" is another loosely used term in the industry. Unscrupulous pros may promise to relocate the animals, but their actual release site could be the bottom of a dumpster. Many animal experts (particularly proponents of wildlife *rehabilitation* as opposed to relocation) believe that relocation is a bad move, citing the spread of disease among other problems. If the general health of the local wildlife population is a concern for you, contact a wildlife rehabilitator in your area; some of these are also animal control operators or can refer you to one.

Helpful Resources

Nuisance wildlife problems often can be solved with a simple do-it-yourself solution. If this works, you'll save money now and will probably learn prevention techniques that could save you more down the road. Urban Wildlife Rescue (www.urbanwildliferescue.org) includes tips for rousting animals from your property, as well as a list of all licensed wildlife rehabilitators in the U.S.

Other helpful sources include your local humane society, your state's department of wildlife (or Fish & Game, etc.), and the National Wildlife Control Operators Association (www.nwcoa.com). These and other animal welfare organizations can refer you to reputable animal control operators should the problem require professional help.

Licenses & Insurance?

States vary widely on regulation of animal control professionals. Some may require licensing, while others have no monitoring of practitioners but may have laws governing the use of traps or poisons. Ask whether your operator is licensed (if required in your area) or whether any permits are needed for the proposed work. An insured pro is recommended because of the potential for accidental damage to your home.

☎ In the Phone Book

Animal Control; Animal Rescue, Relocate & Transport; Pest Control.

APPLIANCE SERVICE & REPAIR

For Help With:

- Repairs & maintenance for major household appliances, including:
  - ☐ Kitchen appliances
  - ☐ Laundry appliances
  - ☐ Hot water heaters
  - ☐ Furnaces
  - ☐ Air conditioners

It's amazing how the failure of one major appliance can disrupt your household routine. Of course, that's why the phone book is loaded with appliance repair companies offering 24-hour emergency service or same-day repairs. It's nice to have the option of speedy service, but if your appliance problem isn't an emergency (such as a gas leak), you'll be better off if you soak the dishes for a while as you check a few things out to make sure you hire the right professional.

When an appliance is acting up, the first thing to check is its warranty. If the warranty is still valid, the repair might be covered, provided you use a factory-authorized repair service. Even if the repair isn't covered under a valid warranty, you could void the warranty altogether by not using an authorized service.

Warranty no longer good? It still makes sense to find a repair service with experience working on your brand of appliance. Unless you need repairs on a wok burner shipped directly from Thailand, you should have no trouble finding a qualified repair pro. You also can contact the appliance manufacturer for a list of authorized service companies and dealers in your area.

Pricing, Parts & Guarantees

Whether you use Ernie's Repair Shop from down the block or Megappliance Super Service, ask about charges during your initial phone call. Most companies assess a trip charge, and some waive the charge if a repair is made. If a technician comes to your house and doesn't have the part she needs on her truck, you might be charged a *return* trip charge. Also ask about warranties on new parts and whom you should contact if there's a problem with a repair part—the repair company or the part manufacturer. Finally, ask about labor guarantees provided by the service company for the repair work.

HOME SCHOOL

The manufacturer of your appliance can be a good source of information on your specific product. Asking them a few questions might just give you an edge when dealing with a repair service. In some cases, what seems to be a problem is actually a normal condition of the product. For example, people are often worried by a little water in the bottom of their dishwasher at the end of a cycle. On most machines, this is perfectly normal—the water is there to keep the seals from drying up.

Licenses & Insurance?

Appliance repair technicians are required to carry licenses in some areas. Unrelated to licensure, many technicians complete voluntary certification programs through trade groups such as the International Society of Certified Electronics Technicians (ISCET) and the Professional Service Association (PSA). Professionals who work with refrigerant are required by federal law to be certified by the U.S. Environmental Protection Agency (EPA). All repair personnel should be insured against accidental damage to your home or property.

☎ In the Phone Book

Appliances (Major) Service & Repair.

ARBORIST

SEE: TREE SERVICE

ARCHITECT

For Help With:

- Custom design services for new construction & remodeling
- Creating project plans & specifications
- Project management
- Cost estimating
- Predesign services
- Job site inspections

Everyone knows that architects design buildings. They're the rock stars of the construction world, making headlines now and then for creating publicly celebrated (or reviled) structures and displaying their unique blend of bravado and artistic quirkiness. But that's Frank Lloyd Wright or Frank Gehry, not Frank, your local residential architect.

Frank takes on jobs like yours and helps you through the entire process, from budgeting, planning, and design through construction and final inspection, if you wish. Frank not only knows how to design homes and additions, he knows how to get them built. So whether you want your new house to be the next Fallingwater or your remodeled space to be something special, hiring the right architect (not all are named Frank) for the job can be the most important first step.

What an Architect Can Do for You

Architects are much more than designers who plan buildings from scratch. They are highly trained problem solvers who listen to the needs and desires of their clients and create custom spaces around those specific criteria. This makes them valuable resources for remodelers, as well as for clients building new homes. Architects are also professional project managers and are often contracted to liaise between clients and their builder, to obtain permits and contract engineering services, to help resolve disputes, and to oversee construction and make sure their plans (and your wishes) are being adhered to.

An architect also can take care of the many details and challenges that arise from a major construction project, including:

- Budgeting and scheduling
- Predesign services such as soils reports and site-use and utilities analysis
- Selection of materials and products
- Building and zoning code interpretation
- Guidance through the permitting process
- Hiring and working with contractors

Of course, an architect's primary service is design. This process begins with a discussion of every aspect of the project and what you hope to achieve with the finished product. Ideas are shared, possibilities and obstacles are considered, and rough sketches are created. Then begins the process of revision, revision, revision. (For a new home project, you might even get a cute little model to show your friends.)

In the end, your architect will supply a set of final drawings and complete written job specifications (see Chapter 2, pages 20 to 25) that will serve as the foundation for all of the construction work. The drawings and specs together are an excellent reference for obtaining bids from contractors, if you haven't done so already. Depending on your project, your architect may supply only basic drawings (floor plans, framing plans, and elevations), or at your request may also create separate plans for the mechanical and electrical systems.

At what point should you hire an architect? In most cases, and especially on large projects, the sooner the better. Architects are expensive, but the idea is that their planning and design expertise will not only help you reach your goals, they'll help you do it efficiently, minimizing wasted time and money. Therefore, it makes sense to consult a professional before heading too far down the planning road. For a list of items you should know before approaching potential candidates, see How to Find an Architect on the following page.

Do I Need an Architect?

This is a question asked by most homeowners considering a new home project or major remodel. And it's tough to get a straight answer because of the many factors involved. Here are a few suggestions to help make your decision.

If you're remodeling your kitchen, bathroom, bedroom, or any other room, and the project does not involve major structural changes or additions, you might be satisfied with the design help of a qualified interior designer and/or an experienced remodeling contractor, rather than an architect. As for basement remodels, these usually don't require much structural planning, and the space restraints limit the design possibilities, so an architect is probably overkill.

On the other end of the spectrum, if you're building a new home, hire an architect. The alternative is to buy ready-made plans and hand them over to your builder, but doing so means you'll not only end up with a cookie-cutter structure, you'll also have to complete the project without the guidance, insight, and creative ideas that an architect offers. And you'll be on your own in fighting battles against your builder and local building officials whenever problems arise.

For those planning a remodel, here are some good reasons to hire an architect:

- You want a truly custom or unique design
- Your project is large or complicated
- Your home has historic value, is a registered landmark, or is subject to approval by an architectural committee
- You desire a high level of architectural continuity and relevance
- Your renovation includes significant changes to the home's exterior
- You have a friend who is an architect, and she would appreciate the work

The local building department might also help in your decision. Discuss your project with the permitting officials and find out whether you'll need drawings with an architect's or engineer's stamp. Some municipalities accept plans created by unlicensed practitioners (apprentice architects, draftsmen, or designers) on certain types of projects. The officials might not care who draws the plans, so long as they carry the required stamps of approval.

How to Find an Architect

Residential architects work for themselves and for firms of varying sizes. For homeowner projects, the scale of the organization is seldom a deciding factor. What's important is that the firm—and the architect who will personally handle your job—has extensive experience with your type of project. Like most professionals, architects tend to specialize in certain types of work; some cater to high-end clientele who like soaring entryways and extravagant detailing, while others are specialists in historic preservation or energy-efficient design. An architect's recent work will tell you the most about her preferred style or specialty.

The best way to learn of a good architect is through—you guessed it—personal referrals. Your friends and neighbors, local contractors, realtors, and even lenders are likely sources for the names of reputable architects. Beyond that, you can contact the local chapter of the American Institute of Architects (AIA; www.aia.org), the nation's largest professional organization of architects (and the industry standard). Many chapters offer referral lists and will help match you with architects suitable for your project. Your state's licensing board for architects may be another good source for names but probably won't endorse any specific professionals.

To expedite your search and get right into meaningful discussions with candidates, you should prepare yourself with as much of the following information as possible:

- A basic description of your project, including the size, look, and function of the new construction
- The services you seek from the architect and firm
- An approximate project budget, including percentages for design and construction
- Financing information (i.e., how you plan to pay for it all)
- Who is doing the construction—your contractor, if known
- Start and completion dates for the project

Narrow the field of candidates by contacting only firms with experience and histories relevant to your project. Then look at their work. If you're planning to add on to your Cape Cod and most of a firm's projects are avant-garde and modern, move on to the next firm. Also ask about the firm's services, to make sure they'll be able to do whatever you need. Once you have a short list of good candidates, interview at least three before making a decision. Be sure to interview the architect with whom you will work and not just a representative for the firm.

Above all, base your decision on the architect herself (her personality, work style, etc.) and on her work. Building or renovating can be a highly emotional and challenging experience, and you'll need a partner you're comfortable with to get through the good and the bad. According to the AIA website, "a good architect is a good listener." Hey, it works for marriages...why not construction projects? You can assume that all architects are pretty well trained but not all are blessed with the same level of talent. Indeed, there are plenty of uninspired designs out there and even more creations that simply wouldn't suit your taste. Again, past projects will indicate what an architect is capable of.

For those candidates who pass the interview stage, run background and reference checks on them before proceeding (see Chapter 1). Your state's licensing board may give you some background information on candidates, such as confirmation of their licensure and whether there have been complaints filed or disciplinary action taken against them.

Fees & Contracts

Architectural fees can easily run to 10% to 15% of a project's total cost, so it's very important to discuss the fee structure and understand what you're paying for. Architects generally charge in a few different ways—by the hour, by a stipulated flat fee, or by a percentage of the total project cost. In a typical arrangement, you'll pay by the hour during the initial planning and design phase, then pay a percentage rate when the project is better defined and construction is ready to begin. Later in the project, you may negotiate for additional management or oversight services, most likely on an hourly basis.

All fees and services and the schedule of payment must be thoroughly outlined in your contract with the architect. Payment schedules usually coincide with the timing of services. In addition to the standard fees for design and management services, discuss the following potential charges with your architect:

Consultants' fees: For specific tests or consulting work, such as engineering, soils testing, and various inspections. Determine whether these fees are included in the architect's fee or whether you'll be charged separately. Usually the architect is in charge of getting these types of outside services done for the project.

Additional fees & expenses: Ask for an estimate of fees such as permits (and paying the architect to obtain them) and expenses related to the architect's work (including travel, etc.). How will these be assessed?

Design changes: Plan revisions are expected on any building project. Changes may be made at your request or your contractor's request, or they may be required to meet the building code. Sometimes changes are made simply for budget-cutting (oops, there goes the indoor swimming pool). Discuss the fee structure for all changes to construction drawings and specifications.

With the services and fees ironed out, it's time to sign the contract. Don't hire an architect without a written contract (see Chapter 2). Some architects create their own contracts, while others use one of the applicable AIA contracts (page 45). Regardless of where the contract comes from, you (or your legal counsel, if you have one) can question or request changes to any part before signing.

Architects' Qualifications

All licensed architects in the U.S. must complete an architecture program from an accredited school or university, followed by three years of apprentice work under a licensed architect. They then must pass a standardized, five-day exam for licensure. States and municipalities may impose additional requirements to practice in their jurisdictions (some people are just hard to please). If you're using an architect who does not normally work in your area, make sure she is up to speed on the local building codes.

Many architects join the AIA, and they're not shy about advertising it. Members must be licensed architects who vow to abide by the AIA's "Code of Ethics and Professional Conduct." They also must complete a minimum number of hours in continuing education each year. AIA membership does not guarantee any level of competence, but it may indicate a certain dedication to the profession and at least some involvement in the community of professional architecture.

Of Architects & Contractors

Being in the same business more or less, architects and contractors get to know one another. This can lead to good referrals and insider advantages for clients, but it can also propagate serious conflicts of interest. If your architect recommends a contractor, put the contractor through the full screening process, just as you would with anyone you hear about on the street. And don't feel pressured to use a contractor simply because your architect likes him. Some remodeling companies and design/build firms have architects on staff, and you hire the design and construction work essentially as a package.

One obvious drawback of using a contractor recommended by your architect is the possibility that the two, if unscrupulous, might work together to favor their own interests over yours. Even if they're completely on the level, the fact that they know each other might make the architect more lenient when it comes to inspecting the contractor's work. Of course, many architects and contractors have good working relationships that benefit their clients by making the whole process run more smoothly. It's just something you should consider.

Building or Remodeling for Retirement?

If you're thinking ahead to a time when it might not be so easy to climb the stairs with full loads of laundry, or if you need to make some changes now to better accommodate someone with limited mobility, look for an architect with Universal Design experience. Universal Design is a realm of professional design that's based on accommodating people of all ages and abilities. Thoughtful planning today is the best way to ensure your home will fit your lifestyle in the future.

Licenses & Insurance?

All states require architects to be licensed. Insurance is not always a requirement, but many architects carry some form of liability insurance.

☎ In the Phone Book

Architects.

ASBESTOS CONSULTING & TESTING

For Help With:

- Home asbestos inspection & testing
- Advice & specifications for asbestos abatement
- Monitoring of asbestos abatement & air quality testing
- Inspection of completed abatement work

There are two groups of professionals who deal with asbestos in the home: Asbestos Consultants (also under the heading of Environmental Consultant or Asbestos Inspector) and Asbestos Abatement contractors.

Consultants are certified specialists who take samples of suspected material from your home and have them tested for asbestos. If they find asbestos, consultants will advise you of your options for dealing with it and recommend appropriate solutions. If a problem calls for complicated or large-scale abatement, a consultant can design project specifications for an abatement contractor to follow. Upon completion of any kind of abatement work, consultants inspect the affected area to ensure the work was done properly and that the air quality in the home is safe for occupancy.

Asbestos abatement contractors handle the actual repair or removal of materials containing asbestos. They use a variety of approved methods to reduce the risk of asbestos contamination in a home, including sealing asbestos-containing materials with special paint or tape, encapsulating them within sealed structures, or removing them completely from the site.

Due to the potentially serious conflict of interest, never hire the same company, or affiliated companies, for both asbestos consultation and abatement. An asbestos consultant may refer you to qualified abatement contractors in your area, but you should check them out just as carefully as you would someone you found on your own.

Don't Mess with Asbestos

Asbestos is a natural mineral fiber that was added to many building materials to increase strength and improve heat insulation and fire resistance. It was commonly used in home construction products from the 1930s to the late 1970s (see Home School, next page). Asbestos is relatively safe if its host material (insulation, floor tile, etc.) remains intact. But when the host material is torn, sanded, or scraped, tiny asbestos fibers become airborne (in what they call a *friable* state). The fibers are breathed in and become permanently trapped in the lungs. That's where your problems start.

The general recommendation of the U.S. Environmental Protection Agency (EPA) and many other expert sources is this: If there are asbestos-containing materials in your home that are in good shape (no tears, breakage, or deterioration), leave them be. Prevent the kids from playing around them, and remove any potential threat of damage, but don't mess with the stuff. The universal rule is that any material suspected of containing asbestos is treated as though it contains it for sure.

If you find suspect material that is damaged, or if you're remodeling and will make alterations in an area with suspect materials, that's when you call an asbestos consultant. They'll check it out and advise you from there. The important thing is not to have any work done or do anything with suspect materials yourself before having them checked out.

Here's a common horror scenario: You hire an ordinary building contractor to move some old, insulated pipe. Halfway into the demolition he mentions that there might be asbestos in the insulation. You call in a consultant, who finds asbestos in the insulation and also, due to the cutting, all over the room. Now you have a hazardous material *spill* situation on your hands. Very bad. You would have saved yourself a lot of trouble and expense, and limited your health risk, by calling the consultant in the first place.

Asbestos Information Resources

- U.S. Environmental Protection Agency (EPA): www.epa.gov
- American Lung Association: www.lungusa.org
- U.S. Occupational Safety & Health Administration (OSHA): www.osha.gov
- Your state or local health department

HOME SCHOOL

Here's a list (incomplete) of common household materials that may contain asbestos:

- Insulation on hot-air ducts, steam pipes, and boilers; also paper duct/insulation tape
- Insulating board or paper used around furnaces, wood/coal stoves, and other combustion fixtures; also the door gaskets on these fixtures
- Floor tile; including rubber, asphalt, vinyl asbestos tile, and floor tile adhesive
- Backing material on vinyl sheet flooring
- Joint compound and patching material (spackle) on wall and ceiling surfaces
- Spray-on wall and ceiling texture (for soundproofing or decoration)
- Roofing materials, shingles, and siding made of asbestos cement

Licenses & Insurance?

Check with your state or municipal health department regarding their requirements for certification and licensing for asbestos consultants/inspectors/testers in your area. Some states require only EPA certification, while others have additional requirements. Some municipalities have their own restrictions, as well. Make sure the consultant you hire meets all applicable requirements and is fully insured.

☎ In the Phone Book

Asbestos Consulting & Testing, Environmental & Ecological Services.

BASEMENT REMODELER

For Help With:

- Start-to-finish basement remodeling/finishing
  - Basement remodelers specialize in turning that cold, concrete box downstairs into everything your house has always lacked:
  - Media room/home theater
  - Kids' bedrooms
  - Home office
  - Workshop
  - Rumpus room
  - Gym
  - Poolroom
  - Wine cellar

…or anything else on your wish list, provided it will fit.

Professionals who remodel basements include independent operators and larger general remodeling contractors who might take on all sorts of home improvements, as well as basement remodeling companies–full-service, design/build firms that do nothing but basements. While qualified pros from each category can get the job done, your best bet in any case is to find someone who has plenty of experience with basements.

Why a Basement Specialist?

Remodeling basements is all about problem-solving, because no other space has the same constraints on floor space, headroom, access, and mechanicals. It takes special design expertise and construction experience to make the most of the limited space available. And because every basement presents its own challenges, the more basement jobs a pro has on his resume, the more problems he's solved and the more solutions he can offer for your basement. When interviewing potential contractors, don't be afraid to ask directly about their basement remodeling expertise.

The Full-service Experience

Most basement remodelers offer turnkey service, meaning you do little other than tell them what you want (and write the checks). Following are some of the initial major steps of a typical remodel, as well as some potential benefits you should ask about:

Consultation: Most pros start with a free in-home consultation, giving them a chance to see your basement and to learn about your goals and wishes for the project. This is a good opportunity for you to ask questions about the contractor's work and to assess his knowledge of basement finishing. If you have design ideas of your own, make sure the contractor listens to them and is willing to collaborate with you on the overall plan.

Preliminary design: If all goes well with the initial consultation, the contractor will take detailed measurements and draft the layout of your new basement space. Some pros will do this for free; others may charge for it or require a refundable deposit before plans are drawn up. In any case, you shouldn't have to commit much money until later–when you approve a set of final plans and are ready to begin construction.

Final plans & bid: You and the contractor revise the basic drawings until they meet your satisfaction. From there, specifications are further detailed, and the contractor should be able to provide a firm quote for the job.

Contract: Any significant basement remodel warrants a full-scale contract (see Chapters 2 and 4). Construction follows the contract agreement.

Job deadline: Many basement remodeling contractors offer guaranteed job-completion deadlines. If yours does so, make sure to read the fine print regarding permissible delays or exceptions to the deadline.

Supplier discounts: Well-established (and well-heeled) remodeling firms often contract with specialty retailers and manufacturers to supply appliances and other goodies, like home theaters, sound systems, wine cellars, and fireplaces. This means you get a discount price if you use the contractor's vendors.

Finding the Right Remodeler

Finishing a basement is a significant and expensive undertaking. Choosing your contractor requires the same due diligence you would follow for a large addition or a kitchen remodel. Check references and backgrounds for all prospective contractors, and make sure to hire someone you're comfortable working with. Most remodeling outfits subcontract much of the construction, while design work is typically done in-house. See Chapter 4 for a detailed discussion of how to find and interview prospective general contractors.

Dealing with Basement Moisture Problems

Moisture is enemy number one for a finished basement. If you've experienced any kind of moisture or water problems in the past, now is the time to deal with them—before you spend thousands of dollars on finishing the space. Even a minor problem, like dampness on foundation walls or a general mustiness or clamminess in your basement, could lead to mold, dry rot, and insect infestation. It's important to note that basement remodelers typically exclude moisture damage from their warranties. And why wouldn't they—their work has nothing to do with how your house reacts to environmental water and humidity.

Basement moisture can be a mysterious and elusive enemy. Causes may be as simple as a faulty gutter system or as challenging as a high water table. Therefore, the best approach is to try the easy solutions first:

- Make sure your gutters are working properly and all downspouts extend at least 4 ft. away from your home's foundation
- Seal minor cracks in foundation walls with hydraulic cement
- Check the grading around your foundation to make sure it slopes down and away from the house
- Cover open window wells that may collect water when it rains

For more ideas, talk to an experienced official at your city's building department, a local home inspector, or other expert to learn about common causes of basement moisture in your area.

If simple measures don't solve your moisture problems, it may be time to call in a waterproofing contractor. These are professionals who specialize in wet basements and foundation repairs. You can find them in the phone book under Waterproofing Contractors or Drainage Contractors. Waterproofing pros use a variety of methods to handle surface and subsurface water, including landscape drains and wells, footing drains, foundation waterproofing, and sump pit systems. The correct method depends on where the water is coming from.

Before talking to local contractors, spend a little time researching the types of waterproofing systems used most commonly in your area. This will give you an edge when discussing solutions proposed by prospective contractors. Next, find at least three local contractors who meet your highest standards in terms of reputation and customer satisfaction. Have each of these contractors evaluate your situation and present a proposal, including a rough cost estimate for the entire job. Because water problems can be difficult to diagnose, it's important to get several opinions at this stage. Don't consider a contractor unless you feel confident that he has conducted a thorough investigation of your moisture problem, your home, and your landscaping.

Contact your city office or building department to learn about permits, building code restrictions, and contractor licensing requirements for waterproofing work. Make sure your contractor will abide by all applicable laws and that he has the insurance and financial viability to honor any guarantees for many years down the road. Get all proposed work in writing, including detailed job specifications and any guarantees against future moisture problems. Once the work is done, it's advisable to put off any finishing work for a year, or at least through the next rainy season, to make sure your problem is solved.

For general information on wet basement issues and waterproofing contractors, visit the website of the National Association of Waterproofing & Structural Repair Contractors at www.nawsrc.org. The NAWSRC certifies waterproofing professionals in the categories of Above-grade Waterproofing Specialist, Waterproofing Specialist, and Structural Repair Specialist. You can find certified waterproofers in your area using their contractor locator.

HOME SCHOOL

A finished basement is great for getting away from it all, but it's not a good place to hide from the local building inspector. Here are some typical code restrictions you and your contractor will have to work around (some may not apply in your area):

- Ceilings must be 7'-6" high in living areas and 7' in bathrooms and hallways.
- Bedrooms need two forms of egress (emergency escape).
- Total window area must equal at least 10% of the total floor space.

Licenses & Insurance?
Your contractor must be fully insured for workers' compensation and liability. Licensing of remodeling pros is common, so make sure your contractor meets all applicable state and local licensing requirements.

☎ In the Phone Book
Basement Remodeling, Contractors–Remodel & Repair, Remodeling Services.

BATHROOM REMODELER

For Help With:

- Complete bathroom re-design & construction

Renovating a bathroom is arguably the single most rewarding home improvement. You get to take out everything you always hated in your old bathroom and replace it with everything you've always wanted (ideally, that is). Like kitchens, bathrooms are relatively small spaces with disproportionately complex systems—not just the plumbing, lighting, and electrical, but also the fixtures, surfaces, colors, and decorative details. You need some good advice for the many decisions involved. That's why experience counts when it comes to hiring a pro to handle a major remodel.

"Bathroom Remodelers" come in all varieties, from small, independent operators to large firms with in-house design services and fancy showrooms. Choosing the right contractor is mostly a matter of matching the remodeler's services and experience with your project. For example, if you're planning to replace some fixtures and surfaces, and perhaps add a window or remove a partition wall, you'll likely be satisfied with any experienced contractor who can talk you through most of the design decisions. On the other hand, if you're thinking about complete reconfiguration of the space for a whole new layout, you'll probably want to start with some professional design help.

Begin with a Consultation

Most bathroom remodelers offer a free in-home or showroom consultation to discuss your existing bathroom and what you'd like to do with it. This is a good chance to get a feel for the contractor's personality, work style, and experience with bathroom remodeling, as well as to ask a lot of questions about your plans. An experienced local pro can be a valuable resource at this stage. For example, she will know how much things cost in your area and should be able to ballpark prices for various materials and features, helping you to refine your goals and think more accurately about your budget.

Do You Need a Designer?

Design help can come from many sources. If you have a creative urge (or you feel "inspired" by a tight budget), you can do your own design work, getting advice from home improvement books, magazines, and industry resources such as the National Kitchen & Bath Association (NKBA; www.nkba.org). On many remodels, the contractor provides enough design advice to get the job done. He probably won't help much with your color scheme, but he can make layout recommendations and tell you where to find fixtures and materials.

For comprehensive design and decorating work, seek the help of a qualified professional designer. Larger remodeling firms often have designers on staff, or you can contract separately with an independent designer. The latter may also become involved with the construction process, if you'd like. Designers can assist with most of the big and small bathroom decisions: drafting a floor plan; cabinet design and layout; selecting fixtures, tile, and flooring; choosing paint and wallpaper; adding windows; and incorporating any specialty or premium items on your wish list. In some arrangements, the designer acts as general contractor, hiring subcontractors and managing the construction project.

The title CBD next to a designer's name stands for Certified Bathroom Designer, meaning the designer has completed the well-respected certification program offered by the NKBA. For more tips on finding and working with designers, see Kitchen Designer (page 121) and Interior Designer (page 118).

Remodeling for Retirement?

Conventional bathrooms can be difficult to use by those with limited mobility. If anyone in your home could benefit from a more user-friendly layout and accessible fixtures, ask your designer or remodeler about Universal Design—a realm of professional design that's based on accommodating people of all ages and abilities. Adding simple features such as grab bars and an easy-access shower now might save you from having to make expensive alterations down the road.

Finding the Right Remodeler

If your bathroom renovation is big enough to warrant hiring a contractor to manage the job, follow the steps described in Chapter 4 to seek out and interview a few potential candidates before making a decision. For a full-scale remodel, you'll definitely need a complete set of job specifications (see Chapter 2, pages 20 to 25) to ensure accurate bids and establish contract requirements. Many bathroom remodelers and general contractors do much of the construction work themselves and subcontract for specialty jobs, like plumbing and wallpaper hanging. Ask about this up front so you know what to expect and who's supposed to be in charge.

HOME SCHOOL

When remodeling a bathroom, you cross a big line, in terms of budget and construction time, when you decide to relocate plumbing fixtures. Moving the tub from one side of the room to the other, for example, can easily cost twice as much as replacing the tub in its current spot. Changes to lighting and electrical outlets are less costly and often can be made using existing circuitry. However, adding a wall heater or other high-voltage appliance may require the installation of a new circuit.

Licenses & Insurance?

Your contractor must be fully insured for workers' compensation and liability. Licensing of remodeling pros is common, so make sure your contractor meets all applicable state and local licensing requirements. Professional designers are required to be licensed in some states.

☎ In the Phone Book

Bathroom Remodeling, Contractors–Remodel & Repair, Remodeling Services.

BLIND & DRAPERY INSTALLER

SEE WINDOW COVERINGS—DEALERS, DESIGNERS & INSTALLERS

BOILER REPAIR & CLEANING

SEE: HEATING, VENTILATION & AIR-CONDITIONING CONTRACTORS

BURGLAR ALARM INSTALLER

SEE: SECURITY SYSTEMS INSTALLATION & MONITORING

CABINET MAKER (CUSTOM CABINETS & MILLWORK)

For Help With:

- Design, fabrication & installation of custom cabinetry, millwork & fine wood creations throughout the home

In the world of building and remodeling, there are three basic levels of cabinets: *stock*, which you buy off the shelf at the local home center or lumberyard; *semi-custom*, which come in stock sizes, but offer a limited range of wood species and door styles; and *custom*, which are built to your size specifications and include all of your style preferences (usually subject to the manufacturer's offerings).

At one end of the custom level are cabinets produced using the maker's standard designs but with the sizes adjusted as needed. These are often manufactured in large production shops or factories, following a standardized process. The quality and consistency of the cabinets may be quite high, but the design options are often limited.

At the other end of the custom spectrum is where you find truly personal creations—cabinets made to order in any size, material, and style, and with unique features like rollout work surfaces and flip-up doors. Custom craftspeople can match any wood species, finish, molding, or decorative detail in your home. They can also design and build things other than cabinets, such as bookshelves, wine cellars, humidors, and interior windows.

Some true custom cabinet makers work in very small shops; others maintain larger operations with dozens of craftspeople and even designers on staff. In general, though, custom shops deal in much less volume than factory-style cabinet producers. It may be months, or even longer, before they can get to your project. But what you wait for are one-of-a-kind products and, usually, top-notch personal service. Many shops also prefer to do their own installations, eliminating the potential for mistakes and the blame game that can result from using a middleman.

Millwork is related to custom cabinetry in that it encompasses all types of architectural woodwork in a home—from staircase parts to raised-panel wainscoting to cornice molding. If your plans call for a range of custom wood features, look for a cabinet maker who can either produce or commission the production of millwork to your specifications. This is the best way to ensure consistency between the millwork and cabinetry and across woodwork in multiple rooms.

Finding the Right Cabinet Maker

Lots of cabinet makers can deliver quality product, but what you really want is someone whose work inspires you. Therefore, the first step is to visit cabinet shops and see what they can do. Woodworkers are creative people who may dabble in different styles, but most specialize in one area or another, and their work often displays a characteristic look and feel.

Of course, price will be a deciding factor in your search, but so should the maker's ability to work with your (or your designer's) ideas. Discuss the materials you like, types of hardware, and other details to make sure the shop can meet your needs. Find out about installation and whether it's included in the price of the cabinets. Also discuss the shop's process. It's not uncommon for fine cabinet makers to outsource aspects of the work, such as the finishing. This is often a good thing, since the outside vendor is usually a specialist and has built his reputation on doing one job very well.

If you like a cabinet maker, ask for references and talk with several recent customers about their experiences. Custom cabinet and millwork shops get a lot of work through referrals from designers and architects, and many shops are happy to work directly with homeowners. Finally, be aware that cabinet shops usually request a substantial deposit—around 50%—for commissioned work. This is to cover materials and supplies that are special-ordered for your project and may not be wholly re-usable if you back out after work begins.

Licenses & Insurance?

Cabinet makers and other woodworkers generally don't need licenses to conduct business. You can always check with your local regulatory office for any requirements in your area. Any pro who will be installing your woodwork should have insurance to cover employee injuries or damage that occurs in your home.

☎ In the Phone Book

Cabinets & Cabinet Makers, Woodworking, Millwork, Moldings.

CARPENTER

For Help With:

- Wood & steel frame construction
- Interior & exterior trimwork
- Custom building projects
- Remodeling & repair services
- Cabinets & shelving
- Deck construction
- Stair building

If you had four children and could selfishly choose their careers to serve your interests, you'd probably want one doctor, one lawyer, one auto mechanic, and one carpenter. Carpenters make up the largest building trade and are arguably the most versatile construction professionals. This is because their skill lies in knowing how to build stuff.

An experienced, all-around carpenter can essentially build a house from the ground up (or from the foundation up). He can frame and sheath the structure; install exterior siding and trim; hang doors, windows, and cabinets; build stairs; add shelving; and trim out the home's interior. Many carpenters will also hang drywall (but are not necessarily expert finishers), lay tile, install wood flooring, build decks... you get the idea.

That said, not all carpenters can do all things, or even want to. In the trades, there are two specialized groups of carpenters: trim carpenters and framing carpenters. Trim carpenters specialize in interior finish work—baseboard and crown molding, paneling, ceiling treatments, shelving and built-ins, custom cabinets and storage units, plus windows, doors, and their moldings. Framing carpenters, or framers, assemble the structural skeleton of a house, starting at the concrete foundation and finishing with the roof decking. They also sheath the exterior walls and build out the interior structural elements that define the home's layout.

Unlike trimwork, framing can't be seen in the finished product. As a result, the importance of quality in framing often is underestimated. But if the frame is poor, every aspect of the finish work that follows will suffer. Cabinets won't fit, doors and windows won't open properly, and your drywall is likely to crack and buckle more than it should (although you can be sure it will crack some, no matter how good the framing is). If you hire a framer, make sure he has a good reputation and that he uses quality, dry lumber for the job (see next page).

A third group of carpenters includes, by default, everyone else. Most of these pros are more or less *all-purpose* carpenters who take on a variety of jobs and may be hired to complete any aspect of carpentry and the related finish work. Some carpenters like to build custom homes or additions by themselves or perhaps with a few helpers. They may work with a general contractor or manage the project themselves, hiring subcontractors (like plumbers and electricians) as needed. This type of carpenter may call himself a builder. If you can find a good carpenter like this, it's probably the best way to go, since the guy in charge is also the guy doing most of the work, and he's likely to place a lot of personal stock in the finished product.

Which Type of Carpenter Should I Hire?

It depends on your project. Framers are good at framing. If your architect has designed a multi-pitched roof with dormers and a turret (in other words, a nightmarish framing job), you'll probably want an experienced framing specialist who can calculate and cut all of the funky angles. Framers are also very fast, since that's all they do. Trim carpenters are all about the fine details and know lots of tricks for making molding lie right and making corners look pretty. They're the appropriate choice for fine interior work, such as paneling a library or finishing staircases (some carpenters specialize in stair building).

For the wide range of other jobs—from constructing a garden shed to tearing out a wall between rooms to adding a garage—your best candidate will likely be an all-purpose carpenter who has a lot of experience with remodeling. In any case, the primary question to ask is whether a carpenter has a background of doing projects like yours.

People Who Know of Good Carpenters

Good carpenters are well-liked people on a job site because their quality product makes everyone else's work a little easier. Carpenters also have to deal with lots of other contractors and demonstrate their personal skills by how well they get along. General contractors rely on dependable carpenters as their right-hand men (or women), so they can be a good source of names for carpenters. Professionals who do finish work, like cabinet installers, drywallers, and trim carpenters, know which framers are good and which should be sent on a slow boat to hell (to use the finishers' sentiments). Homeowners who have hired carpenters, for custom work in particular, will tell you (or preferably show you) when they've had a good experience.

The Proof Is in the Plumbness

For a large project, you should interview and obtain bids from three or more qualified carpenters, as well as run background checks (see Chapter 1), before making a hiring decision. But more important than the usual screening is your inspection of a carpenter's work. Get some references of recent jobs similar to yours, then call the former clients and ask to see the work in person. Are the trim joints clean? Do things appear to be plumb and level? Is the fastening consistent and inconspicuous? Are there any unsightly gaps?

A great test of a carpenter's skill and attention to detail is to see how he's solved difficult construction problems. Plan drawings provide only so much detail, and carpenters inevitably run into things that work on paper but don't pan out in real life—surfaces that won't meet up, stair railings that take a funny turn, or window trim that has to be modified because it's too close to a corner. Carpenters routinely must rely on their judgment and skills to solve these design problems. You can find them in any house, if you look closely.

Check Your Materials

When negotiating a project with your carpenter, thoroughly discuss the proposed materials. For framing (including deck building), find out what grades of lumber will be used (or select it yourself), where the carpenter plans to buy it, and how much he needs to do the job. This is important because not all lumber is of equal quality. Even the pine or fir studs and joists that you'll never see when the job is done can vary significantly in quality and strength. Lumber must be straight for a good finished product and to minimize problems in the future. Construction lumber and decking carries a stamp indicating its species and grade, so you can easily confirm that your carpenter is using the right stuff. For finish work, have the carpenter supply samples of moldings and other trim details.

Licenses & Insurance?

Carpenters are required to carry a license in some states. All should have full liability insurance, plus workers' compensation for any employees on the job.

☎ In the Phone Book

Carpenters.

CARPET INSTALLER

For Help With:

■   Installing new carpets

No matter how much you paid for your new carpet, a quality installation is the key to an attractive, problem-free floor. Proper installation not only makes carpet look good, it helps it wear better and prevents damage to vulnerable areas, like seams and edges. Many carpet dealers have their own installers who are ready to deliver and install your new carpet in one go. Whether you use an in-house installer or find your own, the information here will help you ensure the job is done right.

Questions to Ask Carpet Installers

1. What services are included with the installation estimate?
2. Are there extra charges for moving furniture or removal and disposal of the old carpet and pad?
3. What am I (the homeowner) responsible for regarding the installation?
4. If the carpet will be glued down, what type of adhesive will be used? Is it rated for low VOC emissions? (Note: Glue is used occasionally in specific situations, such as over concrete and other hard-surface subfloors).
5. How will you guarantee your installation?

The industry standard for carpet and rug installation is set by the Carpet & Rug Institute (CRI). For those who are interested in the technical side of laying carpet, CRI's website (www.carpet-rug.org) posts their *Standard for Installation of Residential Carpet, CRI 105*, a scintillating read for all ages, and also a good reference for assessing the quality of your own carpet installation.

As always, check the installer's references, and get the entire job in writing before proceeding with the work. Many carpet installers also install other types of flooring. If you're laying more than carpet, see what kind of deal you can get by using the same installers for both materials.

Preparing for New Carpet Installation

If you're not using an installer who works for your carpet dealer, it's a good idea to check with the carpet manufacturer for installation recommendations or any special instructions.

After the old carpet and pad are removed, vacuum the subfloor thoroughly (or make sure your installers do it) before the new stuff goes down. And always, always use new, high quality pad underneath the new carpet. Never reuse the old stuff.

If you have a standard wood subfloor, replacing your carpet is the perfect opportunity to take care of those squeaks that have been bugging you for years. Make sure to discuss this with your installer, so he'll give you a chance to screw down squeaky subflooring after the old carpet is removed.

People remodeling their homes often ask, Which comes first, the walls or the carpet? That is, whether to finish the painting and trim before or after laying new carpet. And the answer is: walls and ceilings first, then carpet. Finishing the walls first means that you'll probably have to touch up a few spots where the carpet installers accidentally marked the wall, but that's no big deal. If you lay the carpet first in the hopes of keeping your newly painted walls pristine, you have the problem of protecting the carpet throughout all of the subsequent work. And spilled paint on carpet is a lot worse than marks on a wall. Also, carpet is typically tucked under baseboard, so that must be in place first.

Finally, discuss the placement of seams with your carpet installer before he starts the job. Seams should be used as little as possible and should run the length of an area. They should run parallel to main traffic routes and door openings, and should be positioned so that natural light does shine across them. Don't expect seams to be invisible, but they should be properly sealed and glued, and the pile on the mating pieces must face the same direction.

When to Call Back Your Installer

New carpet that buckles or wrinkles may indicate improper installation but can also be caused by humidity, furniture moving, or an unsuitable pad. In any case, the carpet needs to be re-stretched by a professional using power stretching equipment. Seams coming apart or fraying along the edges results from a failed bond or edges that weren't sealed properly. These must be repaired by a professional.

Normal Conditions of New Carpet

- Shedding of random loose fibers
- "Sprouting"—when an isolated area stands a little taller than the surrounding fibers (with certain types of carpet, you can simply trim the ends of the tall fibers, but check with the manufacturer first)
- Color changes or a shading effect caused by variation in the pile orientation, a perfectly normal occurrence

Licenses & Insurance?

Carpet installers should be fully covered for liability.

☎ In the Phone Book

Carpet & Rug Installers, Carpet & Rug Dealers.

CARPET & RUG CLEANER

For Help With:

- In-home carpet cleaning
- Rug cleaning (pickup & in-home service)
- Carpet & rug protective treatments
- Carpet & rug repair & restoration
- Drapery & upholstery cleaning

The Carpet & Rug Institute recommends that you vacuum your carpet at least twice a week. If you think you'll fall short of 104 vacuum days this year, don't worry; you're not alone. But it might be time to get the old shag professionally cleaned. Even with carpet cleaning equipment readily available for rent at the local supermarket, most people agree that a professional cleaning is well worth the money. There are plenty of good cleaning companies, too. Just make sure to avoid the bad ones.

Finding a Good Cleaning Company

An unqualified recommendation from someone you trust is the best way to learn of a cleaning service and will save you the trouble of conducting a search. But if all your friends, relatives, and neighbors have hardwood floors or really dirty carpets, make some calls to well-established local companies and ask about their process. Better companies want to learn about your carpet—as well as inspect and measure it in person—before recommending a cleaning method and giving you a firm price quote.

Find out how long each company has been in business and what type of training or certification their technicians have. The Institute of Inspection, Cleaning & Restoration Certification (IICRC; www.iicrc.org) is one of the leading professional organizations that offers certification programs and continuing education for carpet and rug cleaners. Also make sure you can get the proposed services and costs in writing before any work begins.

Be wary of companies who advertise door-to-door or cold-call you just as you're sitting down to dinner. Low-ball quotes over the phone should also be considered a red flag, along with other pricing scams (see below).

Pricing for Cleaning

As a rule of thumb, a good cleaning company should come to your house and measure the total area to be cleaned, look for tough stains and other problems, then recommend a cleaning process and discuss any extras (normal stains and dirty spots shouldn't be extra). Their basic price should be based on a square-foot calculation. By contrast, when companies quote "by the room" rates, they can't possibly account for the actual sizes of the rooms. Chances are, they'll try to make it up with extras not previously mentioned.

A lot of rummies entice customers with low-ball quotes then push hard for "optional" extras when they show up at your home for the cleaning appointment. A plain discussion of the desired services and a written agreement up front eliminates this kind of annoying sales tactic. A company that balks at doing it this way probably wouldn't perform quality work anyway, so keep looking. Often companies advertise "FREE!" furniture moving, pre-treatment, and stain removal. This is fine, but it's actually quite standard, and you shouldn't have to pay extra for these services.

Many carpet and rug cleaners also clean upholstery and drapes and will probably offer you a good deal if you opt for these services along with a carpet or rug job, especially if the cleaning is done in your home. Again, make sure to get a complete list of services and final pricing in writing before proceeding with the work.

Beware the Warranty Voiders

While a "voider" may sound like something out of a bad sci-fi movie, or a made-up word (which it is), it's here to remind you to call your carpet's manufacturer before agreeing to have any special treatments applied. Stain-proofers, anti-static solutions, and other treatments may just end up warranty-proofing your carpet. Always check first.

What's Different about Rugs

In terms of quality and value, rugs comprise a much broader range than factory-made carpeting. That's why many rug cleaners and restorers offer appraisal and consultation services. If your rug is more practical than valuable, you can probably go with any service and cleaning process that will get the job done. The more valuable the rug, the more diligent you should research cleaning processes and qualified cleaners, as well as restoration services if your rug needs repairs or special attention. The retailer who sold you the rug should be a good source of names for qualified local companies.

Unlike carpets, rugs are typically cleaned at the company's facility. Ask prospective cleaners about pickup and delivery charges and minimum rates for certain services. Common methods of rug cleaning include soap washing, for durable, less-expensive rugs; luster cleaning, a gentler approach than soap washing, using chemical solutions; and hand washing, the gentlest approach, recommended for fine or fragile rugs. Discuss your rug and cleaning options with a few different companies before choosing.

Licenses & Insurance?

A reputable cleaning service will be insured for damage liability—it's a good idea to make sure.

☎ In the Phone Book

Carpet & Rug Cleaning & Restoration.

CEILING CLEANER

For Help With:

- Cleaning:
  - Textured drywall ceilings
  - Acoustical ceiling tiles
  - Plaster ceilings
  - Walls

Professional ceiling cleaners remove dust, grime, grease, smoke, odors, and other contaminants from many types of ceilings and walls. The cleaning process typically involves a non-toxic chemical solution applied with a sprayer. Within minutes, the solution breaks down the fatty (yes, fatty) film that holds dirt and dust on the ceiling's surface, and the particles essentially disappear, at least to your eye. Wiping or rinsing the surface usually is not necessary. The same solution is used to clean walls, which may be wiped down to remove the solution.

Heavily textured ceilings are difficult to clean by hand and are generally too fragile for scrubbing. Acoustical "popcorn" texture—the kind that looks like a snazzy coating of cottage cheese—often is not painted and drops its little curds whenever it's touched. If you have a dirty popcorn ceiling, find a cleaning service that has experience with this type of texture.

Note: Some ceiling textures may contain asbestos, particularly in homes built before the 1980s. This is particularly true of textures that shimmer to the eye—this shininess is achieved through the addition of vermiculite, a mineral substance that sometimes contains asbestos. If your texture material is suspect, and especially if there has been water damage, consider having the material tested by an asbestos consultant (page 48) before having the ceiling cleaned.

Other surfaces that resist conventional cleaning are hand-textured plaster ceilings and acoustical tiles, such as you might have in a finished basement or utility room. The "touchless" cleaning process professionals use is quite effective on these surfaces. In fact, cleaning acoustical ceilings in commercial applications is the bread and butter of most cleaning companies.

Professional cleaning is a cost-effective alternative to painting a ceiling or replacing tiles. If you do plan to paint a very dirty ceiling, you might have the cleaning process done to remove grease and smoke that can bleed through paint—just make sure your cleaner's solution won't affect the paint's ability to stick.

Licenses & Insurance?

Any cleaning service you consider should be insured for liability.

☎ In the Phone Book

Ceiling Cleaning, Ceiling Contractors.

CHIMNEY SWEEP

For Help With:

- Cleaning & inspection of:
  - Wood-burning fireplaces & flues
  - Flues & vents for oil-burning appliances
  - Dryer vents
  - Gas appliance ventilation systems

She's clean as a whistle, Mum! Despite the popular characterization, not all chimney sweeps dance on rooftops and hail from working-class London. Many, though, actually do wear black overcoats and even top hats, perhaps in homage to their English forebears. Whatever their personal shtick, the primary function of a professional chimney sweep is to inspect and clean flues for wood-burning fireplaces. But what they really do is prevent house fires.

Unlike gas, wood is not a clean-burning fuel. Its smoke leaves deposits of creosote that gunk up your fireplace flue (see Home School, on page 66, for definitions of terms). Eventually the buildup of creosote, which is flammable, becomes so great that it ignites–completely ruining your pleasant evening by the fire, to say the least. Chimney sweeps use special brushes to scrub the inside of your flue, while a vacuum placed over the fireplace opening captures all the debris. See why you don't want to do this job yourself?

Chimneys and flues are also popular hideouts for animals like raccoons and birds, who build nests that restrict airflow and are highly flammable (the nests, not the birds). Having a chimney sweep come out prior to burning season is the best way to ensure that nothing is blocking the flue before you start your first fire.

More than a Good Sweeping

An experienced chimney sweep is more than a thorough flue scrubber. He's also a fire safety expert. Creosote buildup is just one of many conditions that can make a fireplace unsafe. Cracks or chunks of missing mortar in the chimney, flue, or firebox create a breach in the thermal envelope designed to contain the extreme heat of the fire and keep it from surrounding combustibles, such as your house. Along with the cleaning, a chimney sweep should inspect: the chimney for damage or deterioration, the firebox for cracks and missing mortar, and the damper for proper operation. He should also warn you of any potential fire hazards, such as piles of newspaper stacked just outside the fireplace opening.

Most chimney sweeps can also replace dampers, install chimney caps and screens (spark arrestors), and make minor repairs to masonry. Some professionals can also install flue liners to get old, unsafe chimneys up and running again. As specialists at sprucing up large pipe-type things, chimney sweeps can clean your clothes dryer vent–another common cause of house fires–as well as vent systems for furnaces and hot water heaters, which can release carbon monoxide into the home when not functioning properly.

Finding a Qualified Chimney Sweep

Considering the specialized knowledge and technique required for quality chimney service, there's surprisingly little official regulation of the industry. Most states do not require licensure of chimney companies, although some municipalities do. The Chimney Safety Institute of America (CSIA; www.csia.org) offers a certification program and continuing education for professional chimney sweeps. Checking out companies with this certification is a good place to start. Also find out whether licensure is required in your area, and if so, make sure any company you consider carries a current license.

Other things to find out about prospective services:

- How many years have they been in business?
- Have there been any complaints filed against the company with the local Better Business Bureau, Chamber of Commerce, or consumer protection office? How were the complaints resolved?
- Are they insured?
- Will they supply references of recent clients whom you may call?

As a basic precaution, you can always set up an appointment for an inspection, then decide whether to proceed with a cleaning based on the professional's recommendation. Granted, most pros will probably say you need a cleaning. But if they recommend extensive repairs or extras, you should get a second opinion before deciding.

HOME SCHOOL

A few terms that are helpful to know when talking to chimney pros:

Chimney—generally refers to the entire structure that carries smoke (or exhaust from appliances) out of the home. The exterior masonry section that extends above the roof on traditional chimneys is called the *stack*. Modern homes commonly have wood-frame chimneys.

Flue—the fireproof clay or insulated metal liner that creates the smoke channel through the interior of the chimney. With masonry chimneys, severe damage or deterioration of the stack often indicates a damaged flue.

Firebox—the open cavity where the fire is built. Like the flue, the firebox must be completely intact and free of holes or cracks for safe burning.

Damper—the adjustable metal plate that permits air flow between the firebox and the flue. Otherwise known as the thing you curse when your living room is suddenly inundated with smoke.

How often should you clean your chimney? The National Fire Protection Association (NFPA; www.nfpa.org) recommends a professional inspection once a year, with cleanings performed as needed.

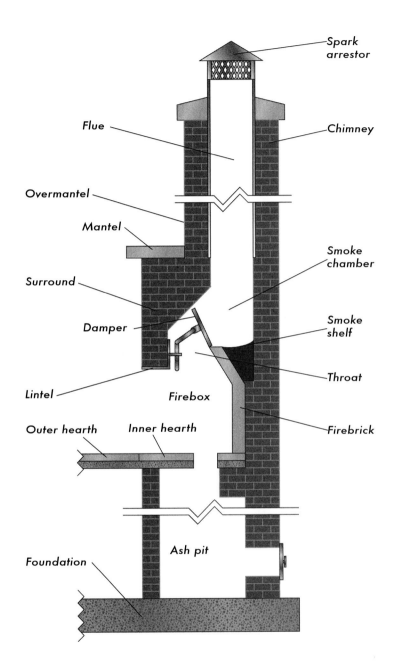

Spark arrestor
Flue
Chimney
Overmantel
Mantel
Smoke chamber
Surround
Damper
Smoke shelf
Lintel
Throat
Firebox
Outer hearth
Inner hearth
Firebrick
Foundation
Ash pit

Licenses & Insurance?

Some municipalities require licensure for chimney cleaning and inspection professionals. Insurance against liability is a must.

☎ In the Phone Book

Chimney Cleaning.

CLOSET DESIGNER (CUSTOM STORAGE SYSTEMS)

For Help With:

- Custom closet & storage systems—design, construction & installation

Let's face it, standard closets are poorly designed. For starters, they have a single hanger rod about 5½ feet above the floor, leaving lots of unused space below your shirts and jackets. But that was before someone (probably in Scandinavia) had the bright idea of hanging two rods, one high and one low, to yield twice the hanging space. This is the kind of thinking behind custom closet design.

Closet designers and custom storage companies are professionals who come to your house, measure your available closet space, look at all your stuff, then design an efficient system of rods, shelves, and drawers that makes the best use of your space. More importantly, the new system is designed around your daily routine, so the stuff you use the most is right up front and ready to go.

Once you approve their design, the closet pros send it to their fabrication team to have the system custom built. Here, "custom" may mean everything from assembling various prefabricated parts and components to creating made-to-order units similar to the operations of a custom cabinet shop. The system is then installed in your home, by appointment and usually taking only one day. And from then on, your life will be a picture of elegance and leisure, as you slip from the day's business suit and into a ball gown without ever having to search on your knees for a lost earring that fell into a dusty corner behind your husband's fishing waders. Pure, organized bliss.

Materials & Features

Getting to the promised land of storage solutions requires a few decisions on your part. Namely, what materials to use for your closet system and whether to treat yourself to a few bells and whistles. (If you already own a lot of bells or whistles, perhaps you can have a custom drawer or pull-out bin made for storing them.)

The basic materials used in closet systems are, in order of plain to fancy: vinyl-coated (or chrome) wire, melamine-covered particle board, veneered wood, and solid wood. You can add crown and base molding for a built-in look, or throw in some specialty knobs and fittings. Not surprisingly, closet designers have also come up with all sorts of clever internal systems, like nifty drawer dividers for tie storage, pull-out belt racks, and see-through plastic shoe cubbies.

Comparing Closet Companies

Start your search by looking through the phone book or online to find companies with showrooms in your area. A little browsing will give you an idea of what's available in terms of materials and design possibilities. Many companies offer free in-home consultations, including a design proposal and price estimate without any obligation on your part. A consultation is also a good way to evaluate a designer's ability.

DECISION FACTORS

1. *Cost*—Prices for similar systems can vary widely among companies. Getting a few quotes following consultations will help you compare your options.
2. *Materials & design possibilities*—Make sure your chosen company has the materials offerings and fabrication abilities to meet your closet dreams.
3. *Installation*—Not all closet companies have their own installers on staff. If they outsource the work, make sure the installers are sufficiently trained and insured.
4. *Warranties*—These can range from limited, one-year protection to transferable lifetime guarantees.
5. *Time*—How long before your new life of organization can begin?

Beyond the Closet

Closet designers can solve a lot more than your wardrobe problems. They'll create organization systems for kids' rooms, pantries, laundry rooms, garages, wine collections, work rooms, entertainment centers, home offices...you name it. Some companies also design and install wall beds (a.k.a. Murphy beds), perfect for visiting relatives and slapstick comedy routines.

Closet professionals design systems around the actual stuff you use every day. But they won't go through your mountains of accumulated possessions and tell you where to put everything. For that you need a professional organization consultant. Yes, they really do exist. They're in the phone book (and online) under Organizing Products & Services.

Licenses & Insurance?

Some closet companies are licensed. All should be insured for liability.

☎ In the Phone Book

Closets & Closet Accessories, Closet System Consulting & Installation.

COMPUTER TECHNICIAN

For Help With:

- New computer installation
- In-home network setup
- Repairs & troubleshooting
- Upgrades
- Data backup & recovery
- Security software & firewall installation
- Computer training
- Virus removal
- Computer equipment sales

When you work in an office and have a computer problem, you call the IT department. They begin by rapidly asking questions about what you did just before the problem occurred, to which you answer, "Yeah...Well, wait. Do I have one of those?" Then they hang up and come over and fix your machine while you chat with the nearest coworker.

As surly as they may be, it's too bad the folks in your IT department don't make house calls. So when it's your home computer that's on the fritz (a very pre-digital expression), you hire a computer technician, or "techie," to save you from your ignorance. Fortunately, along with the rise in the number and complexity of home computer systems, there is now a burgeoning industry of cutting-edge technicians who are also trained in, yes, customer service. This was unthinkable ten years ago, but then again, so was building your own website to share videos of your cats.

What a Techie Can Do for You

Home computer service is not just about getting your computer fixed when it breaks. It's also about optimizing your system (a very digital expression). A good techie can consult with you to discuss how computers are used in your household and how you can get the most from your system. For example, you may decide to link all of the home's computers through a server or wireless connections. This allows you to zip files from one computer to another to access a common printer or other device. But perhaps the best benefit of networked computers is that everyone in your household can use the Internet separately at the same time. The kids can access their personal websites and don't have to wait for grandma to make her Fantasy Yahtzee! picks for the week.

For computer beginners, professional techies give private tutorials to get you started on anything from email to word processing to editing digital photos and video. If you're not in the habit of regular housecleaning on your computer or backing up important files and software, your techie can do it for you, making your machine run more efficiently and safeguarding your data against a complete crash of the hard drive (it can happen). They can also install a new computer, bring you up to date with security software, load new programs and features, and set preferences tailored to your everyday computer tasks. They'll even clean the inside of your tower (the big plastic box that eats and spits out discs) or laptop to remove dust that can foul up the works.

In addition to house calls, many computer services offer help over the phone. They can also try to fix a problem over the Internet by commandeering your machine remotely from their offices. This is a little unsettling at first, but rest assured it all happens over a secure connection.

The Price of Computer Enlightenment

Compared to that sick feeling you get in your gut when your screen suddenly goes blank, paying for professional help is a pleasure. Actually, most services are quite reasonable and are advertised in a straightforward, itemized fashion. If a company's prices for services aren't explicit, ask for an explanation, or choose another service provider.

Most computer technicians and service companies charge by the job or by the hour. Often services are grouped into mini packages, such as "new computer setup" or "security and performance upgrade." Additional charges may include installation of software and any hardware (cables, devices, etc.) your computer needs to achieve your goals. Hourly rates for tutorials and consultation will vary but are easy to compare among different providers. Always ask whether you'll be charged for partial hours or only whole hours at a time.

Finding a Good Service

For experienced techies, the technical demands of helping the average home computer user are nothing. Where they distinguish themselves is in their customer service. You want a service provider who speaks in a language you can understand. No condescension, no questions that require NASA training to decipher.

It's easy to shop around online (unless your computer's down) or in the phone book for computer technicians. Referrals from someone you know are always good because you can ask about the techie's desk-side manner. When comparing services, look at pricing, guarantees, and hours of availability. Some are reachable 24 hours a day. Also find out about charges for follow-up help over the phone or online. You're bound to forget one or two critical steps in a procedure, and you'll want to be able to call for a quick answer without being billed for it.

Some techs specialize in either PC (IBM-based) or Macintosh (Apple) computers. Make sure your pro has experience with your platform (brand of computer).

Practice, Practice, Practice

A final note for those who plan to take a tutorial or learn a new procedure from a professional: Don't wait to apply what you've learned. As soon as your techie takes off in his nerdmobile, head straight back to the computer and run through every step several times. Everyone has difficulty remembering computer processes; repetition is your only hope. A good techie will make sure you know how to operate any new applications or equipment before leaving you to your own devices. But if you don't practice immediately, you've already wasted your money.

Licenses & Insurance?

Computer service companies and independent technicians should have adequate liability insurance to cover accidental damage to your computer equipment and related valuables.

☎ In the Phone Book

Computer Technicians

CONCRETE & CONCRETE CONTRACTOR

For Help With:

- New concrete construction
  - □ Driveways, walkways & curbs
  - □ Patio & porch slabs
  - □ Decorative concrete work
  - □ Basements
  - □ Garage slabs
  - □ Interior concrete floors
  - □ Footings & foundations
- Repair & refinishing of existing concrete structures
- Mud jacking
- Concrete cutting, demolition & removal
- Ready-mix concrete delivery

Concrete is integral to virtually all modern home construction. It's used to build foundations, basement slabs, driveways and paths, deck piers, patios, stoops, and even kitchen and bathroom countertops. Of course, we're talking about poured concrete, as opposed to concrete ("cinder") block or brick-like concrete pavers. Due to the broad applications of concrete, it's no surprise that contractors who work with it are plentiful in most towns. Finding them is no problem. The question is, what kind of concrete work do you need, and what type of pro is right for the job?

The Building Process

Understanding how new concrete structures are built will help you determine the specific services required for your project. With the exception of countertops, most concrete structures are built upon a carefully excavated area of ground topped with a layer of compacted gravel. Slabs, walkways, and other flatwork are meant to "float" on top of the ground, meaning they can shift up and down slightly as the ground below freezes and thaws throughout the year. Concrete foundations for large structures, such as houses and decks, must not move with the ground and therefore are built to extend down below the frost line—the depth to which the ground freezes in a given geographic area (anywhere from 18" to 4 feet and deeper).

So, Step 1 is the excavation and preparing the subbase for the concrete. Step 2 is building the forms—the "molds" that give the concrete structure its shape. Step 3 is installing metal reinforcement (as required by the local building code) for strengthening the concrete internally. Step 4 is the pour—filling the forms with wet concrete and smoothing and finishing the top surface. All of the work up to the middle of Step 4 is pretty standard and is governed by strict engineering requirements. It's in the finishing of concrete where the special skills and a professional's touch are most needed.

In addition to the basic process, you may have an existing concrete structure that must be removed and hauled away before Step 1. In the case of foundations, Step 4 must be followed by a waterproofing treatment appropriate for your area and application. Decorative effects, such as acid staining, are also done after the finished concrete dries, as is sealing of patios and garage slabs. If your contractor isn't taking care of these final treatments, make sure you get detailed advice about when to have them done and by whom. Finally, if you're looking for concrete repair work, you'll need a professional's assessment of the existing structure to confirm that it's stable enough to warrant the expense of repairs.

The pro, or pros, you hire depends on the contractor's range of services and on the needs of your project. For example, let's say that your driveway is so terrible that you can't bear to look at it anymore. You not only want a new slab, you want earth-tone concrete with a stamped finish so the whole driveway looks like adobe pavers (eat your hearts out, Joneses). Some concrete companies in your area may be able to take care of everything; others will have more experience with the demolition and excavation but may not have a crew that can handle the skilled finish work. First determine what you need done, then call around and discuss your goals with different companies. Compare the costs (and hassles) of hiring different contractors for different steps as opposed to going with one full-service outfit.

Concrete Applications & Terms

Here is a brief glossary to help you make sense of the advertisements and websites of concrete contractors:

Flatwork: Generally includes all flat-surface structures, such as driveways, walks, garage slabs, and patios. Sometimes the term is used to distinguish smooth-finished slabs (as in garage or basement floors) from rough-textured surfaces like driveways.

Stamped: A decorative finish treatment created by stamping wet concrete with special tools to mimic the look of tile, brick, or stone. Stamped surfaces may also be colored to enhance the illusion.

Staining: Applying an acid-based or other permanent chemical stain for decorative coloring of the concrete surface. Both flat and stamped slabs may be stained for a range of decorative effects.

Color: Pros use a variety of techniques to color poured concrete. Tint can be added to the wet mix for consistent, through-depth color. Powdered pigments may be applied at different stages of the finishing process for a weathered or aged appearance. On cured concrete, staining is the coloring technique of choice.

Overlay: Resurfacing of damaged—but structurally sound—concrete slabs with a thin layer of new wet concrete. Overlays start at about ¼" in thickness and can receive a decorative or standard finish.

Footing (or footer): A broad, flat curb of concrete used to support vertical structures, like foundation walls. *Piers* are round or square columns or pads of concrete for supporting deck posts or structural columns in a home.

Exposed aggregate: A concrete finish with small stones exposed at the surface.

Specialty structures may include: full-height boundary walls, low patio walls, retaining walls, and mower strips (bordering grassy areas).

Check with the Building Department

Many concrete jobs require building permits and inspections. Before calling any contractors, contact your local building department to find out what's required for your project. Aside from having an expert (architect, engineer, or builder) on-site, inspections are the best way to ensure the job is done properly.

What Is Concrete?

Before you say, "Who cares? That's what I'm paying professionals to know," be aware that familiarity with the very basics of concrete may help you spot trouble with your project. For example, you don't want your pour to commence during a rainstorm or a blizzard, and you always want the finished work to dry as slowly as possible for maximum strength. You also don't want any inappropriate "filler" ending up in the pour, such as scrap wood, lunchboxes, or neighbors in trouble with the local crime syndicate. Impurities, as it were, can seriously undermine the strength of the structure.

Concrete is made up of Portland cement, sand, gravel (aggregates), and water. Other additives may be included for various desired properties. Changing the proportions of ingredients in the mix yields different levels of strength and other characteristics, such as workability. Your concrete contractor is responsible for ordering the proper mix. However, if your project is extensive, or if you're building a foundation for a new home or addition, it's wise to have an architect, engineer, or experienced builder approve the concrete mix specifications and oversee the form building and the concrete pour.

The quality of a concrete pour can be significantly impacted by the weather. Ideally, your pour will take place under overcast skies and a temperature in the mid-50s. When conditions are less favorable, as they usually are, it takes an experienced professional to know what concrete mix to order and how to finish the wet concrete for a perfect final product. The upshot of all this is that your contractor must be responsible for the quality of the work.

Common problems with improperly finished concrete include flaking and chipping on the surface, and cracking in areas other than the control joints the grooves cut into large slabs and along walkways. (Cracking in concrete slabs is normal; control joints are added to direct where cracks occur.) Surface problems may appear after the first winter, when the freeze-thaw cycles have done their worst. Make sure your contractor's guarantee extends well beyond the next cold season.

Hip tip: If you want to sound informed, don't use the terms *concrete* and *cement* interchangeably. Cement is merely an ingredient in *concrete*, while concrete is the complete building material. Calling concrete "cement" is like calling cake "egg." And you'd never do that, at least not in mixed company.

Finding a Good Concrete Contractor

If you know anyone in the building trades, particularly general contractors, home builders, carpenters, and the like, ask them if they can recommend good concrete people. Just as cabinet installers or drywallers can tell you if the framing carpenter who preceded them is good or bad, a framing carpenter knows if a foundation builder does quality work.

After gathering a few names or finding a few good candidates through phone interviews, check the contractors' references. Ask the usual questions about dependability, timeliness, professionalism, and customer service, then check out examples of the contractors' work. This is especially important if your project will include a decorative finish.

Get bids from several prospective companies. Bid should be derived only from on-site consultations, not over-the-phone quotes. As always, make sure everything is in writing before starting the job. In the end, your decision will be based primarily on the following factors:

1. The contractor's experience and reputation for working on your specific type of project
2. Price—as in value, not just lowest cost
3. Quality of work and reports from references
4. How well the contractor guarantees his work

MUD JACKING: REPAIR FOR SINKING SLABS

When a sound concrete slab decides to make its own drop in elevation, professional mud jacking is the answer. Mud jacking, or slab jacking, is a simple process of pumping a special concrete mixture underneath a slab to bring it back up to level. A series of 1½" holes are drilled down through the slab, and the concrete is pumped into the holes under pressure. As the area beneath the slab fills with concrete, the slab rises. The holes in the slab are then filled with a non-shrinking grout to hide the repair.

Sinking slabs are often the result of poorly compacted soils or subbase underneath the slab and are sometimes caused by deeper, unavoidable soil erosion. Mud jacking is an economical alternative to replacing sunken slabs and often runs about half the cost of replacement. Mud jacking pros can repair:

- Patios, drives, and walkways
- Entry steps and stoops
- Interior concrete floors
- Basement and garage slabs
- Pool decks
- Foundation footings

You can find mud jacking professionals in the phone book, under Mud Jacking Contractors or Concrete Repair & Restoration. Contact a few different companies to obtain free estimates, and choose a company based on experience, reputation, price, and their knowledge of your situation.

ORDERING READY-MIX CONCRETE

If you're planning to do your own concrete work and the job calls for one cubic yard or more, you'll probably want to have a batch of ready-mix (or ready mixed) concrete delivered by truck rather than mixing it yourself. Using ready-mix guarantees you'll get the right mixture (or at least the mixture you specified) and ensures consistency and a much quicker pour. But first you'll need to determine the type and quantity of concrete to order.

Personnel at ready-mix companies are usually willing to consult with amateurs and recommend a mixture for their specific application. For your part, be ready to describe your project in detail. Here are the basic specifications outlined in a ready-mix order:

- Maximum size of coarse aggregate.
- Slump—the consistency or stiffness of the mix, which translates to workability in the wet mixture and to strength in cured concrete. The lower the slump number, the stiffer and stronger the mix.
- Entrained air—a concrete additive used when concrete will be poured or cured in freezing temperatures. Air-entrained concrete behaves differently than standard mix, so you'll need a finisher who knows what to look for.
- Strength, rated in psi. A minimum of 3,500 to 4,000 psi is recommended for standard slab construction.
- Additives, such as color, fiber reinforcement, and specific admixtures for desired properties.

Regarding quantity: Most concrete suppliers have a delivery minimum of one yard or more. Order 4% to 10% more concrete than your calculated amount to account for spillage, shrinkage (during curing), and settling into low spots in the excavation. However, be aware that any excess concrete must be dumped somewhere on your site, or the company may charge you to carry off the excess and wash out their truck off-site. Other extra charges may include a short-batch fee (for orders under a minimum size), Saturday delivery, and waiting time if the truck has to sit while you get ready.

Check out three or four concrete companies with batch plants close to your home. The closer they are, the more time you'll have as insurance against problems during the pour. Conduct a background check on your top choice to make sure they have a good reputation with local builders and homeowners. Schedule a delivery day and get an approximate time for the arrival of the truck.

The day before the scheduled delivery, call the supplier to confirm the delivery details, including the quantity ordered. When the truck arrives at your site, read the delivery receipt to make sure the batch was mixed no more than 90 minutes prior to the arrival of the truck (actually, the concrete should be out of the truck within 90 minutes of mixing, or 300 revolutions of the barrel, whichever comes first). It's imperative that the truck has easy access to the site without driving over curbs, the neighbor's yard, or your septic tank. Concrete trucks weigh about 30 tons and can cause a lot of damage down below.

For more information on concrete and concrete applications, visit the websites of the National Ready Mixed Concrete Association (www.nrmca.org), the Portland Cement Association (www.cement.org), and the American Concrete Institute (www.aci-int.org).

Licenses & Insurance?

Concrete contractors of all kinds must be licensed in most areas—check with your municipality about licensing requirements. All contractors should be fully insured.

☎ In the Phone Book

Concrete Contractors; Concrete–Break, Cut, Saw; Concrete–Decorative; Concrete Repair & Restoration; Mud Jacking Contractors; Concrete–Ready Mixed.

DECK MAINTENANCE & NEW CONSTRUCTION

For Help With:

- Cleaning, refinishing & repairing wood decks
- Design & construction of new decks

A deck is a great feature on any home, but like a lawn or hot tub, it is high-maintenance. While a house might get repainted every 10 to 15 years, a wood deck should be refinished every two years, on average. The best approach to keeping up with all the upkeep is to hire a good refinisher and stick to a regular maintenance schedule. In between finishing treatments, cleaning the deck with a hose and spray nozzle will ensure a long life for your precious perch.

If your old deck is too far gone to warrant refinishing, or you want a new deck where there is none, your search is probably two-fold: finding one pro to build the deck (see Building a New Deck, on page 80) and another pro to finish it—soon after construction and, of course, every two years or so down the road.

The Basic Refinishing Process

Every deck maintenance service has its own technique, but most follow these general steps:

1. Inspect for damaged boards and other problems, like rot or overgrown foliage that may be harming your deck.
2. Clean the decking and railings. A thorough cleaning is absolutely necessary to remove built-up dirt and grime and to prepare the wood to accept the new finish. Many pros use a combination of cleaning solution and power-washing (see next page).
3. Brighten—redwood and cedar decks only. A brightening agent, typically oxalic acid, is often used to remove dark streaks caused by fasteners and to bring up the wood's natural coloring. Sometimes a non-chlorine bleach is used for the same purposes.
4. Finish the decking and railings. The new stain/protectant is often applied with a pump sprayer then spread with an applicator pad, rag, or brush. Spreading and blending by hand is essential for a consistent finish and to prevent pools of stain that can leave an unsightly sheen. The understructure (posts, beams, and joists) of a deck typically is not included in a finishing job; be sure to ask if you'd like to have this done.

If your deck suffers from severe neglect, or if you want to remove the old finish completely and start afresh, the pro may suggest sanding to bring the decking surfaces down to bare wood. This must be done judiciously, because a belt sander removes a lot of material quickly and can be a very destructive tool in the hands of a novice. Sanding also brings fastener heads closer to the surface, and they must be driven down again, as needed.

A less invasive approach for getting rid of the old finish is to apply a chemical stripper. This will remove most of the old stuff and usually lighten the color of the wood, but it won't bring the wood back to its natural state, as sanding does.

The Great Pressure Washing Debate

You may not be aware of the fiery discussion raging in the home improvement industry over the use of pressure washers on wood. The issue is this: Many pros use pressure washers (basically a garden hose hooked up to a gas-powered pressurizer) to clean decks, siding, and other exterior woodwork prior to finishing. Opponents of this practice say that pressurized water, in the case of decks, gouges the wood and leaves it more vulnerable to decay.

Well, it doesn't take a physicist to predict that 3,000 psi of water applied directly to a material that you can easily mark with your fingernail may cause some damage. Pressure washers damage wood every day, but usually when they're operated by a novice. In the hands of a careful, experienced professional, a pressure washer is a very effective tool for cleaning a deck, causing little or no visible damage. However, if you're opposed to pressure washing, find a pro who is willing to use an appropriate cleaner and a scrub brush; merely applying a cleaning agent without scrubbing won't do the job.

A Good Refinisher Isn't Too Hard to Find

What you're looking for in a deck maintenance pro is pretty straightforward: someone who does a thorough job, who is careful and respectful of your property, and who uses a quality finish. Like window washers and house cleaners, deck finishers rely on repeat business from loyal customers. It's always in their best interest to make you happy. A reputable pro will also give you honest recommendations about when and how often to refinish your deck.

As for finding the right pro, personal referrals are the way to go. Lots of people have decks, and all those decks need to periodically be refinished. Just ask around. After you get some names, call each candidate to learn about their:

- Preparation and finishing methods
- Cleaning solutions and other agents
- Preferred brand and type of stain/finish material (see below)
- Years of experience working in your area
- Insurance coverage
- Rain policy (if rain halts their progress, how soon will they resume work?)
- Guarantees

Have your top few picks come over to see your deck and give you a firm price quote before you make a decision.

The Finish Is Critical

A deck finish serves three purposes: sealing the wood to repel water, preserving the wood with mildewcide and other chemicals to prevent rot, and blocking UV rays that cause discoloration and slow, steady damage. Most deck pros supply their own finish materials. Again, it's in their interest to use a product that performs well in the local climate, in addition to improving the deck's look. But that doesn't mean you can't check out their preferred finish (by researching through Consumer Reports and the like) or even request a finish of your own choosing. In any case, you want to be sure a high quality product is used (after all, you're paying for it) and make sure you like the color and overall affect it has on your deck.

The most commonly used deck finish is a semi-transparent stain, which contains some pigment to provide UV protection but is only semi-opaque, so the wood grain shows through. The other basic types of finishes are clear sealers and solid stains. Clear sealers have no pigment, so they're the best for showing off new wood. However, they are seldom recommended because they offer little or no UV protection. Solid stains are loaded with pigment and offer the best UV protection. Even though they look like paint, solid stains are okay for decks because they adhere well to the wood (paint doesn't), while also completely hiding the wood grain. The choice is up to you and your finisher.

Deck Repairs

Often, the surface materials (planks) of a deck wear out before the structural framing below. In this case, new decking and perhaps a new top rail make the whole deck look like new. Older decks usually need a few joists replaced or bolstered with "sisters"– new joists sandwiched on one or both sides of the old member. They may also need to have post connections reinforced, and balusters and trim refastened. If your deck requires extensive work, shop for a repair professional following the process described below for finding a deck builder.

Building a New Deck

Adding a new deck can be a fun process of exploring the wide range of materials and design options and coming up with a plan that suits your family and your house. Perhaps the biggest decision these days–aside from hiring a builder–is choosing the decking and railing materials. Not long ago, this was a no-brainer: you used wood, usually pressure-treated lumber for the understructure; and redwood, cedar, or more pressure-treated lumber for the decking and railing.

Most new decks are still built with wood, but recent years have seen a steady rise in the popularity of alternative materials designed for durability and low maintenance. Where they've tended to fall short of wood is in appearance, but that's changing, too. What this means is that, unless you have your heart set on a traditional wood deck, the first step in finding a pro to build your deck is to decide what kind of decking and railing you'd like to have. This is because many deck builders specialize in a limited range of materials and won't build with just anything. Also, some alternative decking products must be installed by a manufacturer-certified installer, which could narrow your search considerably.

A word of advice: Before settling on an alternative decking product, make sure you see it in a real-life installation. Materials that look great on a pristine sample aren't always so pretty when they're screwed in place. Seeing a completed (and preferably weathered) deck is the only way to know what the material will really look like.

Professional Deck Services

The standard process of building a new deck starts with a free consultation at your home. The builder takes measurements and listens as you share ideas, discuss options, and talk about how you intend to use your new deck. Then the builder goes back to her office and draws up a couple of plans for your review. If you like one of the plans, the builder can run the numbers and give you a firm price quote. Then you sign a contract, which should detail the work to be done (including the square footage of the completed deck), all materials, the start date, and a payment schedule. Always sign a contract before proceeding with construction.

This initial part of the process will vary among deck companies and independent builders. Some may require a deposit or design fee to draw up plans; others may do most of the planning in their heads and work out the finer details as they go. Just make sure the important elements are covered in the contract. It's common for deck builders to ask for 10% to 15% of the payment up front. Anything over 15% may indicate that the builder doesn't have a good line of credit with local suppliers.

Things to Check Out

Obtain estimates from a few experienced local builders who specialize in the type of deck you want, then check their references. Look at some recent projects they've done for other clients to get a sense of their handiwork. Also make sure the contractor meets all licensing requirements for your area and is fully insured for liability.

Contact your local building department to find out whether a permit is required for your project. Elevated decks need permits in most areas and are subject to strict code specifications governing railings, stairs, and other features. Your deck builder should obtain all necessary permits for the job and make sure inspections are scheduled as needed.

If you're building a wood deck, ask your builder early in the process about when you should have the deck finished. This will give you plenty of time to find and schedule a finisher.

Wood Decking Resources

The following organizations are good sources of information on building and maintaining wood decking:

Redwood: California Redwood Association
www.calredwood.org

Cedar: Western Red Cedar Lumber Association
www.wrcla.org

Pressure-treated pine: Southern Pine Council
www.southernpine.com.

Licenses & Insurance?

As professional contractors whose work usually requires a building permit, deck builders must be licensed in many municipalities. Liability insurance is a must for all finishers and builders, as is workers' compensation for those with employees on the job.

☎ In the Phone Book

Decks–Construction & Maintenance.

DOOR REPLACEMENT

SEE: WINDOW & DOOR REPLACEMENT

DRYWALLER (DRYWALL INSTALLATION & REPAIR)

For Help With:

- Drywall installation & finishing
- Drywall patch & repair work
- Wall & ceiling texture
- Light-gauge steel framing
- Acoustical (suspended grid) ceiling installation

Home improvement sources love to talk about drywalling as an easy, money-saving, do-it-yourself project. Sure, why not? It doesn't take fancy tools or expensive materials. Go for it. And while you're at it, why not give yourself a haircut? You've got scissors and a mirror...

In reality, drywall work that *looks good* requires skill and lots and lots of practice. It's not a job you can hire out to just anyone—your "pretty handy" brother-in-law, for example (even if he does cut his own hair).

Professional drywallers primarily do three things: hang, tape, and texture. That is, they install new sheets of drywall, tape and finish all of the corners and seams between the sheets, and texture the entire surface for a decorative finish. On the side, many drywallers also install new acoustical grid ceilings, or "drop" ceilings, and most are happy to make house calls for any kind of repair. Pros who do a lot of commercial work may also be skilled framers, typically working with light-gauge steel studs. In residential work, steel framing may be used for custom drywall structures such as curved soffits.

Drywall Materials

Drywall is pretty basic stuff. When it comes to finishing materials, pros use whichever products they like best. But when it comes to drywall panels and fasteners, you'll want to make sure the right stuff is used for each application. Walls and ceilings typically carry ½" thick standard drywall panels. In the old days (and when contemporary builders are being cheap) ceilings were often covered with ⅜"-thick material. But these thinner panels tend to sag over time, especially when the ceiling framing is spaced more than 16" apart.

For new drywall installation, you want ½" panels when ceiling framing is 16" apart, and ⅝" panels when it's 24" apart (or you can use special ½" *ceiling* panels, which are stiffer than regular sheets; they're also recommended for heavy, wet ceiling textures such as hand-troweled finishes). For localized repairs, the drywall used for patching must match the surrounding panels.

Other situations call for specialty drywall products. Attached garages get ⅝"
fire-rated panels on the ceiling and the wall adjacent to the house. Upon request,
⅝" panels may also be used for improved soundproofing in walls and ceilings.
Bathrooms and other damp areas get water-resistant *greenboard* or *blueboard* drywall
panels. However, any wet area that will receive tile must have cementboard or another
approved tile backer. Water-resistant drywall is no longer acceptable for backing tile in
wet areas.

These days, most drywallers install panels with screws. Some still prefer nails, and
some use drywall adhesive as the primary, or as a secondary, fastener. Ceiling panels
should not be installed with nails only; they just don't hold well enough over time.

As for tape and corner bead—the metal or plastic angle that gives wall corners their
hard, clean edge—pros use their preferred products. However, you should discuss the
style of corner bead. Standard bead creates a sharp, square corner, while *bullnose* bead
is rounded. If you use bullnose, be aware that all wall trim (baseboard, crown molding,
etc.) won't have a clean 90° miter joint at the corner. Rather, it requires three pieces of
trim coming together to approximate the shape of the corner, and the resulting small
gaps are unavoidable.

Repairing Drywall

Common drywall repairs include patching holes, reinforcing and refinishing cracks
(tape should be used on large cracks), dealing with popped nails, replacing water-
damaged or rotted drywall, and, of course, filling in the classic doorknob-shaped
depressions that mysteriously appear in every kid's bedroom. Drooping ceiling panels
can sometimes be corrected with refastening, but they won't likely be perfectly flat
again. Any good drywaller can easily handle these repairs. However, if the repairs are
extensive, you should get two or three estimates before contracting the work.

If you've finally decided to do something about that old wallpaper that makes
everyone nauseous, first find a drywaller who is skilled at skim-coating, then think
about removing the wallpaper. Short of replacing the drywall, a good skim coat is
the only way to make an old, ratty wall surface look pristine again. A skim coat is
a thin layer of drywall mud applied with a large drywall knife over the entire area.
This requires an experienced finisher; not all pros can do it well. To be on the safe
side, consult with your finisher before removing the wallpaper, which must be done
properly to make skim-coating feasible.

How to Find a Good Drywaller

The proof is in the mudding. While hanging drywall takes strength and proper technique, it's in the finishing that professionals prove their worth. The best way to check out a drywaller is to ask for references and to see his work. Are the wall and ceiling surfaces smooth and flat? (Shining a bright light across a surface is a sure-fire test.) Are the corners sharp and clean? If a texture was applied, is the pattern consistent and attractive? Also ask the former customers about their experience working with the pro. Did he seal off the work area to control dust?

Aside from friends and neighbors who have used drywallers, talk to local building professionals for references. General contractors know the value of good drywall work, as do painters, cabinet makers and installers, and trim carpenters—people whose work comes after the drywall process.

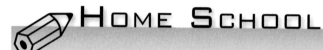

HOME SCHOOL

For more information on drywall products, installation, and applications in your home, visit www.usg.com—the website of USG, the world's leading drywall manufacturer (and the company that gave drywall the name Sheetrock®).

Licenses & Insurance?

Ask your local regulatory agency about licensing requirements for drywallers in your town. All professional drywallers should carry full liability insurance and workers' compensation insurance for employees.

☎ In the Phone Book

Drywall contractors.

ELECTRICIAN

For Help With:

- General household electrical repairs
- Adding new circuits, fixtures & devices
- New system design & installation
- Upgrading a service panel
- Lighting systems
- Voice, data, & A/V cable installation

Assuming everyone knows what electricians do, more or less, let's move right into how you should go about finding a good one. First, consider only full-time, licensed electricians. Avoid handymen and tradespeople who do electrical work on the side. Electricity is just too important to give to someone who doesn't have comprehensive training and experience.

Next, look for a pro who specializes in your type of project. Most electricians are qualified to perform all kinds of electrical work. However, when you're talking to candidates, try to get a feel for the types of jobs they do the most. Someone who does a lot of new construction or additions will be comfortable working with plans and other tradespeople and may even have system design expertise. A specialist in remodeling will have plenty of knowledge for working with existing circuitry as well as the tricky task of running new wiring through finished walls and ceilings. Other pros do mostly service work and are best qualified for basic household repairs.

If you need someone to install specialty wiring, such as high-tech cabling for a home office or entertainment or security system, make sure your electrician is up to date on the latest products and installation protocols. Often an electrician will coordinate with other vendors, such as an audio/video technician, to ensure the various cabling runs are handled properly.

Official Qualifications

The hierarchy of professional electricians is made up of *apprentices, journeymen,* and *master electricians.* In most states, journeymen and masters are licensed and are officially qualified to install wiring and electrical equipment. However, in some areas, journeymen must work alongside a master. General licensure requires passing a standardized test based on electrical theory, the National Electrical Code, and local electrical and building code specifications. Earning a master's license qualifies an electrician to design systems as well as install them.

Hourly rates for electrical work often are based on the pros' qualifications. For example, you'll pay one rate for a master or journeyman working alone on your job. But if the experienced guy brings in an apprentice to help with the simpler stuff, you'll pay a somewhat higher rate.

Identifying Good & Bad Work

How can you assess the quality of an electrician's work when you can't even see most of it? Short of ordering a pair of X-Ray Specs from the back of a comic book, the best strategy is to ask to see a new construction job in process. What you're looking for is neat, orderly installation: cables that are fastened at equal intervals and not twisting and crisscrossing every which way, switch boxes that are carefully installed (if the drywall is up, the boxes should be flush with the face of the drywall), and a general sense of order where the cables run into the service panel (breaker box). An excessively messy job site and haphazard cable runs indicate a careless, imprecise electrician–the very kind to avoid hiring.

If you can't gain access to a work in progress, talk to previous customers about their experience with the pro (actually, you should do this in any case). Ask about the electrician's level of professionalism, and find out whether the customers have had any problems with their systems. If so, how did the pro respond?

Extreme cases of bad electrical work have resulted in house fires. More commonly, though, the problems point to impractical (and improper) design.

True story: After moving in to a beautiful, new custom home, the owners begin to discover some odd inconveniences. The bathroom switches are wired so that the closest switch to the door controls the fan instead of the light. In the kitchen, the lighting circuit is tied in with the countertop GFCI receptacles; when a receptacle is tripped, the whole room goes dark.

Years later, when the owners install a dimmer switch, it takes them 45 minutes to find the right breaker at the service panel. It turns out that the dining room chandelier (the reason for the dimmer) is on the same circuit as the upstairs bedroom, the kitchen pantry, and the bar in the finished basement. Should the electrical inspector have found these problems? Of course. Did he? Nope. That's why you have to be on the lookout.

Licenses & Insurance?
As discussed previously, most states and municipalities require licensure for professional electricians. A valid license is your first safeguard against hiring an incompetent electrician. The second check is the permit process. Permits and inspections are required for most sizeable electrical jobs, so make sure your electrician obtains all necessary permits for your project.

Due to the enormous potential liability of electrical work, and the dangers of the job itself, electricians must have extensive insurance coverage for liability and workers' compensation. Don't hire a pro who isn't adequately covered.

☎ In the Phone Book
Electric Contractors.

ENERGY AUDITOR

For Help With:

- Home inspections for energy efficiency & indoor air quality
- Design, engineering & consulting services for remodels & new home construction
- Qualification for government-sponsored energy programs

Energy auditors, also called *energy consultants* or *energy raters*, perform specialized tests and inspections on your home to evaluate its energy efficiency, among other things. Having your home audited is a little like taking an old car into a trusted mechanic for a comprehensive checkup. The mechanic drives it around, puts it up on the lift, runs some tests, then presents you with options for making the old sled run better. From there, you decide which repairs to make by comparing the cost of each improvement against how much it will contribute to the car's overall performance.

But there's a key difference between a mechanic and an auditor: A mechanic actually carries out the repairs, while an auditor (the *right* auditor) is a completely unbiased, independent source of information and advice. You take the auditor's recommendations and shop elsewhere for pros (and products) to make the improvements.

If your goal is to save money on utility bills, it can really pay to hire an auditor before making major changes. Case in point: A window salesman comes to your house and says you'll save 15% on your energy bills by replacing your old windows with energy-efficient units. Even if those savings are exaggerated—let's say the real number is 7%—you might be looking at a price tag of $10,000 to $15,000 for the new windows. So you hire an auditor. She determines you'll save 5% on your heating bills simply by improving the insulation around your old windows, and that you'll save another 5% by replacing the weatherstripping on your entry doors, installing new trim kits in your recessed light fixtures, and sealing some duct joints. That's a 10% savings for improvements that will cost you well under $1,000.

What Auditors Test For

Auditors' methods and inspection processes vary, but here are the standard things a qualified auditor can evaluate in your home:

- Insulation levels throughout the house
- Air leaks
- Indoor air quality
- Window efficiency
- Air tightness of ductwork
- Heating and cooling performance
- Efficiency of major appliances
- General home and site conditions (orientation to sun, exposure to wind, etc.)

It's also common for auditors to review a year's worth of your utility bills and make recommendations about improving energy-usage habits (don't worry, you can still outdo your neighbors with the holiday lights, but maybe this year your house won't have to be visible from space).

Looking at energy audits a different way, here are some of the common problems auditors help you address:

- High utility bills
- Rooms that don't heat/cool properly
- Drafty areas
- Poor indoor air quality (house feels stuffy)
- Excessive window condensation
- Water heater pilot light won't stay lighted
- Mold and other moisture-related problems
- Ice dams

Building for Efficiency

If you're building a new home or planning a major renovation, an energy pro can help you design and build for maximum long-term energy efficiency and comfort. Consulting with a pro during the planning stage is also a great way to avoid some of the common house problems listed above. Let's face it, most home builders don't give a whit about your long-term energy costs, so you're pretty much on your own. Energy consultants can be hired to review construction plans, conduct tests for proposed and actual energy performance, and inspect construction projects to ensure design specifications are met by the builder.

If you're thinking of buying an existing new home, you can have an audit done to assess its energy performance. Efficiency ratings on new homes can be used to qualify for special government financing offers (see below).

Energy Star® Rating

Through the U.S. government's Energy Star program, you may qualify for special tax incentives and financing opportunities for energy efficiency improvements or the purchase of a new energy-efficient home. To qualify, your home (whether your existing home, a new home you'd like to buy, or, in some cases, your renovation plans) must be audited by a certified Home Energy Rater and meet the minimum efficiency standards. For more information, visit www.energystar.gov.

Finding a Qualified Auditor

Aside from personal referrals, the Internet is probably the best place to find the names of qualified energy consulting companies in your area. Start with these sources:

Residential Energy Services Network: www.natresnet.org
(Includes a contractor locator of energy consultants and home energy raters across the country. Both RESNET members and non-members are listed.)

Energy Star: www.energystar.gov
(Also your state's E-Star affiliate)

U.S. Department of Energy: www.energy.gov

You can also contact your local utility company, which may offer free energy auditing services.

Call a few companies that seem to fit the bill, and discuss your goals and how they might handle your project. Ask about the company's experience with residential work and the qualifications of their auditors. What kind of equipment do they use? How do they charge for their services, and what's included in a standard home audit?

As mentioned earlier, make sure the company is an independent consulting firm and is not associated with any commercial interest. Run a background check on your top choice to see if any complaints have been filed against the company or auditor (see Chapter 1).

Licenses & Insurance?

Licensure for energy consultants is not yet standard, but check with your municipal or state regulatory agency for requirements in your area. Reputable companies are insured against damage liability and carry workers' compensation for any employees–be sure to ask.

☎ In the Phone Book

Energy Management & Conservation Consultants.

EXTERMINATOR

SEE: PEST CONTROL

FENCE INSTALLER

For Help With:

- New fence installation
- Removal & replacement of old fencing

Need a little privacy? Tired of seeing your neighbor mow his lawn in shorts and black dress socks? (Or is it the other way around?) Whatever the reason, a new fence can turn your yard into an attractive oasis, a safe haven for kids, pets, and, well, people who refuse to get rid of their old dress socks.

Finding a good fence installation company shouldn't be a problem. There are plenty of them out there. But before you call around to set up appointments for free estimates, conduct a little background research into your city's regulations, and check out your materials options for the new fence.

Talk to the Building Department

The first step is to contact your city's building department to learn about any and all restrictions that apply to residential fences. Your city may require a building permit for fences over a certain height (6 ft. is typical), and it will likely limit the height of front-yard fences to around 3 or 4 ft. Some municipalities even impose design restrictions. (Government officials with design sense? Yes, it sounds crazy, but those are the rules. At least it prevents your neighbor from building a fence out of old hubcaps.)

Your city will probably have a written document of its fence specifications, which may include any of the following:

- Setback—how far the fence must be set back from your property line
- Fence height—may vary based on the fence's location
- Fence materials
- Depth of post footings
- Easements—areas that must remain free of fences and other structures

Materials & Installation

Once you know the basic legal parameters, you can start shopping for fence materials and styles. Because most fence companies specialize in a limited range of products, this will help you narrow down the list of potential installers. Materials options are abundant–from standards like cedar, vinyl, and chain link to specialty choices like ornamental iron, concrete, and aluminum.

After deciding on a type of fencing, find out what the major manufacturers recommend for proper installation. For example, most fences should have their posts set in concrete for long-term strength and stability. Make sure your fence installer follows the recommended installation procedures. For future reference, also make note of recommended maintenance procedures and protective treatments, such as paints, stains, and sealers.

Choosing a Fence Installer

Now that you have a pretty good idea of what your fence should be, compile a list of local companies with plenty of experience building your specific type of fence. Have any friends, relatives, or neighbors had a similar fence installed recently? If not, drive around some neighborhoods in search of fences you like. Ask the owners of those fences about who did the work and whether they're happy with the results.

With your list in hand, call several companies and conduct a phone interview, or set up an in-home (in-yard) consultation. Check for the following qualifications:

1. Does the company operate a legitimate commercial business that's been working in the area for many years?
2. Will they supply references, specifically for jobs similar to yours?
3. Do they use their own installers and service people, or do they subcontract the labor? Of course, the former is preferable.
4. What are the installation specifications? Are the posts set in concrete?
5. Will they provide firm dates for starting and completing the job?
6. How much money is required up front? Get a sense for the standard down payment in your area. Some states limit down payments by law. In any case, never pay more than 50% up front.
7. What are the guarantees for installation and materials? Are they stated in writing? Warranties on different materials vary widely. Many installations include a labor guarantee of one year.

Licenses & Insurance?

Some states and municipalities require fence companies to be licensed—find out what applies in your area. Insurance is a must to cover the installation work and installers.

☎ In the Phone Book

Fence.

FIRE & WATER DAMAGE RESTORATION

For Help With:

- Damage remediation and restoration associated with fire and smoke, water, sewage, and mold:
  - ☐ Structural stabilization
  - ☐ Emergency board-up
  - ☐ Demolition & debris removal
  - ☐ Cleaning & decontamination
  - ☐ Construction services
  - ☐ Personal property restoration

After fire, smoke, or water has damaged your home, the most important course of action is immediate and rapid response from a qualified restoration team. Safety is, of course, your first concern. But once the emergency is over, the clock starts ticking in terms of how much damage your home will sustain. Water damage experts recommend that cleanup, drying, and decontamination efforts begin within 24 to 48 hours of the flooding. It takes only that long for mold, rot, corrosion, and other destructive forces to begin attacking your home's materials and possessions. Dealing with smoke is just as time-sensitive, as acid residues in soot begin to discolor and damage virtually every surface they touch.

Restoration professionals are trained and equipped to handle every aspect of the restoration process—from shoring up structures to cleanup and decontamination to complete rebuilding and restoration of your property. It's also customary for them to handle the billing through your insurance company. Restoration pros are called in to address everything from widespread catastrophes to ordinary home emergencies, like burst water pipes or damage from roof leaks. Be aware that some companies handle both water and fire damage, while others specialize in water and water-related damage only.

Finding a Qualified Restoration Company

Despite the urgency of responding to damage, the last thing you want to do is panic and turn your home over to an unqualified or unscrupulous contractor who claims to be a restoration expert. Proper restoration work involves much more than just cleaning

up the mess. Both fire and water damage must be thoroughly assessed and inspected prior to cleanup, and the entire restoration process must be monitored continually to ensure all procedures are appropriate and effective.

For this reason, the first things to check out with prospective companies are experience and credentials. Do they have specific training and certification for the type of work you need done? Certification through a recognized industry organization such as the Institute of Inspection, Cleaning, & Restoration Certification (IICRC) can be a meaningful qualification. The IICRC manages the largest registry of inspectors, cleaners, and restorers serving the U.S. and Canada.

Visit the IICRC's consumer website (www.certifiedcleaners.org) for more information on professional inspection and cleaning of various materials in the home (carpet, hard flooring, upholstery, etc.) as well as standard restoration processes. The site also includes a contractor locator for finding certified restoration firms and technicians in your area. Your insurance agent or claims adjuster may be another source for referrals of restoration specialists.

Protecting Yourself

Restoring your home to its original condition can be a lengthy and frustrating process. You may be anxious to get things back to normal, but it's important to follow basic precautions when arranging for the work:

1. Use only licensed and insured contractors. Also run a background check (see Chapter 1) on prospective companies to make sure their record is clean.
2. Get everything in writing, including any verbal agreements or promises made during the initial consultation. Don't allow any work to begin without a signed contract detailing the work to be done and the final cost, as well as any guarantees.
3. Never pay for the entire job up front. A down payment of ⅓ of the total payment is more standard, with the balance of the bill payable upon completion of the work. It's always safer to pay by credit card or check instead of cash.
4. Carefully scrutinize any contractor's recommendation to spend a lot of money on temporary repairs, which leaves less money available for permanent repairs.
5. Avoid part-time contractors or any pro without extensive experience and training with your specific type of problem. Consider only contractors with a legitimate restoration business operating in your area.

Licenses & Insurance?

Your restoration professionals should be licensed and fully insured for liability and workers' compensation. Check with your city's office for specific licensing requirements.

☎ In the Phone Book

Fire & Water Damage Restoration, Water Damage Restoration, Mold Inspection & Removal.

FIREPLACES & FIREPLACE INSTALLER

For Help With:

- Buying & installing:
  - ☐ Fireplaces (gas and wood-burning)
  - ☐ Stoves
  - ☐ Fireplace inserts
  - ☐ Outdoor fireplaces & appliances

Back in the days when all fireplaces were made of brick and mortar, adding one to your home was a major remodel in itself. Now, most new fireplaces are factory-made appliances that can be installed in a matter of hours. The installer you use will most likely work for, or contract with, the retailer who sells you the fireplace unit and all the extra parts needed for your application.

Today's self-contained fireplaces (or *hearth products*, the industry's ironically frigid term) include standard in-wall units, freestanding stoves, inserts for updating old fireplaces, and even outdoor fireplaces and fire pits. Of course, you can still get a traditional masonry fireplace if you want one. But for that you'll need the help of a qualified mason (see page 131).

Choosing a Fireplace

Like cars and computers, fireplaces just keep getting better, both in appearance and performance. And buying a fireplace is a lot like any other shopping experience. First, you decide on a fuel type (wood, gas, pellet, electric, oil, coal, corn...), then you browse all the different models, styles, and features available within the chosen category.

But wait. Before you spend too much time comparing trim details, consult with a qualified installer or salesperson about where you plan to put the fireplace or stove. This is especially important for wood-burning fireplaces. And the reason is combustion. Getting wood to burn and draft properly requires real science (although luck helps, or even a little black magic, if you know any good practitioners). Where you locate the unit and, more importantly, its chimney, largely determines how well the wood will burn and ventilate. For this reason, it's a good idea to have an expert come to your home to review your installation plans. Some retailers and installers will do this for free, so just ask.

Installer Qualifications

As you shop for a hearth product, talk to different retailers about their installation professionals. Are the installers in-house, or does the retailer subcontract the work? If the latter, to whom? Even if the retailer assumes liability and guarantees the work of its subs, you'll want to make sure the installers are qualified and licensed (if required in your area).

Currently, there is no government or nationally standardized regulation of hearth product installers. Rather, installers can elect to become certified through industry organizations. The most widely recognized group is the National Fireplace Institute.

The NFI (www.nficertified.org) offers certification programs for professional installers in three categories: Gas Specialist, Woodburning Specialist, and Pellet Specialist. Installers may also receive specialized training through fireplace manufacturers to become certified for working with a particular brand or product line.

Another safeguard to ensure proper installation of your fireplace is through your city's building department (see Licenses & Insurance?, below). Most municipalities require a building permit for new fireplaces and gas lines.

Blending Hearth (Product) & Home

Depending on your plans, you may need to hire additional pros to create the proper setting for your new fireplace. A fireplace installer might be qualified to add a mantel kit or ready-made hearth, but if you want to bump out a wall, build a chimney chase, or create a custom mantel, you'll need a good carpenter, and probably a drywaller or plasterer. Then maybe a tile setter, wallpaper hanger, painter.... It's just something to be aware of when designing the project. Whatever your plans, it's best to choose a fireplace first, then design everything to the unit's specifications.

HOME SCHOOL

For a good introduction to fireplace options for your home, visit the website of the Hearth, Patio & Barbecue Association at www.hpba.org.

Licenses & Insurance?

Contact your city's building department to learn about their requirements for licensure of fireplace installers, or fireplace-related work, such as installation of new gas lines or electrical circuits. If the city requires a permit for new fireplaces, make sure your installer is licensed to work in your area to avoid problems with the building inspector (who must sign off on the completed job). Any pro involved in any aspect of a fireplace installation should be fully insured.

☎ In the Phone Book

Fireplace Equipment–Retail, Fireplaces.

FIREWOOD SUPPLIER

For Help With:

- Firewood & firewood delivery

Getting a fair deal on firewood is pretty straightforward. Essentially you're looking at four factors:

1. **Type**—Did you get the wood species you ordered?
2. **Condition**—Is the wood well-seasoned and well-split?
3. **Quantity**—Measure the stack to make sure you weren't shortchanged.
4. **Price**—Considering the quality of the wood and your experience working with the supplier, did you get a good value?

Now, to elaborate:

Wood Type

You're pretty much limited to the species of wood available in your area, which can change from one season to the next. Different species have different burning characteristics. Generally, soft woods, like pine and fir, are easier to start and burn more quickly than hardwoods, such as oak, maple, and hickory. Hardwoods produce more heat than softwoods and typically are more expensive.

At a deeper level of comparison, wood species are rated for qualities like coaling, ease of splitting, and Btu output. But most people prefer one species over another because of the way it burns (and sometimes the way it smells; fruitwoods, like apple, actually give off a fruity fragrance when burned). Firewood is commonly ordered in mixtures–half pine and half oak, for example–to get the desired qualities of each species. Whatever you order, make sure you're getting what you paid for (see Quantity, next page).

Condition

Regardless of its species, wood must be well-seasoned (i.e., dry) to burn efficiently. Inadequately seasoned, or "green," firewood has too much moisture in it, resulting in a smoky fire that produces less heat than dry wood. Green wood also deposits more creosote into your chimney (for an explanation of why this is bad, see Chimney Sweep, on page 65).

Under proper conditions, seasoning takes 6 to 12 months after the wood is cut. Visual clues can help you distinguish dry wood from green: Dry wood develops a grayish color, and its bark becomes loose and falls off easily. The ends of dry wood show cracking and checking, while the ends of green wood look freshly cut and may even be moist to the touch. Wet wood is considerably heavier than dry pieces of the same size, and it makes a heavy, dull thud when pieces are struck together. But if you miss these clues, you'll know green wood once you try to burn it. It won't light easily or will burn out quickly without constant intervention (how relaxing!). It will also smoke a lot and may hiss–as the water inside turns to steam.

It's your supplier's responsibility to season the wood before delivering it to your house. However, there's no guaranteeing what you'll get, no matter how much you insist on dry stuff. The best way to ensure seasoned wood is to order it at least six months before you plan to burn it. Store the wood where it gets some air and is protected from snow and rain (an outdoor shelter with cross-ventilation is best). Don't store it indoors or up against the house, as this can invite vermin, like mice and termites, to move from the woodpile to your home.

Splitting is another job that some suppliers do well and others don't. You're looking for a majority of medium-sized split logs, which will start fairly easily and burn well on their own. Overly split wood burns too quickly, and under-split stuff is a bugger to start. Of course, you should expect to split your own kindling from the regular pieces.

Quantity

The standard measurement for firewood is the cord, which can be divided into a ½-cord and a face cord. Here's what these terms mean:

Cord = a neat stack of firewood that measures 128 cubic ft. Standard length for firewood pieces is about 16", so the classic cord dimensions are 4 ft. high × 8 ft. long × three rows deep. A ½-cord is exactly half that size, or 64 cubic ft.

Face cord = a stack that measures 4 ft. high × 8 ft. long × one row deep, or ⅓ of a cord (based on 16"-long pieces).

The only practical way to measure a load of firewood is to stack it and measure it. The stack should be neat, with all pieces parallel and with minimal gapping, and arranged in even rows. If the stack doesn't measure up to the ordered amount, you got gypped. One good reason to have the supplier stack the wood for you (aside from avoiding back pain) is that you can measure the stack before you pay him.

Any supplier who tries to sell you wood by the truckload, the "rick," or the pile is probably trying to sell you a pile of something else right along with the firewood. Because trucks come in all sizes, buying by the truckload is like choosing the mystery prize on a game show: you get what they give you. The only true standard for measuring firewood quantity is the cord or fractions thereof.

Finding a Good Supplier

Unfortunately, this usually takes some trial-and-error. In other words, unless you get references from someone you know, you'll have to take your chances and try a supplier who can meet your predictable criteria (wood offerings, price, etc.). Once you get the delivery, evaluate the wood as best you can, then see how it burns throughout the season. If everything goes well, you've found yourself a good supplier. When you call for orders in the future, just make sure to do it early enough to season the wood yourself. If you don't like the wood or the service, find another supplier. There's no sense in giving a bad supplier a second chance.

When your wood is delivered, be sure to get a receipt that includes the supplier's name, address, and phone number; the type and amount of wood delivered; and the price. Pay the supplier to stack the wood, or stack it yourself right away. If you find any discrepancies in the order, contact the supplier immediately.

☎ In the Phone Book

Firewood.

FLOORING

SEE: CARPET INSTALLER
CARPET & RUG CLEANER
TILE INSTALLER
WOOD FLOORING INSTALLERS & REFINISHERS

FURNACE MAINTENANCE

SEE: HEATING, VENTILATION & AIR-CONDITIONING CONTRACTORS

FURNITURE REPAIR & RESTORATION

For Help With:

- Wood furniture refinishing
- Reupholstering & recaning
- Antiques restoration
- Refurbishing of cabinets, interior woodwork, doors & paneling
- Estimates for restoration & refinishing work

Furniture repair and restoration professionals work on everything from plastic-laminate coffee tables to kitchen cabinets to Chippendale chairs. Their services can range from simple stripping and refinishing to rebuilding pieces almost from scratch. Whatever pieces you have, there's probably someone in town who can help. The challenge lies in matching the right craftsperson with your project.

Start by seeking personal referrals. People you know who have had work done, furniture dealers you trust, and local appraisers are often the best sources for names of good refinishing pros. Next, contact the pros on your list and ask about their experience and expertise with your type of project.

Most refinishers tend to be generalists who work with all sorts of pieces, finishes, and even period styles, but you'll still find plenty of specialization, particularly in the realm of fine restoration. Also inquire about additional services. Many pros offer pickup and delivery service, while some may do the work in your home—for delicate pieces or for quick touch-ups on ordinary furniture, or when the items can't easily be moved, as with wood paneling.

Is It Worth It?

How much people are willing to spend on refinishing naturally has a lot to do with how much their furniture is worth. For extensive work on valuable antique pieces, estimates are recommended and are usually worth the cost, regardless of what you decide to do.

Proper estimates are conducted in your home and include a discussion of how the pro intends to finish the piece. This also gives you a chance to assess the pro's knowledge level. Many refinishers apply the charge of an estimate toward the final repair cost or will charge a standard fee if you don't use them for the work.

If you're considering refinishing a prized antique or any piece that may have historical significance, it is very important that you first have it appraised by one or more qualified pros. Although owning something of rare value and not knowing it is indeed rare, it's better to be safe than sorry. Even the finest refinishing work can degrade the value of furniture that has miraculously survived the years with its original or near-original finish.

Licenses & Insurance?

Your refinisher should have enough insurance to cover the value of your furniture. Make sure to check this out if you have expensive stuff.

☎ In the Phone Book

Furniture Repair & Refinish.

GARAGE DOOR REPAIR & INSTALLATION

For Help With:

- Garage door repairs & routine maintenance
- New door and opener installation

"We Fix Broken Springs!" Look in any phone book and you'll see this heroic proclamation in dozens of ads for garage door companies. Indeed, *every* garage door service fixes broken springs. If they didn't, they'd be like a dentist who could identify a cavity but couldn't do a filling.

Granted, a broken spring is a real bummer, and probably scary if it broke while you were in the garage. (That's why extension-type springs have safety cables running through them—to prevent a loaded spring from becoming a projectile when it breaks.) Springs act as a counterbalance to carry most of a door's weight. If a spring breaks, you can still open the door manually (don't use the automatic opener), although it may be quite heavy. Don't leave the door in the UP position—someone unaware might try to close it, not expecting to have to support the full weight of the door. When a spring breaks, it's best to keep the door closed and call a service technician.

Garage Door Services

These are the main things that garage door technicians check or repair on service calls:

- Door hinges, rollers, locks, and hardware
- Door tracks
- Springs (replacing broken springs, adjusting existing springs)
- Pulleys and cables (for lifting door)
- Safety cables (extension springs only)
- Automatic opener (mechanical parts, mounting system, switches, transmitters)
- Opener auto-reverse and other safety mechanisms

Having a door serviced usually makes it quieter, smoother, and easier to open. When the springs are properly adjusted, the door is "balanced" and will stay in position when opened about 3 to 4 ft.

Getting a New Door

If your old door or opener is in terrible shape, a technician might recommend replacement, in which case you can get an estimate from the technician's company, then do some comparison shopping before making a decision. Garage doors come in a range of materials, finishes, and styles and now have special features like weather seals between door panels and no-pinch panel joints (good for the kiddies). New doors include the track system and all the hardware—everything you need to open the door the old-fashioned way. An automatic opener is a completely separate system.

Considering the wealth of available brands and options, it makes sense to research the latest products then look for a local garage door company that offers what you want. Otherwise, you're limited to the brand and product offerings of a single business.

Selecting a Garage Door Company

For service or new installation, look for a company that's been in business for a long time. Well-established businesses are likely to have the staying power and financial stability to honor warranties down the road. Most companies service "all major brands" of doors and openers, but always confirm that they can service your door and opener model. Compare pricing, of course, and find out what a basic service call or maintenance checkup typically costs. Companies that offer free estimates for service usually have to make up the lost trip charge elsewhere and may pressure you into paying high prices once they're at your house.

Doing your research and pre-selecting a model of new door or opener makes it easy to comparison-shop for the best price and warranty. Make sure all equipment and labor are included in your contract for any new installation or service work.

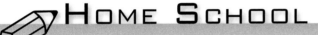

HOME SCHOOL

In case anyone asks, here are the two main types of garage door springs; your door should have one or the other:

Extension—long springs mounted parallel to the upper (horizontal) door track; typically with one spring on each side of the door.

Torsion—super heavy-duty spring(s) mounted along a steel rod over the door opening (parallel to the face of the door).

Both types of springs may be under tension at all times and are fully loaded—at greatest tension—when the door is closed.

Licenses & Insurance?

Licensing is common for garage door service and installation professionals. A quick call to your city's building department will tell you what's required in your area. Any company you use should be fully insured for liability and workers' compensation.

☎ In the Phone Book

Garage Doors & Openers.

GARBAGE COLLECTION

For Help With:

- Removal & disposal of waste not collected by ordinary trash service
  - ☐ Construction & remodeling debris
  - ☐ Yard waste
  - ☐ Household goods (furniture, appliances, etc.)
  - ☐ Hazardous materials

Just as Native Alaskans have seven words to describe different types of snow, the modern homeowner draws from a range of terms to identify trash: there's yard waste, construction debris, chemical stuff, and old clothes. Then there's "crap"—a generic term for once-loved-but-now-reviled household items such as worn-out couches, outdated computers, and perfectly good espresso machines that haven't been used since the mid-90s.

What's common among much of this rubbish is that the garbage man (your weekly trash pickup service professional) won't take it. He simply refuses to collect some refuse. So what do you do with it? Fortunately, you have a couple of easy options: 1) rent a dumpster, or 2) hire a collection service for a one-time pickup.

Renting a Dumpster

Dumpster rental (also called "roll-off" service, because dumpsters are often rolled off of a truck) is now a popular trash solution for all types of home improvement projects. The dumpster service parks the bin in your driveway or yard (or on the street if the city allows it), you fill it up and then call them when you want it taken away. Rental periods vary. As an example, you might pay a flat fee to get the dumpster for a week then pay an additional daily fee if you want to extend the rental. Renting a dumpster is the way to go if you don't have space to store the garbage temporarily and you need it out of the way for your project.

Dumpster rentals come with many restrictions, so be sure to read your agreement carefully. By law, dumpster companies can't collect hazardous materials, and they'll charge you if they find any in your bin (they may even require you to pick up the "hazmats" at their site). Other common restrictions include weight limits, which are usually determined by volume. For example, you may be allowed to fill the bin only 12" deep with concrete, dirt, or sod. And most services will not pick up a dumpster that's overfull, with junk sticking out of the top of the bin. Dumpsters are available in a range of sizes from 3 cubic yards and up. Ask the dumpster company for help with estimating the best size for your job.

A new type of dumpster coming into vogue isn't a dumpster at all, but rather a large, hammock-like sling made of very strong nylon fabric. You request delivery in the same fashion as a roll-off dumpster, then simply spread the sling out and fill it with all your junk. After you call for pickup, a truck comes and hoists the reusable sling back into the truck bed for disposal. Because of its light weight, this system can be significantly less expensive than metal dumpsters, if you're lucky enough to have this service available in your area.

One-time Collections

Collection service professionals come to your house, load your refuse into their truck, clean up the site, then drive away, ridding your home of decades of accumulated crap. They'll even schlep the junk up from your basement. What could be better (besides getting back all the money you spent on that stuff in the first place)? This type of garbage removal is a good option for major spring cleaning efforts or even construction or yard projects when you have room to store the garbage until the pickup date.

Like dumpster companies, garbage collectors won't take hazmats, and only some services will haul away old appliances. Pricing is typically based on the amount of trash you have. This means the pros have to see the stuff before giving you a firm quote. Many services take a progressive approach to trash by recycling appropriate materials and donating reusable goods to charity organizations.

Getting Rid of Hazardous Materials

How can it be that the same paint used in your baby's nursery is considered a public health hazard when sitting in a can at the landfill? This is one of those questions for which there is no satisfying answer. So don't ask. Instead, call your city or county government to find out how to dispose of your extra paint and other household hazmats. Some towns have a free pickup or drop-off service for residents. Otherwise, they can tell you where to bring the nasty stuff or will provide names of local collection companies who deal with hazmat disposal.

Common materials and items that are considered hazardous include:

- Paint, oil, stains, and solvents
- Antifreeze
- Lawn and garden chemicals
- Toxic cleaning solutions
- Batteries
- Appliances (particularly cooling appliances that contain Freon)
- Propane tanks
- Pool chemicals
- Thermometers
- Florescent bulbs
- Gasoline and other fuels

Obtain a complete list of specific hazmats from your city office or collection professional.

Licenses & Insurance?

Be sure to discuss insurance with your rubbish professional. Make sure they have liability coverage for any damage done to your property and workers' compensation for any employees working in your home. Check with your city office about licensing requirements, as well as any permits needed for dumpster rentals. It's important to follow the law when dealing with garbage.

☎ In the Phone Book

Garbage & Rubbish Collection, Waste Disposal, Waste Disposal–Hazardous.

GARDENER

For Help With:

- Garden design & consulting
- Regular & seasonal garden & landscape maintenance
- Diagnosis for sick plants
- Greenhouse tending

A beautiful residential garden usually tells you one of two things about its owners: Either they have lots of time or they have hired help. As any green-thumbed enthusiast knows, creating and maintaining a thriving garden requires not only a great deal of time and care but also knowledge—of horticulture, the local climate, and when and how to respond to specific plant behaviors. It's a professional gardener's job to provide these services, but how much and how often they tend to a garden is up to the client.

Some people hire gardeners for design expertise. They want to get a new garden off to a good start and to avoid wasting money on plants that won't do well in a given location. Once the garden is established, the clients take over the maintenance. Other clients want nothing to do with the regular digging, weeding, and watering, so they retain a gardener for scheduled, full-service caretaking. As for the gardeners, individuals may specialize in any number of areas, such as organic gardening, greenhouse growing, or container plantings.

How Should Your Garden Grow?

The first step in finding the right gardener is to decide what you want to achieve with your garden and landscape and how much help you need to reach your goals. Make an assessment of your landscape, considering such factors as:

- Style of garden you have or would like to have. Do you prefer the rugged, earthy look of Xeriscape or the lush splendor of an English garden?
- High-maintenance or low-maintenance?
- Would you like to contribute ideas for designing the garden or give the gardener total creative authority?
- Will the garden support herbs and vegetables, or just flowers and decorative plants?
- What's your feeling on environmental issues, such as water efficiency, chemical use, pest management practices, fertilizers, mulching, and composting?
- Do you need lawn care and tree services along with garden tending?

Thinking about your goals and establishing priorities are essential steps for finding a gardener with the right qualifications and experience. If you decide against an ornamental garden and just need someone to keep the lawn in good shape, any reputable "mow and blow" company will likely meet your needs (see Lawn Service, on pages 129 to 130). On the other hand, a dynamic garden that delights the senses will require a pro with extensive horticultural training and proven creative ability. For the latter, you'll definitely want to see several examples of the gardener's work.

Conducting Your Search

Seek the names of good gardeners through friends, neighbors, and colleagues, all of whom can report on the personal as well as professional qualities of a gardener they've worked with. Other sources for referrals include Extension agencies at local universities and quality garden centers and landscape suppliers. Non-professionals who have completed Master Gardener programs (through Extension agencies) may also be familiar with the work of local gardening pros.

When interviewing candidates, discuss their qualifications and gardening philosophies. Are they a good fit with your goals, priorities, and style preferences? Be as clear as possible about the work you would like to have done, both on a regular and an as-requested basis. Find out who will be doing the work–the principal gardener, full-time employees, or subcontractors? You'll want to make sure that anyone working regularly at your home is well connected to the business and has a clean background.

Licenses & Insurance?

Gardeners and landscape professionals must be licensed in some areas; check with your city or state office for local requirements. General liability and workers' compensation insurance are important, especially considering all the work done with mowers and trees.

☎ In the Phone Book

Gardeners, Landscape Contractors, Lawn & Grounds Maintenance.

GENERAL CONTRACTOR

SEE: CHAPTER 4

GUTTERS & DOWNSPOUTS

For Help With:

- New gutter installation
- Adding gutter covers
- Gutter cleaning & repairs

Neglecting gutters is one of the great American pastimes. Okay, that may be an exaggeration, but gutters certainly rank high on the list of things that don't get any attention until there's a problem. Fortunately, gutter professionals are never in short supply, and they can be hired for everything from seasonal cleaning to new installation.

Gutter cleaning and repair pros take care of that dreaded semi-annual task of mucking out the gutter troughs and flushing out the downspouts. They also patch holes, seal leaky joints, and refasten loose connections to the house. For maximum performance, gutter runs must have the proper slope (typically $1/16$" per foot, with the high point at the beginning of the run and the low point at the downspout. Checking for slope and straightness of runs is a critical aspect of any cleaning and repair job. Low spots or damaged sections of a run cause water to pool and spill over the top of the gutter, rendering the system useless.

By the way, here's why gutters are so important: They keep excess water from saturating the ground along the home's foundation and from splashing up onto the siding. Without gutters, there'd be a lot more leaky basements, moldy crawlspaces, peeling paint, and rotted siding. Also, whenever it rained, you'd have to walk through a sheet of falling water to reach the front door.

If your gutters need more than a cleaning and spot repairs, it's time to look for an installation professional. But first, spend a little time deciding what type of gutter you want so you can narrow the field to installers who specialize in your chosen system (don't worry, gutters aren't complicated).

Gutter Specs

A brief overview of gutter materials, sizes, and fasteners:

Standard gutters come in aluminum, galvanized steel, and vinyl. (Specialty materials include wood, copper, and stainless steel. For any of these, you'll need a highly qualified specialist and lots of money.) Most experts agree that aluminum is the best all-around material, especially if you're hiring out the installation. Vinyl is easy to install and therefore good for do-it-yourselfers, but it doesn't last as long as aluminum and comes in a very limited range of colors. Steel gutters are strong and durable, but untreated joints and damage to the finish lead to rust. Aluminum is not quite as hardy as steel but plenty strong for most applications. And aluminum never rusts. This is important: Use only heavy-duty aluminum that's at least .032" thick. Anything thinner may be too flimsy.

The standard gutter size is 5", but 6" gutters are commonly available for situations that require more capacity. Discuss sizing with your gutter installer. If your old gutters have been overloaded during heavy rains, you probably need to upgrade to 6" gutters, at least in problem areas. Another way to increase capacity is to use larger downspouts (standard 2×3" downspouts move 6 sq. inches of water, while 3×4" spouts move 12 sq. inches) or install double downspouts where needed.

The type of fasteners used to hang a gutter usually isn't a critical decision, but you might prefer one over another for aesthetic reasons or because it seems to hold better in your application. The old standby is the spike-and-ferule (the spike being a giant nail and the ferule a metal sleeve that the spike goes through). Some say these loosen over time and that they don't allow expansion of metal gutters, but they've worked pretty darned well on lots of gutters over the years. Other fasteners include various screw-on "hidden" hangers and straps that mount to the roof deck. In any case, it makes sense to see what's available before deciding.

Seamless vs. Sectional

Seamless gutters are the preferred standard for professional installations. Fabricated from large coils, gutter runs can be made to any length without a seam. No seam means a nice, smooth path for the water without the potential leakage problems of joints between pieces. Of course, seamless gutters still have joints at corners and downspouts, but so do sectional gutters. Sectional systems include gutter runs in lengths up to 20 ft. (although some pros can get them longer than that) and are best for do-it-yourself installations or when a professional job requires only short runs.

Gutter Covers (Leaf Guards)

Covers are the industry's attempt to create maintenance-free gutters. Is this possible? Maybe. But it's certainly true that covers can reduce the amount of leaves, twigs, and seedlings that clog your gutters every year. There are several products and designs available—from basic screens to near-fully enclosed systems that rely on liquid adhesion to collect rainwater while keeping out debris. Covers can be installed onto existing gutters as well as new systems. Some installers are so confident in their covers that they guarantee you'll never have to clean your gutters again. Just make sure to read the fine print on such claims.

Getting the Right Contractor & a Good Deal

Once you've looked at some products and know what type of gutter and features you want, compare gutter installation companies based on the following criteria:

1. Quality of product. If aluminum, make sure they use .032" or thicker material.
2. Workmanship. Ask for references and check out the company's work on recent jobs.
3. Guarantees. A one-year guarantee on labor is standard, while warranties on gutter materials range from 20-year to lifetime.

Schedule at least a few free estimates at your home, and get firm quotes for comparing companies. Make sure to ask about repairs on damaged or rotted trim boards and whether this is included in the estimate. As always, run a background check on your top choice (see Chapter 1). Ideally, the company should carry special insurance to cover your gutter warranty even if the company goes out of business.

Licenses & Insurance?

Licensure is common among gutter installers; contact your city or state office to learn about requirements in your area. Considering the nature of their work, it's especially important that gutter professionals carry liability and workers' compensation insurance.

☎ In the Phone Book

Gutters & Downspouts.

HANDYMAN

For Help With:

- General household repairs & maintenance, including:
    - ☐ Plumbing, electrical & fixtures
    - ☐ Some appliances
    - ☐ Walls, ceilings & trimwork
    - ☐ Paint & wallpaper
    - ☐ Flooring
    - ☐ Doors, windows & locks
    - ☐ Exterior home repairs
    - ☐ Fences
- Remodeling services

With apologies and no intent to offend, it must be said that "handyperson" never made it into common usage. This versatile professional is still known as a handyman (despite the heading in the phone book).

So, putting language study aside, what exactly is a handyman? A jack-of-all-trades, an odd-jobber, a home improvement generalist? Yes, just like in the old days. Except that now a professional handyman isn't necessarily a white-haired, avuncular fellow who takes on jobs in his spare time. Many of today's handymen (and handywomen) are full-time service people who work for polished organizations with plenty of marketing savvy and freshly uniformed crews. This change offers several potential benefits for you, the consumer.

First, your handyman is likely to be insured through his company. Second, he's probably been trained in customer service. And third, by contacting a company with many employees, you can request someone with experience specific to your job.

This is not to say that trusty old Harold, your neighborly handyman, is no longer a good option. But if you don't know a Harold and you're flying blind when searching for a pro, it might be less risky to go with a handyman organization than with an individual who's name came to you without references.

Let's say you have a laundry list of repair jobs needed around your house: a couple of bad light switches, a leaky faucet, a hole in some drywall, and new shelves waiting to be installed in your home office. Nothing major, but also nothing you want to tackle yourself. Looking at your list, you need the skills of an electrician, a plumber, a drywaller, and a carpenter. You can hire all four of those pros or hire a single qualified handyman (and skip the second mortgage on your house).

Traditionally, handyman services have been great for odd jobs and "honey-do" lists. But these days, many handymen advertise complete remodeling services, including basement finishes, bathroom remodels, and additions. This begs the question: Should you hire a handyman for a complex job like building a garage or wiring an addition? That depends on the handyman. If he worked as a full-time carpenter or electrician before becoming a Johnny-on-the-spot, he might have the right skills and experience. But if you're not sure your handyman is fully qualified for the job, you probably shouldn't take the chance.

Choosing a Handyman

An experienced full-time handyman is likely to have a broad range of general skills, but that's no guarantee that he can do everything or even wants to. Therefore, start your search by defining the jobs you need done. When interviewing candidates, plainly ask about their experience with your types of projects. The one who offers the most expertise at a fair price (not necessarily the lowest price, of course) may be your next handyman—provided he passes a background check (see Chapter 1) and possesses adequate customer service skills.

For standard small-job work, handymen often charge by the hour. Discuss the pricing for your job before any work starts, and get a total-cost estimate from the handyman. Most importantly, set up a communication plan so your handyman can reach you in the event that someone opens Pandora's box (in home repair, the box is full of expensive surprises that reveal themselves only after the work begins). Make sure your handyman stops working and contacts you if the job threatens to go way over budget.

Licenses & Insurance?

Licensing requirements for handymen vary widely. Contact your city or state office to learn about the local licensing laws. Liability and workers' compensation insurance are a must for handymen and/or their companies. The more things they work on, the more chances there are for something to go awry, and you don't want to be liable for accidents or to be stuck with the bill for a professional's mistake.

☎ In the Phone Book

Handy Person Service, Home Improvements.

HEATING, VENTILATION & AIR-CONDITIONING CONTRACTOR

For Help With:

- Furnaces
- Boilers
- Air-conditioning units
- Evaporative (swamp) coolers
- Heat pumps
- Air ducts
- Attic vents & fans
- Thermostats
- Humidifiers
- Indoor air quality
- Air filtration systems
- Maintenance, repairs, remodeling & new installation

Heating, ventilation, and air-conditioning (HVAC) pros work on all types of home heating and cooling systems. Typical jobs range from simple repairs, like replacing a thermocouple (when a pilot light won't stay lighted) to complete design and installation of new systems. Indoor air quality is another function of HVAC that contractors may specialize in.

Start your search for a qualified HVAC pro by first identifying what type of heating or cooling system you have (see Home School, next page, for the main types). Also note the brand of equipment and try to remember how old it is. This basic information will help you narrow the field of prospective contractors (don't worry, you'll have more than enough to choose from; there's about one HVAC pro for every 1,000 people in the U.S.). Look for a contractor who has extensive experience with your type of system. The phone book is as good a resource as any for this search.

Contact only licensed and insured contractors with a long history of service in your area. A quick background check (see Chapter 1) is also a good idea to make sure your candidates have clean work records. For a basic service call, get several estimates before setting up an appointment. Replacing your system or having any new installation work done requires a more thorough interview process.

Servicing Your System

Like your car, your heating and cooling systems need regular cleaning and maintenance to perform efficiently. This can be handled in several ways: You can ignore all maintenance and wait for something to break (what most people do), you can call in an HVAC pro for a system checkup (a good technician can give you honest advice about how often to service your system), or you can sign up for a service plan that includes regularly scheduled maintenance appointments.

Your utility company may offer low-cost service plans aimed at maximizing the efficiency of your equipment and thereby lowering your energy bills. Some plans work like an insurance policy for your major appliances (furnace, air conditioner, refrigerator, stove, etc.) and include maintenance visits and free repairs for a set monthly fee. Before signing any service contract or guarantee, understand the fine print, particularly regarding what you must do to uphold the agreement.

Installing a New System

Adding new ductwork, branch lines, zones, or entirely new systems is where a pro's experience and qualifications really count. There's a lot of science and even a little art to designing HVAC systems. All systems use a combination of mechanical equipment and natural air currents (hot air rises, cold air drops) to keep your home comfortable. System design involves a lot of calculations, as well as learning from the homeowner about what's wrong with their current system (bedroom too hot, kitchen too cold, etc.). A good contractor will consult closely with you before recommending a system change. In most cases, the contractor should present more than one option for meeting your heating and cooling needs.

Before having any new work done, get a few design proposals and cost estimates. It's usually better to negotiate a flat fee for the entire job rather than a parts-and-labor arrangement. Make sure everything is detailed in the contract, including the exact model and specifications of major equipment. The biggest challenges to designing or replacing HVAC systems are in the sizing of the equipment and in the layout of the duct or pipe networks. You want the right size and capacity for your home—no more and no less. System alterations and new installations usually require a building permit and inspections. Make sure your contractor follows the local laws.

Indoor Air Quality

Today's super-insulated and airtight homes often require mechanical ventilation and air circulation to keep the air fresh and healthful. Without it, a home can start to feel like an airplane cabin. A qualified HVAC contractor can assess your system and home for air quality and recommend equipment for reducing pollutants, controlling humidity levels, introducing fresh air into the system, and increasing operating efficiency. For more information on indoor air quality, contact the U.S. Environmental Protection Agency's IAQ INFO service at 1-800-438-4318.

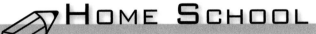

HOME SCHOOL

Here are the three main types of heating systems:

Forced air—Standard system with a gas-fired furnace and network of ducts. Some systems use a heat pump to draw heat or cold from the outdoor air. Though rare, it is also possible that your forced-air system uses an electric heating element.

Hot water (or hydronic)—System with a boiler that sends heated water through pipes and fixtures (convectors or radiators). Old systems (prior to 1940) use steam circulated through radiators. In addition to HVAC pros, many plumbers have the expertise to service hydronic systems.

Electric—Electric units are typically baseboard heaters used for supplemental heat, although some homes rely on electricity as the primary heat source. Work on electrical heating systems may require the help of an electrician rather than an HVAC pro.

Zone system—Heating system that divides the home into several areas, or zones, each with its own thermostat. By focusing heat where it's needed most, a zone system is often more effective and efficient than a standard system.

For more information on HVAC systems in your home, visit the website of the Air Conditioning Contractors of America (ACCA) at www.acca.org.

Licenses & Insurance?

Licensure of HVAC contractor and service technicians is required in most areas, and all should carry liability and workers' compensation insurance.

☎ In the Phone Book

Heating Contractors, Air-conditioning Contractors/Repair; Boilers–New & Used; Boilers–Repair & Clean; Furnaces–Cleaning; Furnaces–Heat, Sales & Service.

HOME BUILDER

SEE: CHAPTER 4

HOME INSPECTOR

For Help With:

- Pre-purchase home inspections

If you're buying a house, you must have it inspected. It doesn't matter if the house is brand spanking new, 20 years old, or 200 years old. Buying a house without a thorough inspection report is like buying a used car without driving it. That said, there are good inspectors and bad inspectors, and all kinds in between. The following tips will help you find a good one and help you get the most from your inspection.

What Inspectors Do

Home and building inspectors (also called property inspectors) are independent, trained professionals who conduct a detailed visual examination of a home's physical structure and systems. Following the visual inspection, an inspector completes a detailed report of her findings. This report gives the buyer an overview of the house's condition and alerts him to any major problems in addition to small defects. If warranted, the buyer can use the report to negotiate a price reduction or obtain a credit from the seller to cover the cost of repairs or replacements. Or the seller may be required to remedy the problems before the closing.

Inspectors examine homes of all types, including single-family homes, townhouses, condos, and co-ops. All types of dwellings should be inspected. In the case of condos and other multi-unit housing, you're buying into the building as well as your individual unit. Your inspector should assess the condition of the entire building and all common areas.

A standard pre-purchase home inspection includes an examination of the following:

- Foundation
- Basement or crawlspace
- Structural framing
- Exterior siding and trim
- Roof and gutters
- Chimneys and roof penetrations
- Insulation and ventilation
- Interior walls, ceilings, and floors
- Bathrooms and kitchens (including all fixtures and appliances)
- Plumbing and electrical systems
- Heating and cooling systems

- Windows and doors
- Smoke detectors
- Water pressure
- Common problems such as mold, mildew, leaks, and insects

Following a standard inspection, your inspector may recommend further inspections, such as a pest-control inspection to check for termites, carpenter ants, dry rot, and other destructive things. These are commonly recommended in warm climates. Your inspector may also refer you to a trade specialist, such as a roofer, for a more in-depth assessment of specific elements of the home that need repair.

Home inspectors won't pass or fail a house. Their job is to provide an objective, comprehensive report on the home's condition and note defects that currently need attention or are likely to need work in the near future. A thorough inspection typically takes between two and four hours to complete.

Inspector Qualifications

Surprisingly, professional home inspectors are not licensed or regulated in most areas, so you have to be especially diligent in seeking a pro with the right training and experience. The closest thing to certification in the field is membership in the American Society of Home Inspectors (ASHI; www.ashi.org). Bear in mind that membership is voluntary and doesn't guarantee quality work, but ASHI's requirements for membership are rigorous enough to indicate a decent level of proficiency and experience. To qualify for membership an inspector must have completed at least 250 professional inspections and pass a written technical exam administered by ASHI. Members must also agree to abide by a code of ethics (most associations require that) and participate in continuing education, currently at least 20 hours each year.

In addition to direct inspection experience, many inspectors have backgrounds in related fields, such as architecture, engineering, and the construction trades. If, for example, your inspector used to be an electrician, he'll be great at spotting wiring problems. But any related professional experience is likely to broaden the scope of the inspector's review in one way or another.

Finding & Interviewing Candidates

You're looking for an objective, independent, full-time professional inspector who has no connection whatsoever to the purchase of the home. So how do you find that person? A reference from a friend or trusted acquaintance who used an inspector recently is a good place to start, provided the inspection was thorough and the inspector was a good source of information. But if your friend liked the inspector because the whole process was "quick and easy," then their referral might not count for much.

Other sources for names are the ASHI website (which has a locator for finding member inspectors in your area), the phone book, and real estate agents. There is a big caveat with agent referrals, though, because some inspectors get more insider referrals because they're known to go soft on inspections to make the closing process a little easier. But if you know and trust your agent, going with his or her recommendation can eliminate a lot of guesswork.

THE INTERVIEW

It's a good idea to interview several candidates to find the best fit for your home. Here are some of the important questions to ask:

1. How long have you been a full-time inspector? How many inspections have you done?
2. What are your qualifications? Building-related background? Professional associations?
3. Where do you perform most of your inspections (what towns/areas), and on what types of residences? (The idea here is that you want an inspector who is familiar with the local building codes and regulations and with your type of dwelling.)
4. Do you carry errors and omissions insurance? (This insurance helps to cover repairs and expenses resulting from an oversight or mistake on the inspector's part.)
5. Do you contract for repair work on homes you inspect? (The answer to this must be No. An inspector who does repair work on clients' homes reeks of self-guaranteed job security—the practice is actually forbidden for ASHI members.)
6. How much do you charge? (You want someone with competitive pricing but generally not the lowest bidder. Saving $100 or so by going with a lousy inspector could cost you many thousands down the road.)
7. Do you have a list of recent customers whom I may contact?

Also ask how long a typical inspection takes, and request to see one or two sample reports done on homes similar to yours. A thorough report describes each area of the home in detail. Photographs of damaged or cited areas of the home are helpful, too. If the sample reports you get are simplistic checklists with little written description, look for another inspector. The ASHI Standards of Practice, available on the ASHI website, features a detailed list of what an inspection and report should include.

Finally, make sure the inspector is comfortable with you being present during the inspection (more on this on the following page). You're not required to be there, but if the inspector discourages your presence, consider it a red flag.

When to Hire an Inspector

In most cases, the actual inspection takes place after the buyer signs the contract for the house purchase. The buyer is then allowed a specified amount of time (typically 3 to 10 days) to get their inspection done. Considering this short allotment of time (and the usual craziness of home transactions), some experts recommend looking for an inspector at the beginning of the house-hunting process. You won't actually hire the inspector until a house contract is signed, but having a pre-screened pro on deck means you won't be pressured to hire just anyone when you're under the gun.

Tip: Your real estate agent should tell you this anyway, but make sure the sales contract includes an inspection clause specifying that the final agreement is contingent upon the results of the inspection.

Getting the Most from Your Inspection

You've done your research, you've asked all the right questions, and you've hired your top candidate. Now, if you don't show up for the inspection, you'll be missing out on a lot of good advice. Chances are you'll end up buying the house, so why not get a guided tour to help you become familiar with its systems? Of course, the inspector must get her job done, but it's perfectly acceptable for you to tag along and ask questions about inspection notes you don't understand. You may even spot some potential problems yourself and can point them out to the inspector.

It's usually beneficial—for both the buyer and seller—if the seller's agent is also present at the inspection. This lends credibility to the inspector's findings when they're brought to the negotiating table.

Read the completed inspection report as soon as you get it. Make sure it includes every important item discovered or discussed in the inspection. If you think something is missing or you have any questions about the report, contact your inspector right away; you probably won't have much time to iron things out before your deadline.

Licenses & Insurance?

As mentioned, licensure of home inspectors is not required in most areas, but it's a good idea to ask your city or state licensing office about the local laws. If licensure is required, make sure to use a licensed inspector. Liability insurance, as well as errors and omissions coverage (mentioned earlier), is recommended.

☎ In the Phone Book

Home & Building Inspector.

HOUSE CLEANER

For Help With:
- Weekly, bi-weekly & monthly cleaning service
- One-time cleanings
- Preparing a home for moving in/out

Professional house cleaning is one of the most highly valued of affordable luxuries. And why wouldn't it be? You're letting a pro take care of the dirty work, who will likely do it much better than you. But more significant for most people is the idea that paying for house cleaning is essentially buying time. A pro can do in 6 hours what the average homeowner—who's subject to interruptions by kids, phone calls, etc.—can do in perhaps 10 hours or more. So what's 10 hours of your time worth? When you think of it in those terms, regular cleaning service can be a real bargain.

Okay, you're probably not here to be convinced that you need a cleaning pro; you want to know how to find a good one. The best way to start is to ask around. Lots of people hire house cleaners and most of them will give you a detailed report of their cleaner's professionalism and personality—maybe even too much detail. (The difference between house cleaning and other home-related trades is that with house cleaning, everyone's an expert.) However, don't be surprised if you meet with some resistance. People who love their house cleaner may be wary of giving out too many referrals, lest their cleaner become overbooked and inflexible with scheduling. It's ugly but true.

The phone book and Internet are also standard sources for finding cleaning pros. When you've gathered some names or selected a few local cleaning companies, call to discuss their pricing and standard cleaning services. Basic packages typically include:

- Complete kitchen and bathroom cleaning
- Vacuuming
- Dusting
- Cleaning fixtures and removing cobwebs
- Linen change

To these services you might add specific items or tasks, such as:

- Windows
- Laundry
- Furniture and drapery
- Floor waxing
- Wood polishing

Ask each candidate about service contracts and how they handle cancellations or changes to regular cleaning appointments. Make sure the cleaner or company (and all of its employees) is insured, and discuss the process for dealing with damage or theft in your home. Also ask about equipment and supplies—most cleaners provide their own tools and cleaning supplies, but not all do. If you're sensitive to strong chemicals or cleaning agents, you might request that the cleaners use your supplies.

After talking with a few candidates and getting price estimates, decide which services you want, then decide which cleaner or company best fits your needs. Schedule a cleaning appointment and plan to be home when the cleaners arrive. It's a good idea to start with a quick walk-through of the rooms to be cleaned and to discuss particulars like where to leave garbage and what to do if the dog tries to attack the vacuum.

HOME SCHOOL

Here's a cleaning tip: This may sound crazy, but you have to tidy up around the house before each cleaning appointment. Professional cleaners are there to clean, not to pick up your kids' toys or to file your stacks of paperwork. As any house cleaning customer will tell you, your cleaners will be much more thorough if they don't have to work around your clutter.

Licenses & Insurance?

As mentioned, insurance is important to protect you from property damage and other problems. Licensure of cleaners is not standard but may be required in your area; check with your city or state licensing office.

☎ In the Phone Book

House Cleaning, Maids & Butlers.

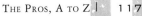

INTERIOR DESIGNER
(& INTERIOR DECORATOR)

For Help With:

- Complete home interior design & decorating, including:
  - ☐ Space planning
  - ☐ Paint, texturing & wallcoverings
  - ☐ Window treatments
  - ☐ Molding, woodwork & built-ins
  - ☐ Floor surfaces
  - ☐ Furniture selection
  - ☐ Custom upholstery & fabric creations
  - ☐ Lighting design
  - ☐ Renovation project management

Interior design has been around as long as the home itself. And while most home-owners take it upon themselves to decorate their own living spaces, professional designers and decorators offer the potential of creating something extraordinary. Will they make you glamorous and witty, a commanding presence in elite social circles? Probably not. Of course, you may already possess those qualities, or you might just feel that way in your newly designed rooms.

What a designer can definitely do for you is:

1. Help you define your own likes and dislikes;
2. Provide creative vision and technical expertise for achieving your project goals; and
3. Make it all happen with insider connections, professional shopping skills, and (hopefully) an uncanny knack for knowing what looks good.

And today's designers can do a lot more than choose colors and patterns. Many are trained in special arts, such as historic restoration, interior building design, and complete kitchen and bathroom planning. If you're building a house or addition from the ground up, you might hire a designer along with your architect to refine the interior spaces for a truly custom home.

Note: If your project involves kitchen or bathroom design, see Kitchen Remodeler (page 121) or Bathroom Remodeler (page 53) for more information on working with professionals specifically trained in kitchen and bath design.

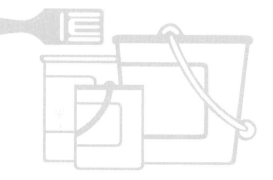

What Happened to Interior Decorator?

While it may seem that Interior Designer is just the fashionable contemporary name for an interior decorator (just as *secretary* evolved into *assistant*, and *carpenter* is often upgraded to *builder),* the two titles describe fairly distinct professional groups. Interior decoration focuses on all of the standard ornaments and surface stuff that make up the look of a room: paint and wallpaper, window treatments, flooring, upholstery, furniture, and artwork. Interior design includes the same decorative elements but goes beyond that to encompass floor plans; lighting design; architectural details and built-ins; and the placement of doors, windows, and even staircases. In terms of technical expertise, designers as a group span the gap between decorators and architects.

Which one is right for you depends on the scale of your project. If you're making cosmetic changes or just need some color recommendations, a decorator may be the better choice. At the other end of the spectrum, if you're building a new house or a large addition and you want the space to be characterized by the artful use of natural light and a unique floor plan, you'll need the help of a highly trained interior designer.

Interior designers are required to pass a nationally accredited exam and complete a minimum number of work hours, while interior decorators need no formal training before setting up shop. Talent, of course, is something that can't be tested, and it's up to you to judge a professional's ability, regardless of what her title is. (For the record, "designer" is such an inclusive word that you'll often hear it used in place of "decorator." And the truth is, designer is a bit more fashionable these days.)

Design for Modest Budgets

There is a popular misconception that interior designers work only on large projects with 5- or 6-digit budgets. In reality, design is like any other field, where work is work, and small jobs help pay the bills right along with big ones. As a client, you might need only a few hours to sit down with a designer to discuss your project. Even if you're planning to complete the work (shopping, installation, etc.) yourself, you'll gain valuable advice by consulting with a designer or decorator beforehand. Many (not all) designers will be happy to work with this type of arrangement.

Finding a Compatible Designer

Searching for a "compatible" professional may seem a little artsy-fartsy, but it's appropriate when talking about design. You don't really care if your septic tank service guy is a little surly (and who could blame him?), but planning and decorating your home is different. It's an emotional process that hinges on the intangible and irrational notions of personal taste (imagine telling the septic guy that you don't like his work because it's "just a little too billowy"). Therefore, it's important to find a designer who has similar ideas to yours about what looks good. You also want to make sure this person is someone you can get along with through the many discussions and disagreements that decorating usually involves. It's true that designers are trained to work within a range of styles, but they're human, too, and are likely to be more interested in your project if they're comfortable with your style.

The best way to learn about a designer is to see his work. Looking through a portfolio of recent projects will give you a sense of his personal style and abilities. Some designers impart a recognizable "signature" style on each project (and some clients desire this), while others let the client's vision lead the way. Make sure you and your designer see eye-to-eye on this point. Other ways to see a designer's work include visiting show homes and looking through local home magazines. Also, if you like a room in an acquaintance's home, ask who designed it.

Personal referrals are always the best way to hear about a designer's work ethic and professionalism, which are just as important as his design sense. Conduct a background check on all potential candidates (see Chapter 1) to look for customer complaints. Checking designers' qualifications is less cut-and-dried than with other professions. Some states require licensure for interior designers. There are also certification programs offered by the American Society of Interior Designers (ASID) and the National Council for Interior Design Qualification (NCIDQ), but most professional designers choose not to participate in the certification. So, beyond checking for a license (if required in your area) and checking references, you'll have to rely on examples of a designer's work to inform your decision.

Before you decide to use any designer, be sure to discuss budget and timing. The designer needs to know how much you're willing to spend on the project, and you need to know when the designer can fit you into his schedule.

Designers' Fees
Paying for design services can be fairly complicated, and you should discuss the fee structure openly with your designer before signing a contract. The contract must spell out the services requested and the fee structure and include a timetable for the project.

Designers charge in a few different ways:

Pure design fee: This may be on a flat-rate or hourly basis. It's used when a client seeks only design advice and/or plans, or when the next step (making purchases and contracting labor) is undetermined. Some designers require a retainer or down payment fee before any design work is done.

Product fee: A large portion of a designer's revenue comes from supplying clients with all the decorating elements (furniture, fabrics, rugs, etc.) and charging a markup for each item. This is often a good value for clients, because designers have access to the good stuff at wholesale prices, even after the standard 30% to 35% markup is added by the designer. Often, a portion of the initial design fee is applied toward product fees on the same project. Note: The standard markup applies to new products. If you're planning to redecorate with antiques, discuss this thoroughly with your designer. Pricing by antique retailers is often variable and negotiable, and you'll want to make sure you're getting a good deal.

Management fee: Designers who serve as general contractor for a remodeling project typically charge a set percentage–often around 10% to 15%–of the total project cost. Designers may also charge for commissioning and overseeing the work of fabricators and craftspeople to create items for your project, such as upholstery and custom furniture.

☎ In the Phone Book
Interior Decorators & Designers, Designers–Home & Commercial.

KITCHEN REMODELER
(& KITCHEN DESIGNER)

For Help With:

- Complete kitchen remodeling design & construction services

With its pristine surfaces, gleaming appliances, and custom layout, there's nothing quite as fabulous as a newly remodeled kitchen. Then again, there's nothing quite as involved as a kitchen remodel. No other room in the house requires such complex orchestration of fixtures, materials, utilities, and decoration to create a work space that is both beautiful and functional. That's why it's important to plan the remodeling process carefully and to find the right professional help for your job.

Generally defined, a qualified kitchen remodeler is an experienced construction contractor who works from a set of design drawings to complete every aspect of a kitchen remodel. Most likely, this contractor hires subcontractors for specific aspects of the work, like plumbing, electrical, and countertop fabrication. In a typical scenario the kitchen remodeler acts as general contractor and is responsible for organizing and overseeing the work of all subcontractors. In other situations, though, the contractor or his direct employees may do much of the work.

There are plenty of experienced kitchen remodelers in every sizable town, but be warned that "experienced" is not used lightly here. A kitchen remodel is not a good time to give a new kid a chance. Kitchens are just too complicated and too easily require expensive changes when things don't go as planned. The bottom line: don't even consider a remodeler who hasn't done plenty of kitchens similar in scale to your project.

Finding the Right Professionals

To find a good remodeler for your kitchen project, follow the process described in Chapter 4 to interview several candidates. A large kitchen remodel also necessitates written job specifications to use for obtaining bids from prospective contractors. In order to be as clear and complete as possible, the specifications are best drafted after the bulk of the planning and design work is done.

Designing Your New Kitchen

When industry people talk about kitchen design they mean everything from the utility lines and floor plans to cabinet pulls and paint color. The design is the master blueprint of the entire space, and it's something every homeowner should get help with. How much help you need usually depends on the scale of the remodel.

Professionals who provide kitchen design advice (not all are professional designers) may work for cabinet dealers, home centers, lumberyards, remodeling firms, or other kitchen-related businesses. There are also independent professional designers who specialize in creating, or re-creating, an entire kitchen plan from scratch and are often involved in shopping for fixtures and supplies. Some, but not most, independent designers can be hired to act as general contractor for the remodel construction.

If your remodel is relatively small in scale—for example, replacing appliances and surfaces but making no significant changes to the floor plan—you might get all the design help you need from materials suppliers, manufacturers, or your remodeling contractor. Advice from these sources is likely to be free, provided that you're buying some related product or service. If your remodel goes a step further and includes a whole new set of cabinets, your cabinet supplier will probably have a designer on staff who can give you advice and create design drawings based on your cabinet specifications.

For a major remodel—that is, significant redesign of the floor plan and a whole new look or style—an experienced professional designer is almost always worth the money. At this level, some designers work for large remodeling firms or for design firms (either as contractors or direct employees), while others are self employed as independent businesses. See pages 118 to 120 for additional tips on finding and contracting a designer for your project (the focus is on interior designers, but most of the same information also applies to kitchen designers).

The National Kitchen & Bath Association (NKBA), the leading professional organization for the kitchen and bath remodeling industry, has a designer locator on their website (www.nkba.org). It provides a list of each designer in your area who has completed the NKBA's highly respected certification program to become a Certified Kitchen Designer (CKD). Certification requires seven years of work experience in addition to NKBA coursework and exams. The CKD title won't guarantee you'll have success working with a specific designer, but it is a meaningful professional qualification.

Finally, if you're planning a major-major remodel—for example, putting on an addition to make room for a new kitchen—it might be more efficient to use an architect for everything rather than hiring a separate designer for the kitchen plan. Of course, an architect who specializes in kitchen design is the best choice (see pages 43 to 47 for help with finding a qualified architect).

Working with a Kitchen Designer

What you hope to get by using a kitchen designer is, quite simply, good design. A lot of people can lay out a functional, efficient kitchen space, but it takes real ability to present creative ideas, apply distinctive (or architecturally appropriate) styling, and devise a truly custom plan tailored to your family's use of the kitchen. It's okay to expect a lot from a good designer, but your role is important, too. Be up-front with your opinions and with budget concerns, and don't make the designer wait for weeks while you agonize over every decision.

Most design processes start with an initial consultation—under the gloomy, inadequate lighting of your old kitchen. You'll discuss your ideas, goals, and wishes for the project and probably show the designer all kinds of clippings and dog-eared pages from glossy design magazines; i.e., examples of your dream kitchen. The designer will (or certainly should) ask about how and when the kitchen is used most and what you like and dislike about the current setup. In the end, the designer will leave with a page full of measurements and a better feel for the overall project.

Next comes a set of preliminary drawings, followed by your review and, typically, a few rounds of refinements. Then you get a set of final drawings. At that point, the designer's work may be done, or she may proceed to shop for materials and supplies and/or make construction plans. It all depends on what you've agreed upon at the outset. The final drawings are what your contractor will follow to carry out the actual remodeling work.

You don't have to secure a contractor and designer at the same time, but some overlap can be beneficial. For example, if you're working with an independent designer (one who doesn't work with the remodeling contractor's firm), you should show your plans to the contractor before finalizing everything with the designer. This is a good way to get a second, construction-focused opinion of the project before the design is set in stone.

TAKE-OUT TRAUMA (OR SURVIVING A KITCHEN REMODEL)

Your remodeling contractor estimates that your kitchen will be out of commission for about three weeks during the remodel. Thinking ahead, you and your family plan to make do with TV dinners, take-out meals, and a few restaurant outings a week.

But before you call in that first order of "Rotisserie Chicken with Two Sides of Mashed Potatoes," you will be well advised to apply some basic math: Three meals per day for three weeks equals 63 primary meals. Now double that (your remodel could easily take twice as long as estimated). That's 126 meals. Now add up how much it will cost to buy many of those meals from restaurants. Also consider the price you will pay in spiritual trauma for having to eat dozens of Salisbury steak TV dinners on your lap (not to mention what the microwave will do to the already gummy cherry cobbler dessert).

The point is, your family will endure the upheaval much better if you prepare for the long haul:

- Set up a makeshift kitchen in a convenient place where it won't interfere with the remodel. A refrigerator, microwave, coffee pot, toaster oven, and hot plate will get you through most everyday meals.

- Rely on a large, sturdy table for holding appliances and preparing food. Flimsy card tables (or the backs of couches) are not safe places for cooking.

- Use paper plates and plastic cups and utensils as much as possible (unless you like washing dishes in the bathtub).

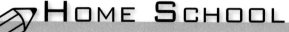 Home School

Kitchen remodeling has become nothing short of an obsession for American homeowners. As a result, the variety and availability of cool products and fancy equipment for kitchens are seemingly endless. This is a good thing. However, before you hit the showrooms with a stainless-steel gleam in your eye, keep in mind that the kitchen is a place for work; it's not just for show. If you choose a cooktop because it looks good with your countertop material without considering whether is has the right features for the type of cooking you do, you'll be sorry.

And don't assume there's any correlation between price tag and performance. High-end appliance manufacturers are notorious for over-engineering their products without much thought given to basic practicality. Case in point: Those futuristic vent fans that slide up automatically behind your stove—great idea, but not so great in practice because the fan sucks all the burner's heat to the rear half of your pan. The only way to know whether an appliance, product, or material is right for you is to give it a test drive.

Licenses & Insurance?

Make sure your contractor is fully insured for workers' compensation and liability. Licensing of remodeling pros is common, so make sure your contractor meets all applicable state and local licensing requirements. Professional designers are required to be licensed in some states.

☎ In the Phone Book

Contractors–Remodeling & Repair, Kitchen Cabinets & Equipment, Kitchen Remodeling, Remodeling Services, Designers–Home & Commercial.

LANDSCAPE DESIGN & CONSTRUCTION

INCLUDING:

- LANDSCAPE ARCHITECT
- LANDSCAPE DESIGNER
- LANDSCAPE CONTRACTOR

SEE ALSO: GARDENER, LAWN SERVICE, SPRINKLER SYSTEM CONTRACTORS, TREE SERVICE

For Help With:

- Complete landscape design & consulting services
- Landscape construction & installation, including:
  - Walls & fences
  - Patios & paths
  - Boulders, berms & contouring
  - Trees, plants & flowers
  - Ground covers & loose materials
  - Arbors, trellises & shelters
  - Sprinkler systems
  - Water features
  - Outdoor lighting
- Landscape maintenance

If you've ever seen a home "makeover" show featuring the transformation of a backyard, you've witnessed television's sleight of hand at its most profound. After a scathing review of the homeowner's pathetic landscape, the design and construction pros descend upon the scene. Approximately 9.4 minutes later (including commercial breaks, of course), the work is done. Meanwhile, the homeowner has barely had enough time to fill the tiki torches in preparation for the celebration party.

In reality, completing a major landscaping project takes at least two months and often up to a year. And when the initial work is done, the setting looks more like *Little House on the Prairie* than *Fantasy Island*. This is because well-designed landscapes need time to mature. Over-planting a yard for instant gratification (or to satisfy a TV audience) is expensive and ultimately unhealthy for the plants.

The point to be made here is that success in landscaping requires patience and long-term planning. With that in mind, you're ready to start looking for the pros who will help you transform your own outdoor home.

The three groups of professionals to consider are *landscape architects, landscape designers,* and *landscape contractors.* Which pros are right for your project depends largely on how much design work is required and how much of the physical work you plan to do yourself—both in creating the new landscape and in maintaining it for years down the road. While each of these groups offers its own set of core services, you'll find that the professions overlap quite a lot (particularly in the area of design). Yet it's likely that you'll end up hiring more than one type of pro. For example, you might work with a landscape architect to develop comprehensive plans for your property then hire a landscape contractor's crew to carry out the work. You may also decide to retain the architect to oversee the construction process.

Landscape Architect

Landscape architects are highly trained and licensed practitioners who design everything from backyard gardens to city parks. On a residential job, an architect can help plan and engineer all sorts of hardscape elements, like retaining walls, water features, arbors, and patios, as well as the complete range of softscape features: trees, shrubs, turf, loose materials, and garden plants.

Because of their comprehensive knowledge of outdoor environments, landscape architects often are hired during the early design stages of new-home projects. They can be instrumental in making decisions affecting the entire property, including the home's orientation on the site, the location and configuration of driveways and parking areas, the size and placement of decks and patios, and specifications for grading, drainage, and irrigation.

Like conventional architects, landscape architects offer a combination of technical expertise and creative thinking. They design projects on paper, using hand-drawn sketches and computer-aided design programs. Their completed plans are used for obtaining permits from city building and zoning departments and to serve as the blueprints for work crews to follow. Landscape architects are also experienced construction consultants who can advise clients when obtaining bids and choosing a landscape contractor, and they can represent the client to ensure that all work meets the standards of the original plans and the client's wishes.

In addition to licensure at the state (and sometimes local) level, landscape architects may enhance their qualifications by joining the American Society of Landscape Architects. Members must have at least three years of professional experience as licensed architects and abide by the Society's Code of Professional Ethics. For more information, visit www.asla.org. Fees for architects' services typically are based on the time spent on the design (or consulting services) and may be assessed by the hour or by the job. Depending on the geographic area, architect fees typically range from 7% to 15% of the total cost of construction.

Landscape Designer

If landscape architects are similar to conventional architects in their ability to conceive the master plan of a space, then landscape designers can be likened to interior designers—professionals who have much less technical training than architects but who are conversant in the vast range of materials, colors, and textures that give a space its character and beauty. Designers may work independently or work with a landscape contracting company, nursery, or garden center.

Experienced landscape designers know how to analyze soil and climatic conditions, design complete exterior spaces to suit clients' needs, and select appropriate plant materials and hardscape elements for a given design. A designer should be skilled at drafting landscaping plans to convey her ideas and outline construction details and plant specifications. In other words, if hiring a landscape architect seems like overkill for your project, a good designer is probably a better fit for your needs. Keep in mind that a designer's drawings and construction specifications may not be adequate for obtaining certain permits and permissions from building and zoning departments, although in many cases they are more than adequate.

Landscape designers are not required to be licensed and come from a variety of educational backgrounds. Many have college degrees in horticulture or related disciplines or have received most of their training on the job. As a result, qualifications among individual designers vary widely. The Association of Professional Landscape Designers sponsors a certification program for its professional members. Certification requirements include at least two years of professional design experience and acceptance by APLD's certification committee based on a review of submitted plans and other data, as well as participation in continuing education.

How do you know if a designer has the right qualifications? Ask about her education, experience, and design strengths. And most important, look at her work; that's where real ability shows through. Designers' fees are assessed in a number of different ways. Independent designers may charge by the hour or the job, while designers who work for contractors or nurseries may roll their fee into the total project cost. This can make it difficult to compare designers based on cost. With package deals, you'll have to consider the designer's ability and services as part of the overall value of the contractor's bid.

Landscape Contractor

Landscape contractors are the pros who bring your plans and ideas to life. Most are full-service providers who supply everything for the job—trees, plants, sod, and other softscape materials—as well as build all types of hardscaping, like retaining walls, patios, paths, fences, water features, and sprinkler systems. Larger firms often have landscape designers on staff and offer complete design/build packages. Once the work is done, you might hire the same contractor to take care of ongoing maintenance of the new landscape.

If you're creating a totally new landscape or making significant improvements to an existing one, the job is likely to be complex and expensive. It's not uncommon for homeowners to spend 10% or more of the total value of their property on the landscaping. These big-ticket jobs require a full-scale bidding and hiring process, such as you would conduct for a major remodel or addition (see Chapter 4 for more information on preparing for a major project). Spend some time thinking about what you hope to achieve with the landscaping, and define your goals as clearly as possible.

Of course, if you're working with a landscape architect or designer, your dreams and goals will be represented in detailed plans and job specifications, which are valuable tools for obtaining accurate bids from contractors.

If you're hiring a landscape contractor for maintenance services, start by listing everything that needs care. For example, how often should the lawn be mowed? Are there trees and shrubs that need pruning, and how often? Would you like to have annual flowers replaced on a regular basis? Next, determine your budget. How much do you want to spend on monthly or yearly fees? When it's time to choose a contractor, interview several candidates and obtain bids derived from on-site consultations. Make sure your contractor is fully insured as well as licensed if required in your area. Also make sure that any workers sent to your house will be pre-screened employees of the contractor.

Before Hiring a Landscape Design Professional

Designing an outdoor home is a collaborative process. And whether you have plenty of ideas to share or you're planning to give your designer total creative authority, you'll be better equipped to hire the right design help if you first answer a few questions about your project:

1. *What is your goal?* How do you envision your new landscape? Do you want distinct areas for specific uses or just a beautiful composition that looks great from the house? Do you have any long-term plans for add-ons, such as a greenhouse, a swimming pool, or an outbuilding? What do you expect from the landscape in 5 years? 10 years?

2. *What is your style?* Start a collection of magazine clippings and book pages showing what you like and don't like. Take photos of other landscapes in the area that suit your taste. Be on the lookout for plants, flowers, trees, and structures that strike your fancy. The more you have to convey your sense of style to your designer the better.

3. *What is your budget?* It helps designers to have a rough idea of how much you're planning to spend on the entire project. But be careful here: Much of the cost of landscaping comes after the initial design and construction work is done. The costs of fertilizers, tools, water, etc., add up over time. If you plan to hire out the maintenance to a contractor, how much will that cost each month?

4. *What are your maintenance concerns?* Ongoing maintenance is a critical aspect of landscape design. Be realistic about how much time and money you're willing to spend on regular upkeep—whether you do the work yourself or hire a service. Discuss this with your designer at the beginning of the creative process.

Landscape Lighting

Landscape lighting is a constantly evolving realm of exterior design, as more and more people understand the benefits of a thoughtful, creative lighting plan for their outdoor spaces. Lighting should be considered along with any landscape improvement. Pros who create outdoor lighting plans include landscape architects and designers and many landscape contractors. You may also choose to work with an independent lighting consultant or lighting designer who specializes in outdoor applications.

Licenses & Insurance?

Landscape architects currently are required to be licensed in 47 U.S. states. Licensure is not standard for landscape designers. As for landscape contractors, they must be licensed in many areas, sometimes depending on the type of work they do. Check with your state or city licensing office for specific requirements in your area. All landscape professionals should carry liability insurance. As for landscape contractors, make double-sure that all employees are covered by workers' compensation, since injuries are all too common with these jobs.

☎ In the Phone Book

Landscape Architects, Landscape Contractors, Landscape Designers, Lawn & Grounds Maintenance.

LAWN SERVICE

For Help With:

- Lawn fertilization & pest control treatments
- Complete lawn maintenance services

Need a little help maintaining your lawn? What, you don't like spending your free time pushing a noisy mower and crawling around on your knees digging up dandelions (which, incidentally, have the most steadfast and elusive root system known to mankind)? Let's face it, lawns are great for sports and picnics, but they're hell on your social life.

So, to whom do you turn for help? Professional lawn service companies, which cover the full range of treatments and maintenance tasks for turfgrass (as the fussy green stuff is known among experts). There are two basic levels of professional lawn service: treatment services and complete lawn care. Which level is right for you may be directly related to how much those dandelion roots have broken your spirit.

Lawn Treatment Service

The core function of lawn treatment services is to spray your grass with chemicals to control weeds, insects, and disease and to apply fertilizers to make the lawn thick and green. The rest of the work—watering, mowing, and general maintenance—is your responsibility. And it's important to keep your end of the bargain, because inadequate care between professional treatments will render them useless (unless you just enjoy having a fresh coating of chemicals on your property).

Complete Lawn Care

Full-service lawn care can be like having your own groundskeeper. Mowing, trimming, fertilizing, and tree and shrub care are blissfully whisked from your weekly schedule, leaving you time for more noble pursuits, like laundry or cleaning out the garage. Many service providers also take care of occasional lawn treatments, including power raking, aeration, and sprinkler system service. In snowy climates, companies may also contract for snow removal.

Choosing a Lawn Service

To select a company for any level of lawn service, talk with several candidates about how they fertilize, control pests, and treat turf diseases. In most areas, a lawn needs to be fertilized at most three or four times per year. Some lawn companies over-fertilize to beef up their numbers—and profits. Pest control is more complicated. Some companies advertise "healthy" treatments, which may or may not be an accurate description. If you're concerned about the chemicals and treatments used on your lawn, find out what the companies use, and check it out on your own.

Often, routine pesticide treatments can be excessive and ultimately less effective than a more targeted approach of monitoring the lawn and using pesticides only when pests are found. It's also important that lawn professionals know what specific pests they're treating for, rather than employing a scatter-bomb attack against any pests that *may be* in the area. For more information about fertilization and pest control practices in your location, contact a local Extension agency (these typically are affiliated with major universities).

Obtain price quotes from several companies, and check references by talking with some of their current clients. All quotes should include a detailed schedule of services and treatments proposed for your lawn. Ask about the companies' experience and training for working with grasses and pests in your geographic location. Someone new to the area or new to the lawn business may lack sufficient knowledge to solve problems and administer effective treatments on local grasses, plants, and pests. Finally, make sure any service agreement is bound by a written contract signed by both parties.

Licenses & Insurance?

The most important license held by lawn service providers is for pesticide use. Most states require certification and licensure for anyone who applies pesticides (including insecticides, herbicides, and fungicides). Make sure your contractor has the required training and credentials. Lawn service companies should be insured for liability and workers' compensation. Lawn services have been known to *spread* diseases with contaminated chemicals, so make sure they have insurance to repair any damage they might cause.

☎ In the Phone Book

Lawn & Grounds Maintenance.

MASON

For Help With:

- Building new walls & other structures of brick, stone & concrete block
- Brick repair & restoration
- Stone & brick veneer
- Stone, brick & concrete paver patios, drives & paths
- Interior stone flooring
- Fireplace & chimney construction & repair
- Glass block construction

When you hire a mason to build or repair an authentic masonry structure, you're buying into a time-honored tradition of craftsmanship that has changed very little over the centuries. Try to remember that when you see the contractors' estimates. Building with natural brick and stone is expensive for several reasons: namely, the cost of the materials and the amount of time and skill it takes to create a quality structure. But if you've chosen your mason and materials carefully, you'll enjoy your investment for many years to come–and, most likely, so will your grandchildren.

Choosing a Mason

The professional masonry trade includes specialists in bricklaying (and concrete block), stone work, and masonry restoration, as well as more specific areas of expertise, such as fireplace construction. Some masons are experienced in several types of building, while others focus on only one or two specific techniques. Another defining characteristic of a mason is his personal style. Traditional masonry, and stone work in particular, involves artistry as well as technical skill. Thus, not all masons' work looks the same.

Before contacting prospective masons for your project, conduct some research to get an idea of what you want in the finished product. Visit local brick and stone suppliers to see what materials are readily available, how much they cost, and what options you have for applying them for different effects. Many suppliers may have sample structures erected, allowing you to effectively "window-shop" for styles and effects. While you're there, ask for names of local masons who specialize in your preferred materials and building techniques.

Contact several masons who seem to fit the bill and ask about their experience with your type of project. Ask for several references of former clients, and make sure to include some projects that were completed many years ago. Older structures will show how well the mason's work has held up over time. It's important to see the mason's work firsthand, to get a sense of his personal style and attention to detail. If you're hiring a mason to build a fireplace, ask former clients about how well their fireplaces work. The design of a fireplace and chimney has a direct effect on how well the fire burns.

After interviewing candidates, have three or more of your top picks come to your house to inspect the project site and submit a formal bid. An on-site review of the project is important because many masonry applications require a concrete substructure or other type of support. Make sure this is discussed during the bidding process. Another thing to find out is whether a building permit is required for your

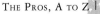

project (you may have to call your city's building department). Permits are standard for many masonry projects, including fireplaces, fire pits, and walls and structures over a certain height (typically 3 or 4 ft.). The official inspections that come with a building permit are one of the safeguards for the consumer, ensuring that basic structural criteria are met. If a permit is required, make sure your mason gets one.

Tuck-pointing & Other Brick Repairs

Tuck-pointing and *re-pointing* are the common terms for a standard brick restoration process in which loose, cracked, or deteriorated mortar is carefully removed and the joint is repacked with layers of fresh mortar. (Just in case someone tries to get fancy with you, true tuck-pointing was an old English technique of applying a thin veneer of mortar over brickwork, then cutting in fine, decorative mortar joints to make the brick look perfectly uniform.)

If you have a brick house or structure that needs repair, get a few professional opinions about your options for correcting the problem. Why? Because tuck-pointing is quite expensive, and it won't do you much good if the source of the damage (such as a leaky roof, structural settling, or excessive dampness) isn't dealt with first. If the structure has little or no historical value, the experts might recommend rebuilding over re-pointing.

For historic homes, it's important to find a qualified restoration professional. Re-pointing old brickwork requires accurate matching of the original mortar's formula and coloring. Getting it wrong can result in an ugly repair and can even damage the bricks. Experts on historic restoration—and possible sources for names of good contractors—include historic architects, architectural conservators, your state's historic preservation office, and the local chapter of the American Institute of Architects (www. aia.org).

Licenses & Insurance?

Licensure is common among masons, so check with your city office to learn about local regulations. Liability and workers' compensation insurance are a must.

☎ In the Phone Book

Mason Contractors, Stone Setting, Brick Cleaners & Finishes, Fireplaces, Glass—Block.

MORTAGE BROKER & MORTGAGE LENDER

For Help With:

- Shopping for & obtaining a home mortgage

First, some quick definitions: A mortgage lender is the person or institution that sells you a home loan. A mortgage broker is a professional who helps you find lenders and loans. Another type of broker you might run across in a home transaction is a real estate broker (see page 148). And now, a disclaimer: The following tips and information are intended to help you find qualified professionals in the home loan business. It is their job to steer you toward appropriate loans for your needs. Finding a good broker or lender is just one step to getting a good loan.

Do You Need a Mortgage Broker?

Technically, no. That is, it's perfectly feasible (and common) for ordinary borrowers to find a mortgage lender on their own. But it does take a fair amount of research and comparison shopping in the local market. Mortgage brokers do the shopping for you, and for that you pay them a fee based on a percentage of the loan amount, typically in the range of .5% to 2%.

A good broker can also guide you through the jungle of loan options and translate all the fancy mortgage-speak, like "assumability," "negative amortization," and "periodic cap." If your credit score isn't exactly stellar, a broker can help you make your loan application as flattering as possible and should know some lenders who are used to working with higher-risk borrowers.

Choosing a Mortgage Broker

In addition to the fee a mortgage broker receives from you, her client, she also earns a commission from the lender from whom you ultimately secure a loan. Usually you can get the same loan terms (interest rate and points) from the lender whether you use a broker or find the lender yourself. But this isn't always the case.

Which brings us to one of the key questions you should ask all prospective brokers: What's your commission rate? (In other words, what will you charge the lender for brokering the deal with me?) If a broker's commission is higher than the going rate for your size of loan, lenders might feel compelled to offer you less favorable terms to cover the broker's commission. Keep in mind that brokers' commissions usually are negotiable, so it makes sense to ask for a lower rate.

Another important thing to find out from prospective brokers is which lenders they deal with. A good, active broker will have a full roster including many major players in the industry. Be wary of brokers who represent only a few small-time lenders; the shorter their list of lenders, the more limited your exposure to the market. Finally, try to get a feel for the broker's acumen and her bank-side manner. Is she the kind of person who will patiently explain and advise you on pertinent loan details? Does she have the experience, the up-to-date knowledge, and the brains to know what's in your best interest?

One trick commonly used by unscrupulous brokers is to give you low-ball quotes to get your business. While they may be quoting you actual loans available through real lenders for real borrowers, it's possible that you're not the kind of borrower who qualifies for those loans. If you know who the lender is, you can contact them directly and ask them to confirm the broker's numbers.

Looking for Lenders & Loans

Tracking down a good, low-cost loan for your needs requires a basic knowledge of mortgages and lenders and, most importantly, lots of comparison shopping (enter, mortgage brokers). That said, here are some sources for finding lenders in your area and educating yourself about the wonderful world of mortgage lending:

- Your trusted real estate agent. Most agents will provide one or more names of lenders they've had good results with. This is a good place to start. However, every expert recommends that you also talk with additional lenders to compare with your agent's people. Your agent and her lenders will probably tell you to do the same.
- Friends, relatives, and coworkers. Pretty much anyone who owns a home has a mortgage on it.
- The real estate section of a major local newspaper. Many papers publish comparison charts of current interest rates offered by a group of local lenders. Because the rates and pricing information are incomplete and sometimes unreliable, these charts are better as a source for picking up lenders' names than for comparing actual loan costs.
- The Internet. As with most online information, it's important to take mortgage help with a grain of salt (or whatever spice that will help remind you of the considerable limitations of some electronic content). Many real estate professionals discourage borrowers from obtaining loans online, particularly from non-local lenders. Their reason (a good one) is that local lenders serve their clients best because they understand the local real estate market and property values. So why use the Internet? It's a good source for learning about mortgage types and for comparing the long-term costs of various loans and packages. It can also help you stay abreast of changes and trends in the marketplace. A few helpful websites to check out:
  - ☐ HSH Associates: www.hsh.com
  - ☐ Fannie Mae: www.fanniemae.com
  - ☐ E-LOAN: www.eloan.com
- The phone book. Here's what you'll find: a somewhat frightening section of blaring, full-page ads followed by names, names, and more names. Not much help, but it's there.

What to Look for in a Lender

Most mortgages are offered through one of three types of organizations: mortgage bankers, savings and loans, and traditional banks. These are called mortgage or loan "originators" because they are the folks who actually put up the money for your loan. To get a sense of the market, it's a good idea to compare loans from all three types of originators, although it's likely that you'll purchase your mortgage through a mortgage service company, which in turn will secure the loan through one of their preferred originators.

When it comes to the actual person who will handle your loan, look for someone who speaks plainly about the available products and can answer any questions you have. An honest lender will encourage you to comparison shop rather than try to convince you that his offers are unquestionably the best in town. You also want someone who knows the local market, even down to specific areas of town or neighborhoods. And he should be in the practice of seeking appraisals and loan approvals from local vendors. For the most part, lenders approve loans based on the perceived value of the home as much as on the borrower's creditworthiness. They need to understand the local market to know when a home is fairly priced.

If you found your lender through personal referrals, ask those who recommended him whether he got things done at the appropriate times. You don't want a deal to go sour because your lender procrastinates. And finally, after you've done some comparison shopping, you can try to negotiate a better rate from your preferred lender. If you're up-front about finding a lower-priced loan through a local competitor, your preferred lender may be willing to match it.

☎ In the Phone Book

Mortgages & Contracts.

MOVER

For Help With:

- Full-scale moving services

According to numerous personal accounts, working with a professional moving company can feel a lot like dealing with a foreign government. Despite your best efforts to state your needs and desires clearly, you're never quite confident that you're being understood, or even that *your* wishes are of any concern whatsoever. In the end, you cross your fingers and hope for a reasonable outcome. All too often this includes ugly surprises: "We're sorry, Ma'am, but because you were the one who packed your Fabergé egg, we can't be blamed for the television falling on it during the move."

Consumer complaints about movers are so common that the federal government has set up a 24-hour hotline for filing grievances (see below). But of course, your true objective is to avoid a grievous situation in the first place. And the best way to do that is by informing yourself. In addition to considering the general tips given here, visit the website of the Federal Motor Carrier Safety Administration at www.fmcsa.dot.gov. The FMCSA regulates interstate transport and shipping and grants licenses to moving companies. It's also the agency that operates the complaint hotline mentioned above, at 1-888-DOT-SAFT (1-888-368-7238).

On the FMCSA website you can find the following document: *Your Rights & Responsibilities When You Move*, which includes detailed information about:

- Preparing for a move
- Obtaining estimates
- Making sure all contracts and documents are complete and accurate
- Laws regarding charges, payments, insurance, and liability
- How to handle complaints and inquiries

Interstate movers are required to give you a copy of this document, but gaining the information early will increase your chances of finding a good mover to begin with. Most of the advice will be helpful whether you're moving in-state or out of state. However, for complaints and some specific information, the FMCSA is the appropriate contact for interstate moves only. If you're moving within your home state, contact the state's public utilities commission or other regulatory authority for information, complaint resolution, and local laws regarding moving and transport. Another source for general information about professional moving services is the American Moving and Storage Association at www.moving.org.

Estimates & Costs

Moving companies generally offer two kinds of estimates: binding and non-binding. A binding estimate is a complete written description of all proposed services and costs for your move, including the total price you will be charged. The total charge is what you can expect to pay, plus any charges for extra services you request (or that become necessary) during the move. Many companies charge a fee for binding estimates. A non-binding estimate also is a written description of the proposed services, but the cost estimate is approximate and may be higher or lower than your actual total cost.

For in-state service, moving charges typically are assessed on an hourly basis and may include minimums for labor hours or distance traveled. For interstate moves, charges are based on the weight of the stuff and how far it has to go. How do they weigh an entire household of goods? They weigh the moving truck twice—with and without your stuff.

Before you make your move, be sure to fully understand your contract's payment requirements (moving companies have their reasons for not participating in today's easy-pay culture). Standard payments include cash, money order, or bank check handed over at the time of delivery. Only some companies take credit cards. If you're not prepared to pay upon delivery, the movers may haul your stuff directly to a storage site, where it will sit until you pay the principal charge and any extras for storage and handling.

Licenses & Insurance?

Absolutely. Don't even consider using an unlicensed or uninsured mover. Contact the FMCSA (for interstate movers) or your state's regulatory agency (for local movers) to confirm a mover's licensure.

☎ In the Phone Book

Movers.

10 STEPS TO A SMART MOVE

1. *Hire only licensed and insured professionals.* Also run a background check to see if they have a history of complaints and how the complaints were resolved (see Chapter 1).

2. *Get accurate estimates.*
Make sure the movers see everything that has to go before they calculate your costs. If, for example, you forget to show them your shed full of blacksmithing tools, your final cost will be much higher than estimated.

3. *Choose insurance carefully.*
Movers typically offer several insurance packages (the four basic levels of insurance are outlined in *Your Rights & Responsibilities When You Move* available at www.fmcsa.dot.gov). Whatever insurance you choose, make sure you know exactly what's covered and what isn't.

4. *Get everything in writing.*
This may include:
   - Estimates
   - Inventory of goods
   - Bill of lading (your moving contract)
   - Order of service (specifying dates for pickup and delivery)
   - Freight bill and weight tickets

5. *Supply your own packing materials.*
Most movers charge a huge markup for basic items like boxes, packing foam, tape, etc. Moving equipment, such as blankets, dollies, and tie-downs, typically are provided by the movers at no charge.

6. *Have the movers pack the fragile stuff.*
Under most contracts, the movers are liable for damage to your stuff only if they packed it. But having the pros pack *everything* gets expensive. Instead, you can arrange to have them pack the dishes, furniture, and other breakables, while you pack all of the durable things. If something has great sentimental value—in other words, is truly irreplaceable—the safest option is to pack it yourself and move it in your own vehicle.

7. *Avoid peak moving times.*
If you can be flexible regarding when you move, ask prospective movers about discounts for scheduling on weekdays and during the slower season, generally October through April. Moving during the summer is usually more expensive, and the better moving companies in your area will have limited availability.

8. *Be ready for delivery.*
Make sure the movers can reach you when it's time to deliver your load. Also have the money—in the appropriate form—to pay upon delivery.

9. *Inspect your stuff before signing.*
Don't sign an inventory or any kind of receipt until you've seen all of your items and have inspected their condition.

10. *File complaints right away.*
You may be allowed up to 90 days to report damaged goods, but when you're dealing with customer service issues (and possibly arbitration), the sooner the better.

MUD JACKING

SEE: CONCRETE & CONCRETE CONTRACTORS

PAINTER

For Help With:

- Interior & exterior house painting
- Decorative (faux finish) painting treatments

While basic painting is something most amateurs can do themselves, the services of a good professional painter rank among the best home improvement values. The primary reason for this is labor. It takes a lot of time and effort to prepare a home for a new paint job—cleaning the surfaces, masking the windows and doors, covering the floors or ground with tarps, scraping and sanding old paint, and applying a primer. That's *before* any paint goes on.

When it comes to the actual paint job, high quality results require a lot more skill than most people realize. For example, amateurs think that the best way to get a clean edge—such as along a corner between a wall and ceiling—is to use tape. Pros know that paint seeps right under the tape, resulting in a sloppy line. Instead, they use their best brushes to freehand the edge, giving them total control of where the paint goes. This technique, called "cutting in," takes longer than taping, but it's a key difference between a homeowner job and a professional's work.

Because of the extensive labor involved, what you're looking for in a good painter is someone who simply takes the time to do it right. Sprayers and other modern equipment may speed up the process, but a good painter who uses a sprayer always follows up with detailed brush work. Even more important is the time and care a painter devotes to the preparation. This rule goes double for exterior jobs. So whether you're hiring a pro to paint the inside or outside of your house, knowing what to expect in a quality job is the first step to finding a good painter.

The All-important Prep Work

For interior painting, preparation includes:

- Cleaning the surfaces to remove all grease, dirt, dust, mildew, and other elements that don't take paint well.
- Patching and filling holes and cracks.
- Removing old caulking and applying new caulk as needed.
- Applying a stain-blocker and/or primer as needed.
- Masking doors, windows, woodwork, fixtures, switches, and outlets, and covering floors.

Exterior work is more complicated. Here are the basic steps (with notes about things to check out with your painter):

1. Cleaning all surfaces. This typically involves a chemical solution applied and rinsed off with a pressure washer. Do not hire a painter who wants to use a pressure washer to strip paint from your siding. It's too hard on the wood. Stubborn spots should be worked on by hand, not blasted with extra pressure. See page 146 for more warnings about the use of pressure washers on your home.
2. Scraping and sanding. All flaking, loose, and bubbling paint must be removed from the old paint job. Pros may use hand scrapers and/or

power tools to do this. Areas where scraping has left the surface uneven must be sanded smooth; otherwise, you'll get an ugly, bumpy finish like the kind you see on old houses.

3. Repairing damaged wood. Split and cracked boards should be caulked or replaced. Boards with rotted wood must be replaced or have the affected area removed, the surrounding wood stabilized, and all cavities patched.

4. Priming and caulking. Some painters prime first; others caulk first. The important thing is that they do both, as needed. If the old paint is in good condition, and you're not changing the paint color, priming may not be necessary. Don't let your painter caulk the undersides of windows or the horizontal seams between siding boards. Airflow is needed at these points to ventilate the interior of the house wall.

Keep in mind that you'll pay more for a painter who does a thorough job on the prep work, but it's the only way to get it right. And it's the only way to get your money's worth on the paint.

Use Good Paint

Everyone who knows anything about paint will tell you the same thing. Unless you're whitewashing the inside of a rental property in a college town, you'll get more value out of high quality paint than bargain stuff. Good paint promises richer color, better coverage, and greater longevity. And since most of the cost of professional painting is in the labor, you're actually wasting money by using cheap paint that will need another coat in a few years.

When you hire a painter, you can either choose the paint yourself (if the painter is amenable to the idea) or use one of the painter's selections that meets your standards of quality. Make sure all primer and paint materials are specifically noted in your written contract for the job. For more information on paint products, check out the Consumer Reports website at www.consumerreports.org, or pick up their most recently published paint reviews.

Things to Discuss with Prospective Painters

Finding a painter requires the standard process used for any big job: gather names of experienced local contractors, call several and interview them on the phone, then set up three or more on-site consultations to obtain accurate estimates for comparing the costs and services provided by each. Carefully check references, and have a contract drawn up before any work begins.

Here are a few things to discuss when interviewing candidates:

- Preparation and painting process. Does the painter routinely perform all of the steps discussed above?
- Paints used and number of coats required.
- Who will be on the job? Ideally, you'll meet with the painter or painters who will do the work. If there will be additional workers on the job, make sure a supervisor will be present or will visit the job frequently to inspect the crew's work.
- Lead paint. If your house is old and you think it might contain lead paint, ask the contractor about how he plans to deal with scrapings and dust.

- Liability. Will the painter be responsible for any damage and messes that occur in and around your home?
- Start and finish dates. Let the painter know that once the work starts, you expect him to be on the job every day until it's done.
- Labor-only bids. Ask whether the painter can provide a labor-only bid so you can isolate the cost of the paint from the price for the work.
- References. For exterior work, ask for references of jobs that are several years old; these will show how well the paint job has held up over time.

Contracts for Painting

Before any work begins, be sure to have a written contract that includes:

- Details of preparation work
- Exact paint materials, methods of application, and where each paint will be used
- Start and completion dates
- Payment schedule
- Warranties for the work and materials

Decorative Painters

So far, we've talked only about professionals who do standard, solid-color paint jobs. But what about those creative pros who specialize in faux finishes and other decorative paint treatments? The faux finish craze is still alive (actually, it's been around since antiquity), and there are plenty of skilled practitioners who work their magic with paint to create everything from weather-beaten stucco effects to dazzling full-wall murals. Where do you find them? Ask local interior designers and decorators or knowledgeable staff at quality paint stores. Also, you can tour show homes to see painters' work firsthand.

When interviewing decorative painters, ask to see a portfolio of their work, and find out if you can get samples of different paint treatments to take home with you. Fees for decorative work may be assessed on an hourly basis or be calculated into a single-cost bid.

Licenses & Insurance?

Painting contractors are not licensed in many areas. Ask your city's or state's regulatory office about the local laws. If licensure is required, you're better off using a licensed pro than an unlicensed one. Any painter you use must be insured for liability and workers' compensation.

☎ In the Phone Book

Painting Contractors, Faux Finishes.

PEST CONTROL

For Help With:

- All types of problem insects
- Mice, rats & other small rodents
- Termite inspections

Pest control operators (a.k.a. exterminators) rid your home of ants, spiders, bees, wasps, termites, roaches, bed bugs, and other destructive or just plain creepy things. Most pest control pros also take care of small nuisance rodents, like mice, rats, and voles. If your problem involves wildlife (squirrels, skunks, raccoons, snakes, etc.) that have taken up residence in your home, contact an Animal Control operator (page 40).

To find the right pest control service for your problem, first ask local pros about their experience in dealing with your particular pest. General household treatment methods usually eliminate ants, roaches, spiders, and seasonal invaders, while termites and other highly destructive pests require special knowledge and experience. Also ask about their methods of eradication. Some services like to set up automatic monthly or annual treatments, while others respond only when you call with a problem. Your comfort level with chemicals is another matter to discuss with contractor candidates.

Serious pest control requires expertise and thorough work. Keep this in mind when comparing services and prices. The cheapest estimate won't necessarily yield the best value.

Contracts & Guarantees

Many pest control operators guarantee their work. This generally means they agree to perform future treatments for free if bugs come back. Some guarantees cover damage to your home caused by returning pests. Make sure to read and understand any guarantee fully before signing up. It's common to find clauses outlining responsibilities that you must fulfill to maintain the guarantee. For example, if a pro treats your kitchen for roaches but you continue to decorate the room with old pizza boxes, the roach treatment won't last for long, and neither will the guarantee.

Contracts for pest control services are common in some climates where insects are a persistent problem. While many operators offer contracts for monthly visits, the current industry trend favors more extensive treatments with fewer return trips. It pays to shop around for contract terms that work for you. You might prefer to have monthly inspections as a preventive measure; on the other hand, do you want scheduled treatments to occur whether you need them or not?

As with guarantees, make sure you fully understand the terms of a contract before signing. Important contract items to look for include:

- Name and address of company
- Description of services (and costs)
- Length of service agreement
- Exclusion clauses
- Cancellation policy and penalties
- Errors & Omissions clause (who's responsible for accidental damage)
- Arbitration clause
- Signatures by both parties

For more information on pests and pest management in your area, contact your county's Extension office (look up your county in the phone book). Educating yourself is especially recommended if you live in an area prone to termite problems.

Licenses & Insurance?

Many states license qualified pest control operators. Insurance is highly recommended due to the liability of damage to your home caused by improperly managed pests or accidental operator damage.

☎ In the Phone Book

Pest Control, Exterminators.

PLASTERER

For Help With:

- Repair & restoration of plaster walls & ceilings
- Plaster moldings, medallions & other ornaments
- New plaster surface installation

When it's in good condition, traditional plaster is arguably the best interior wall finish. It's extremely durable, has good soundproofing and insulating qualities, and, when applied with a skilled hand, can be far more attractive than plain, old drywall. But when plaster starts to fail, things can get ugly. Often the visible damage on the surface is only the beginning, especially in old houses. That's why rule no. 1 of plaster repair is this: Don't do anything before carefully inspecting the damage and surrounding areas. In other words, the first step is to call a professional.

Plasterers use a variety of techniques to repair and restore old plaster walls and ceilings. The best approach in each case depends on several factors, including the condition of the existing surfaces and underlying structure, the historical importance of the home and the plaster elements, and the cost of restoring the plaster compared with tearing it out and starting over. For any major repair work, start by getting a few free estimates from full-time professional plasterers. These consultations, which must be done in your home, will help you to identify your options and give you a chance to assess the expertise of each contractor.

Historic Preservation

If your home has historical importance, your search for a plasterer will be more focused than for someone seeking basic repair work on an ordinary pre-WWII home. Preservation work requires a professional with a proven background in restorations. An experienced restorer can determine what type of plaster and application techniques were used on your home and present you with various options for matching the existing work following the original methods or using modern techniques to replicate the old plasterwork. You can find the names of qualified restoration pros and ornamental plaster shops by contacting your city's or state's historical society, architects and builders who specialize in historic preservation, or a local plasterers' union.

For more information on restoring traditional plaster surfaces and moldings, visit the website of the National Park Service at www.npa.gov. Search under the keyword "plaster" to find these two documents:

- Preservation Brief 21: Repairing Historic Flat Plaster—Walls & Ceilings
- Preservation Brief 23: Preserving Historic Ornamental Plaster

New Plaster Work

Drywall has all but replaced plaster in new construction, but custom builders and homeowners who want to pay a little more for the hand-troweled texture of real plaster find it in the relatively inexpensive technique of veneer plastering. Veneer plaster starts with a special drywall, commonly called *blue board,* which is fastened to the wall and ceiling framing just like regular drywall. The joints between panels are taped to create a flat surface, then the entire area is coated with one or two thin layers of real plaster applied with trowels.

As for plaster moldings and other ornamental work, you can still have custom pieces cast using traditional methods, or you can choose modernized versions made with foam-core construction for lightness and easy installation. If you're considering new plaster work for an addition or remodel, compare the costs and finish quality of veneer plaster (and modern moldings) to traditional 3-coat plaster. Be sure to visit actual jobs of prospective plasterers to see their work firsthand.

Licenses & Insurance?

Plasterers generally don't need licenses as proof of their training (as with electricians or architects), but they may have to carry a license to work in a given area; check with your city or state regulatory office. Any professional plasterer should have liability coverage to insure the quality and safety of their work.

☎ In the Phone Book

Plastering Contractors, Stucco & Texturing.

PLUMBER

For Help With:

- Repair, replacement & new installation of:
  - Water supply & drain systems
  - All fixtures that use water
  - Hot water heaters
  - Heating, ventilation & air-conditioning systems
  - Septic & sewage systems
  - Supply & ventilation lines for gas appliances
  - Water & gas appliance hookup

When you consider that a plumber is called in virtually every time a faucet leaks, a toilet backs up, or an expensive earring drops down a drain, it's easy to see why plumbers make up one of the largest building trades. And the fact is, the modern world just couldn't get along without plumbers (which might help to explain why they can charge so much; in truth, plumbers are among the highest-paid tradespeople, but who's in the mood to complain when their toilet won't flush?).

An experienced plumber who is trustworthy immediately becomes a key member of your home maintenance team. In some ways, it's like knowing a good doctor: Once you're a regular customer you generally receive better service. The plumber gets to know your house and its systems, and you can be confident using him for ordinary repairs as well as larger projects (depending on his training and experience, of course).

But before you set out in search of the perfect, all-around professional who handles every type of job, be aware that plumbers, like most skilled tradespeople, tend to specialize. Some focus on new construction and remodels, while others spend most of their time making house calls. The right pro for you will most likely be determined by your current needs.

Plumbers for House Calls

Most of the plumbing work needed in a home includes basic repairs (hopefully) and the occasional fixture upgrade or appliance hookup. For these jobs you need a plumber who is a good service professional, one who is courteous, prompt, respectful of your home, and honest. The plumber must be insured but may or may not be licensed; it depends on the local city or state laws.

Ideally, you'll have time to look for a good service-type plumber under normal circumstances—that is, not at 4:00 a.m. when a frozen pipe has just burst. Once you've established a relationship by hiring the plumber for a job or two you'll have someone to call in a real emergency. Tracking down a plumber like this is pretty much like finding most other service pros: ask around. Friends, relatives, neighbors, and coworkers can tell you about plumbers they've used and what their experiences have been like.

Plumbers should be up-front about their pricing. Usually they can give you a rough estimate for ordinary jobs and, when appropriate, present more than one option for solving your problem. Most plumbers charge an hourly rate for service calls (plus parts, trip charge, extra fee for weekends and off-hours, etc.). If you hire a pro based on a rough estimate and the final bill is substantially higher without a good explanation, look for another plumber next time. As always, a background check (see Chapter 1) is advisable.

Tip: When you've found a reliable plumber you like, don't forget about the trip charge (or the plumber's hourly fee for getting to and from your house). People often make the mistake of calling their plumber out for one repair then remembering two other things that need attention only after the plumber has left. To avoid this, spend some time listing every plumbing need in the house before setting up your next appointment.

Plumbers for New Construction & Remodels

If you read the entries for Electrician or HVAC Contractors in this book, you'll see the same advice: Installing a system requires different skills than maintaining a system. In other words, a good service-type plumber isn't necessarily the right guy for your major kitchen remodel. If you're planning a large project, what you need is a pro with plenty of design experience—someone who has worked in the area for a while and knows all the ins and outs of the local building code.

You can ask around for personal references of plumbers with design expertise, or you can talk to trade professionals. Experienced residential builders and general contractors have already hand-picked their plumbers and know firsthand the quality of their work. You might also ask at a well-established local plumbing supply house for names of good plumbers who have accounts with them.

Get bids on your job from a few qualified plumbers before deciding. Also consider each plumber's design ideas and recommendations for your project. Plumbing installations are strictly governed by local codes, but often there are many different *legal* ways to build a system. If you mull over the different design plans you might get a sense for which candidate offers the most expertise for your project.

Checking New Installations

One indication of a plumber's attention to detail is how he makes cuts into framing and other structural elements to run his pipes. Of course, to see this you would need access to a current new project or possibly an unfinished basement. But if you get the chance, check it out. When cutting into joists, for example, plumbers know exactly how much wood they *need* to remove and exactly how much they *should* remove. Good plumbers cut judiciously, while careless ones hack away at the wood, leaving a tattered, gaping hole for a relatively small pipe (they also fail to use a shield when soldering fittings, letting the flame from their torch burn up the wood framing). What you should see are clean, consistent holes with pipe insulators used at every penetration through wood.

HOME SCHOOL

The key to minimizing service calls for ordinary plumbing problems is to learn more about your home's plumbing system. Even if you're not inclined to make minor repairs yourself, being able to diagnose a problem, at least roughly, often will help you judge the urgency of having it repaired and will give you an edge when hiring a plumber for the job.

How do you learn? Whenever there's a plumber in the house, pay attention. Talk about the repair and why the plumber chose a particular solution. Most important, find out what caused the problem and how it might be avoided in the future.

If you've owned your home for a while, you've probably experienced something like this: A plumber comes over to solve your mysterious and seemingly significant plumbing problem. He takes a few minutes to assess the situation, grabs some simple parts out of his van, and completes the repair in 20 or 30 minutes. Afterward, as you look over the $175 bill, you think, "If I had known it was going to be that easy, I would have done it myself." That knowledge (which you lacked, of course) is primarily what you paid the plumber for.

Licenses & Insurance?

There is no national licensing requirement for professional plumbers. Some states and municipalities require all plumbers to carry a license; others require licenses only on jobs that need a building permit. About half of U.S. states offer a Master Plumber license, with qualifications based on criteria such as years of experience, completion of a written and/or practical exam, and continuing education. Insurance coverage is important for any type of plumbing work, especially because faulty work or equipment can cause extensive damage before it's discovered.

☎ In the Phone Book

Plumbing Contractors.

PRESSURE WASHER

For Help With:

- Occasional cleaning of your home's exterior & other outdoor elements

Pressure washer machines get a bad rap, and when they're in the hands of a careless or inexperienced operator, they deserve it. With the potential to deliver upwards of 3,000 psi of water, pressure washers can quickly cause a lot of damage to pretty much anything in their path, including concrete, brick, roofing, and all types of siding. That alone may be the single best reason to hire a pro for your cleaning job.

Professional pressure washers—the technicians, not the machines—use a combination of pressurized water and cleaning solutions to clean and renew all sorts of things around the house, including:

- Patios and decks
- Walks, driveways, and stoops
- Siding, gutters, and trim
- Roofing
- Awnings
- Swimming pools
- Fences
- Materials including concrete, brick, wood, vinyl, aluminum, steel, and plastic

Indeed, if it's durable enough to be outside, a pressure washing pro can probably clean it for you.

Selecting a Pressure Washer

Given the potential for damage to your home and the environmental impact of many gallons of chemicals pouring into the storm drain, it's important to choose a reputable, experienced pressure washing service. First, look for insured companies that specialize in residential work (some do mostly, or all, commercial work). Find out how long each company has been in business and run a quick background check (see Chapter 1) to look for unresolved customer complaints.

Finally, ask about their cleanup procedures. Good services offer "environmental" cleanup, meaning they capture all of the contaminated water produced in the cleaning process, preventing it from going into your sewer or storm drains. This is important, because many municipalities will slap you with a big fine for dumping into drains.

Need more information? Well, then, look no further than the Power Washers of North America. Aside from being further proof that there's a professional society for positively every line of work, the PWNA has a website (www.pwna.org) with answers to frequently asked questions, as well as a contractor locator for finding members in your area. The PWNA offers certification in the specialties of Wood Restoration and Preservation, Environmental Awareness and Cleaning, and Kitchen Exhaust Cleaning.

Things to Avoid with a Pressure Washer

Windows—One sure way to ruin a big, expensive, double-glazed window is to spray too close to the glass, either breaking the seal along the sash or forcing water in between the glazing where the seal is already broken. You'll never get that moisture out of the window.

Stripping paint and other finishes—Even though lots of people do it, spraying with enough pressure to strip paint from wood siding (and other soft materials) is a bad idea. Along with the paint comes little splinters of wood. It's unavoidable.

Spraying underneath siding—Water is supposed to flow down, not up. When you spray upwards onto a house wall, the water can go right between the siding boards and get inside the wall. Too much water in the wall leads to mold and rot. The same concept applies for roof shingles.

Some masonry—Old, fragile brick and masonry structures are too vulnerable to damage and can easily let excessive amounts of water into wall cavities. Pressure washers also should not be used on any brick with a sand or slurry finish.

Licenses & Insurance?

Professional pressure washers are required to be licensed in some areas; check with your city's office to learn about the local laws. Liability insurance, and workers' compensation for those with employees, is essential.

☎ In the Phone Book

Pressure Washing Service.

REAL ESTATE AGENT

For Help With:

- Buying or selling a home

Selling your house or buying your next dream home is a complicated process, to say the least. Success requires having a keen understanding of local home values and knowing the rules of the real estate game from start to finish. You also need access to as broad a market as possible, to make sure that the perfect buyer or house doesn't slip through the cracks and disappear before you get a chance to make an offer. For these reasons, most people wouldn't even consider selling or buying a home without the help of a qualified real estate professional.

A good agent not only does 90% of the legwork of finding a home or buyer, she represents you throughout the bidding and negotiation process and can advise you on everything within her realm of expertise. When a question or problem requires additional skills, a good agent refers you to an appropriate specialist, such as a lawyer or insurance expert. An active agent with a good track record can also be a source for names of other professionals you may need for your home transaction, like inspectors, lenders, and appraisers.

An Agent by Any Other Name...

So far, we've referred to the person who helps you buy or sell a house as an agent. Depending on where you live, this person may be called a "broker," or even a "realtor," if she's a member of the National Association of Realtors. Real estate professionals are licensed and regulated by their home state, and each state has its own rules and classifications. In some areas, separate licenses are issued for agents and for brokers. Other states license only brokers, and there are no agents, per se. In the case of separate licensing, a broker's license usually requires more experience and training and generally (not always) represents a higher level of expertise in the real estate process. Brokers are officially qualified to handle complete transactions independently, while agents may be required to work with a broker to conduct business. In some firms, one or more brokers will supervise several agents, while other firms may consists only of brokers. It all depends on how your state regulates the industry.

If you're selling your home, the agent (or broker) you contract with becomes the "seller's agent" and is bound by law to act in your best interest, within the confines of state law, of course. A "buyer's agent" does the same for a home buyer. Agents are usually free to represent either sellers or buyers on separate transactions, but some tend to specialize in one side or the other. There is also such a pro as a transaction broker, who is not an agent for either party but may be hired by the buyer or the seller, or both, to facilitate a home transaction. As an example, if your friend or neighbor makes a serious offer to buy your home and you therefore feel no need to put it on the market, the two of you might work with a transaction broker to guide you through the deal.

For help with making sense of all this, and to learn the specifics of real estate services in your area, contact your state's real estate commission or licensing bureau. This office will probably offer lots of additional tips on finding and working with real estate professionals.

Finding the Right Real Estate Professional

Considering the money involved, buying or selling your home is likely the most important home-related hiring decision you'll ever make. Start your search for a local pro by asking around. Personal referrals mean a lot in the real estate business. Also take the time to interview several candidates to find the best person for your needs. Here are some of the primary questions to ask candidates:

Do you work full-time as an agent?

Active, full-time agents are your best bet. You should be cautious about using agents who have another day job and are moonlighting in real estate. Years of experience in real estate may be another factor for you, but that doesn't mean that a newer agent can't provide great service. In fact, sometimes rookies are more motivated to please clients than their seasoned colleagues, and they often have more time to spend on individual projects.

Where do you do most of your work?

An agent's territory, as it were, is a critical consideration. You want an agent who works primarily in the area or areas you are selling in or hope to buy in, because she will know those markets and neighborhoods best. Agents who try to work everywhere may be stretched too thin and will probably lack expertise in your preferred areas.

What's your background and experience?

This question may include several aspects, such as how many years the agent has been in the business (and how long in her current territory) and whether she has any certification or titles obtained through professional organizations like the National Association of Realtors. An agent's license type is good to know and may say something about the agent's experience and education, but it's really no indication of her typical quality of service.

Is this a good time for you?

In other words, does the agent have time in her schedule to take your business. Real estate pros are used to working odd–and long–hours when required and are good at handling multiple clients. However, if you need to settle a deal quickly, make sure the agent knows this and is comfortable working under the time constraint.

What sort of office do you work in?

Some agents and brokers work independently, while others belong to large firms that employ a variety of specialists. You may have a preference for one over the other. If an agent works as part of a team, you may want to meet the other team members. As a seller, you should try to get a sense of a firm's market presence: Does it market itself well? How large is its listing inventory? What types of additional services does it offer?

Finally, and perhaps most importantly, ask yourself this:

Do I like this person?

You should feel completely comfortable with, and trusting of, your agent. In the emotional and often mysterious world of real estate, good communication and rapport go a long way. Remember, an agent should be a patient and informative advisor throughout the process, not a pushy salesperson. An agent who relates to you and your goals will be well equipped to represent your interests.

Activity Lists

An activity list is a complete record of an agent's listings and sales for the past year to date and can be a good resource for learning about an agent. It's not always customary for agents to show their activity lists to clients, but you can ask if you're interested. An activity list can tell you where the agent has been working, the type and prices of homes she tends to list, and whether she represented the buyer or seller in each case. What you're looking for are sales of homes similar to yours, indicating that you would be a typical client for the agent. The list also gives you a year's worth of recent clients whom you can call to ask about their experience with the agent.

Licenses & Insurance?

All real estate agents must be licensed by the state in which they work.

☎ In the Phone Book

Real Estate.

ROOFER

For Help With:

- Installing new roofing
- Complete roofing replacement
- Major roofing repairs

Installing new roofing requires two important decisions: the roofing material and the roofing contractor. If you take the time to make the right choices, you'll be sitting pretty for 15-20 years, on average. But compromising on either the roof or the roofer could mean that many years of seasonal headaches (and playing every homeowner's favorite game, Find the Leak).

Fortunately, there's plenty of information available to help you choose a new roofing material and find a good roofer. Start by visiting the website of the National Roofing Contractors Association at www.nrca.net. The site's Consumer section leads you to all sorts of tips and information on roofing systems, roofing materials, how to screen contractors, and making sure your job contract is ironclad. The NRCA's *Residential Roofing Contractor Qualification Form* is a handy, two-page document you can print out and use for making side-by-side comparisons of prospective contractors. The form also serves as a list of the basic questions to ask contractors and includes many details that will end up on your written job contract.

With some background information under your belt, you can start researching roofing materials and manufacturers. If you're looking for asphalt or fiberglass shingles, Consumer Reports (www.consumerreports.org) is a good resource for learning about current products and comparing their performance ratings and warranties. There are only a handful of major manufacturers of shingles. Since shingles warranties last so long (from 20 years to lifetime, accounting for depreciation, of course), it's generally recommended that you go with one of the big names when buying asphalt or fiberglass shingles. You want the company to be around and have the financial stability to back your warranty for its duration.

If you're breaking with convention by choosing a different roofing material, such as cedar, metal, slate, or tile, this will narrow your contractor search to companies that specialize in your chosen material. The more experience they have with your material the better.

Is a Re-cover an Option?

If your old roofing is standard shingles and you're using the same for the new roof, you may have the option of installing the new shingles right over the old–called a "re-cover" in the business. The only real benefit of a re-cover is that by leaving the old roof in place you save the expense of tearing off and disposing of the old shingles. Having two layers of shingles does not guarantee that your roof is any more weatherproof than a single-layer installation.

Assuming that the old shingles are in good condition and are flat (not curling or cupping), most building departments will allow one re-cover (two total layers). Many do not allow more than two layers, and most experts discourage this anyway, due to reduced performance and the cumulative weight of three complete roof coverings. If you're thinking about a re-cover, first get the go-ahead from the local building department, then discuss the plan with prospective roofers. Also make sure that the installation won't jeopardize your warranty from the shingle manufacturer.

Finding a Roofer

Nothing personal, but roofers as a professional group have a somewhat less-than-sterling reputation. This may be because there are more than a few fly-by-night companies who don't care to answer your complaints and probably won't be around to honor their labor guarantees. You just need to be careful to weed out the losers and land a solid contract with one of the many good companies.

Personal referrals are the best way to get the names of good roofing businesses. This allows you to ask your fellow consumers how well the job went: Did the roofers start on time, and did they finish quickly once they started? Were all of the contract specifications met? Were the roofers respectful of your property, and was the cleanup thorough (including a careful sweep of your yard with a magnet to pick up stray nails)? Have there been any leaks or other problems since the installation?

Obtain bids from three companies, using the NRCA's Contractor Qualification Form (mentioned above) or other bid sheet to make sure that each bid includes the vital details. If you've chosen a roofing material from a major manufacturer, you should have no problem finding roofers who are certified by the manufacturer for proper installation. Ask each company how your job would be supervised, and make sure there will be at least one supervisor or journeyman on the job at all times. And by all means, discuss start and completion dates. Bad roofers are notorious for juggling jobs, pulling crews off of houses and leaving roofs unfinished for days.

If roofers are required to be licensed in your area, use only licensed contractors. Also run a background check (Chapter 1) on your top candidates to review their track records. Finally, check with the local building department for installation requirements. These may include important details like nailing schedules, building paper (underlayment) specifications, flashing, and roofing performance minimums. If a bid doesn't conform to the local code, the contractor could become a problem

for you when it comes to inspections. By the way, new roofing commonly requires a building permit, which should be addressed in the roofers' bids and your job contract. If your state or municipality has a roofing contractor's association, this may be a good source for additional information about materials and installation techniques specific to your climate.

Contracts Are Critical

Getting everything in writing is especially important for roofing jobs. Here are some of the main points that should appear on the contract, in addition to any relevant information found on your Contractor Qualification Form:

- Materials.
  Including the roofing manufacturer's product details (shingle type, color, etc.), flashings, drip edge, valleys, vents, building paper, ice dam membrane, etc.
- Scope of work.
  Detailing re-cover vs. total roof replacement, replacement of flashings vs. re-using of existing flashings, installation of new roof vents (if applicable), repair work to roof structure or house trim, etc. Also debris removal, disposal, and final cleanup.
- Installation details.
  Including fasteners used (demand that the roofer uses nails, not staples).
- Damage liability.
  Who is responsible for any damage to your home (interior and exterior) or outdoor property as a result of the work?
- Warranties.
  Roofing manufacturer's warranty and the roofer's guarantee for workmanship. Roofers' guarantees typically cover their installation for one to two years. They generally do not cover replacement of defective roofing product.
- Approximate start and completion dates.
- Payment schedule.

Licenses & Insurance?

Licensure for professional roofers is required in some areas. Complete liability and workers' compensation insurance coverage are essential, given the potential for expensive damage resulting from faulty work and the hazardous nature of roofing. Ask your contractor for insurance certificates for both types of insurance.

☎ In the Phone Book

Roofing Contractors.

SECURITY SYSTEMS INSTALLATION & MONITORING

For Help With:

- Burglar alarms
- Fire & carbon monoxide (CO) detection
- Video surveillance
- Security monitoring service
- Home automation

The evolution of electronics and wireless technologies has made high-tech home security affordable for a wide range of consumers. And burglar alarms are just the beginning. Fire detectors, carbon monoxide sensors, and video monitors can now be combined with a traditional security system, and everything is linked to a service center that's ready to respond 24 hours a day. By integrating home automation devices, you can also control ordinary systems, like lighting and heating, or keep tabs on your house from anywhere in the world via the Internet or cell phone ("Darling, before we head off to the Louvre, would you mind peeking in on the kids to make sure the babysitter isn't keeping them up too late?").

Choosing a Security Company

The effectiveness of a security system lies much more in the design of the system and the ongoing monitoring than in the manufacture of the system's equipment (sensors, keypads, cameras, etc.). Therefore, your most important job is finding a good security company. Many companies handle both installation and monitoring; others do just the installation and leave the monitoring to someone else. If you choose the latter, make sure the installation company will be available for customer service and maintenance issues in the future. Also ask whether you can use any monitoring company of your choice.

Finding the best system and monitoring company for your needs is mostly a matter of careful comparison shopping. Start by asking friends, neighbors, your insurance agent, or the local police department for referrals of good companies. If you don't know anyone with home security, drive around the neighborhood looking for houses with the familiar "Protected by..." signs in the yards or windows. Ask the owners if they're happy with the service.

Next, find out whether your state or municipality requires security companies to be licensed. Then make some calls to your list of potential candidates. Ask whether they are licensed (if required) and whether they run background checks on their employees. This is important, because you don't want to open up your home to creepy technicians who will ultimately have access to your security codes, etc. You might also ask if the company is a member of the National Burglar & Fire Alarm Association (NBFAA; www.alarm.org), the industry's leading professional association. The NBFAA sponsors training and certification programs and requires members to agree to their code of ethics (of course, membership is voluntary).

Set up in-home consultations with three or four of your top picks (the NBFAA recommends asking all company representatives for identification before letting them in your door). Your goal is to get a detailed, written estimate from each of the companies so you can make accurate comparisons. During each interview, the representative should conduct a thorough inspection of your home and recommend a complete system layout. He should also discuss any additional services offered by the company and let you decide how much protection you want. Home security is all about peace of mind; the system that's right for you is the one that you're most comfortable with.

Don't accept quotes for a system over the phone, and don't use a company that provides only a quickie quote written on the back of their business card. Other things to discuss (and get prices for) in your consultation:

- Will I own the system equipment or lease it from the company?
- Is the monitoring service included in the quote?
- What's the minimum required length of contract for monitoring service?
- What is the cancellation policy?
- Can I use a different company for monitoring?
- Are there warranties or maintenance plans available?

Also, you may be able to negotiate for a lower price on the installation, monthly monitoring fee, or length of contract. It never hurts to try.

Be aware that the best company for your needs may not be the cheapest. As you compare prices, systems, and plans, also consider the layout and usability of the system each company proposes. Which one will work best for your home and family? You should also have plenty of confidence in the customer service of the company you choose. Finally, be sure to read and fully understand your contract—for both installation and monitoring service—before signing.

Special Features to Consider

Without going into detail about specific pieces of security equipment (which undoubtedly will be obsolete by the time you finish reading this paragraph) here are a few bells and whistles you might like to have:

Wireless devices—For easy installation without having to run wires inside the walls. These also make security a viable option for people who rent their home or apartment, as you can take the system with you when you move.

Battery backup—Provides power to your system during power outages.

Alternate communication paths—Connect you to the monitoring service via cell phone, Internet, email, or two-way radio. These are good safeguards against losing communication with a conventional phone line, and they keep you in touch when you're away from home.

Video monitoring—Some companies watch your house via closed-circuit television. This also lets you view your home over the Internet.

Home automation—Includes a range of futuristic devices for controlling home systems remotely.

Know Your System & Use It

Window stickers and yard signs aside, a security system that's not activated is about as effective as a rubber crowbar (used by only the dullest of burglars). Many homeowners who have systems installed turn them on only when they go on vacation, by which time they've forgotten how to activate the system properly. Or they simply grow complacent and neglect to arm the system while they're gone during the day, which happens to be one of the most common times for home burglaries.

Another problem occurs when only one or two people in the house really know how to use the system. The result is that the others leave the house without arming the system, or they trip the alarm coming into the house and don't know how to turn it off (see False Alarms, below). Fortunately, the solution to these problems is simple: Make sure everyone in the household is present when the security technician teaches you how to control your new system. Then, get used to arming the system as part of your daily routine.

False Alarms

False alarms are the bane of the home security industry, and they're usually the fault of the homeowner. In addition to wasting the time and resources of local law enforcement, false alarms can cost you money. Fines for repeated false alarms can run into several hundreds of dollars in some areas.

The best way to prevent false alarms is to make sure everyone in the house is proficient at operating the system. Another safeguard is to opt for what the NBFAA calls "enhanced call verification." Under standard protocol, a monitoring company calls your home phone whenever your system sounds an alarm. If you don't answer, the company contacts the local authorities. With the enhanced feature, the monitoring company calls your cell phone after failing to reach you at home, giving you a second chance to verify that the emergency is legit.

5 STEPS TO SUCCESSFUL HOME SECURITY

1. Get referrals. Consider only companies who are licensed (if required) and whose employees have been screened and fully trained.

2. Interview three to four companies and get written bids from each.

3. Compare companies based on matched criteria, including system design and usability, customer service, monitoring contract, guarantees, and price.

4. Read and understand your contract fully before signing.

5. Make sure everyone in your home knows how to operate the security system.

Licenses & Insurance?

Some states and municipalities require licensure for home security installation and monitoring services. Insurance is a must for installation crews.

☎ In the Phone Book

Security Equipment Systems & Monitoring, Burglar Alarms & Monitoring, Fire Alarm Systems.

SEPTIC TANK SERVICE

For Help With:

- Septic system cleaning & repairs
- Septic system inspections & certification
- Design & installation of new septic systems

A septic system is like having your own backyard sewage treatment plant (every homeowner's dream!). This means that you don't have to pay annual sewage fees to the city. It also means that all maintenance and repairs are your responsibility–not an especially prestigious role, but isn't it nice to know you're keeping all the waste management in the family?

If you're new to septic systems, it's time to learn about the professionals who will keep your backyard plant running smoothly:

- *Pumping/cleaning service technicians* perform periodic cleaning of septic tanks and limited routine inspections.
- *System designers* conduct site evaluations and locate and design new septic systems according to local building and zoning codes.
- *System installers* construct new systems and make major repairs and alterations to existing systems.
- *Inspectors* thoroughly test and evaluate existing systems, perform compliance inspections for permits, and issue compliance certificates and inspection reports.

Your state or municipal licensing board may issue licenses separately for any of the above services, or it may license for a combination of disciplines. One advantage of hiring, and getting to know, a full-service contractor (one who handles cleaning, inspection, design, and installation) is that the same pro or company can correct any problems that are discovered during routine cleanings and inspections.

Choosing a Septic System Professional

As always, interview at least three candidates before hiring an unknown contractor for any type of septic service. Find out how long the company has been in business and how much experience they have with your type of project or service. Contact references and run a background check (see Chapter 1) on each candidate. If applicable, obtain written bids for repair, installation, or design work.

Compare candidates based on experience and expertise, reputation, cost, and the scope of their services. Automatically choosing the lowest bidder is dangerous with septic systems, because incomplete service or poor design work can go unnoticed for a long time and end up costing you a lot more in the long run. Here are some additional considerations for each type of septic service:

Pumping/Cleaning–Pumpers should visually inspect the leach field (drain field) for signs of problems, such as seepage above ground (major problem) and tire tracks or other indications of heavy traffic (major problem waiting to happen).

The pumping should be done through the tank's maintenance hole, not through the inspection pipe. Before pumping, the technician should visually inspect the contents of the tank to look for non-biodegradables and other items that clog the system (and give you a stern talking-to if he finds them). He should then completely pump out the tank and backflush it. After the tank is clean, the pumper should check the tank baffles to ensure they are properly positioned.

Design—Designers must visit your property and conduct soil tests to evaluate the site in detail. The final design and system specifications are based on the site evaluation and test data, the size of your home and how many fixtures it has, and any additional elements required by local regulations.

Installation—All installation work should be outlined in a written contract and should specify who is responsible for restorative landscaping work, if applicable. A one-year guarantee for installations is standard, but be sure to discuss this with your contractor. Any warranties on parts or equipment installed should also appear in the contract. New systems must be inspected to ensure compliance with state or local code requirements.

Inspection—Inspections of existing systems may include the following tests (plus any additional points required by your local government):

- ☐ Ensuring the tank is watertight
- ☐ Checking for surface water or effluent in the leach field
- ☐ Flushing a full tank with water, then pumping to check for any backflow from the leach field
- ☐ Estimating the tank's size and inspecting the baffles
- ☐ Inspecting the distribution box and measuring the length of the field drains
- ☐ Testing the soil to determine the depth of seasonal water tables and confirming adequate separation from the drain area
- ☐ Confirming that the system poses no threat to public health

Note: Standard home inspections typically do not include a thorough evaluation of septic systems. If you're buying a home and want to make sure the septic system is in good shape, hire a qualified septic inspector.

Recordkeeping—In some areas, local government offices keep records of inspections, cleanings, and design specifications on every home's septic system. If this is done in your area, ask your contractor how your records will be handled.

Licenses & Insurance?

Contact your local or state office of utilities, health, or water/sewage regulation to learn about licensing requirements of septic service professionals. All contractors should carry adequate insurance for general liability and workers' compensation.

☎ In the Phone Book

Septic Tanks & Systems—Cleaning; Septic Tanks & Systems—Contractors, Designers & Dealers.

SEWER CONTRACTOR & CLEANER

For Help With:

- Sewer pipe cleaning, inspection & repair
- Sewer line replacement

Oh, the feeling of heading down into your basement and finding it awash in sewage ... Nothing makes you wish more that you had remained a renter. So, your house is filling up with waste. You need help, fast. Whom do you call? Believe it or not, your city government.

Here's why: Sewer backups occur in one of two places: 1) between your house's drain and the city's sewer main in the street, or 2) in the sewer main itself. If the backup is in the sewer main, it's the city's responsibility, and hiring a plumber or sewer contractor right away will likely be a waste of your money. Most cities and municipalities will send out a technician to determine where the backup has occurred. A problem in the main will be handled by the city, but if the main is found to be clear, it's your baby; time to call in a pro. Either way, you get to clean up the mess in your house after the drain is working again.

Even if the city exonerates itself, it may have a law requiring you to hire a registered or certified contractor for your sewer problem. If so, the city office should have a list of all registered contractors in your area, which gives you a place to start. Beyond city requirements, your contractor search should be guided by the type of service you think you'll need. Most residential plumbers have equipment for clearing and inspecting sewer lines, so your trusted family plumber might be the person to call. Another option is a drain-cleaning service, which specializes in clearing and inspecting sewer and household drains. However, if your drain lines are especially problematic and backups are a recurring problem, you might need the help of a full-service sewer contractor.

Introducing Your Local Sewer Contractor

Sewer contractors generally handle all aspects of sewer drain maintenance, including cleaning, inspection, repairs, and complete sewer line replacement. These days, clearing drains is often done with pressurized water, and inspections are made with video cameras. Video inspections can accurately pinpoint damage and other problem areas anywhere from your house to the sewer main, and they make for interesting home movies. Sewer contractors are also experts at dealing with tree and shrub roots—the most common cause of sewer backups.

If an inspection reveals major problems with your sewer drain, you might opt to have it lined or replaced. The traditional method of replacement is to dig a trench, remove the old drain, and lay in a new one. Today, trenchless technology offers a less-invasive alternative. The trenchless technique starts by breaking up the old drain, using a splitter head drawn through the pipe. New plastic pipe is then inserted into the path of the old drain. The beauty of it is that the pipe goes right underground, without disrupting your yard, driveway, patio, etc.

Hiring a Drain Cleaner or Sewer Contractor

For a basic drain cleaning, call several local drain specialists (or plumbers; see pages 143 to 146 for hiring tips). If a city representative comes out to your location, she should be able to tell you the distance between the sewer main and your house. This will be helpful for obtaining over-the-phone estimates from prospective service pros. Select only licensed (if required in your area) and insured pros with a solid reputation and clean complaint record (see Chapter 1).

Before hiring a sewer contractor for extensive repair or replacement work, get detailed, written bids from at least three licensed contractors. Prices can vary widely for sewer work, so make sure you're comparing similar services and guarantees. Since there's usually more than one way to solve a sewer problem, try to gather a range of opinions and proposals before choosing a contractor. You also might want to discuss your options with your family plumber, if you have one.

Licenses & Insurance?

Plumbers and sewer contractors must be licensed in most areas; again, check with your city office for specific requirements. Liability and workers' compensation insurance are essential.

☎ In the Phone Book

Sewer Contractors & Cleaners, Plumbing Drains & Sewer Cleaning, Sewer Inspection, Plumbing Contractors.

SIDING CONTRACTOR

For Help With:

- New siding installation & siding replacement
- Additional services offered by siding contractors:
  - Window & door replacement; see page 180.
  - Installing gutters & downspouts; see page 105.
  - Roofing; see page 150.
  - Carpet installation; see page 60.

A quick browse in the phone book gives you the sense that siding contractors are the old-time vaudeville actors of home improvement: they do it all. You want new windows? I do windows. You want doors, gutters, trim, a patio cover? Heck, you want new carpet? I can do carpet. Ha cha cha!

The question is, Are they *good* at all those things? That's what you'll have to figure out before hiring a contractor for multiple improvements. Chances are, any additional service you need is covered in this book (see the page references above), so you can start there to find tips for assessing the quality of a contractor's work and the value of his services.

Unfortunately, it's not safe even to assume that all siding pros are good at installing siding. Most are, but not all. Since a quality installation is absolutely critical to the performance of any type of siding, it's important to choose your contractor carefully. Above all, make sure he has a good reputation and plenty of experience working with your siding material.

Choose Your Siding First

As with most projects involving expensive new materials, it's best to start with some product research. Once you've selected a siding material, then find a contractor who specializes in that type of siding. The alternative is to meet with different contractors and let them try to convince you to use their products, but that's certainly no way to get unbiased information. Learning about siding materials on your own will also teach you about proper installation techniques, which will help you when inspecting the work of prospective contractors and managing quality control on your own project (don't worry, siding installation is pretty simple).

Siding options are extensive. And, as with flooring and roofing materials, each product has its advantages and disadvantages. Here are the main types of siding, along with some good resources for more information on applications and installation:

- *Vinyl*—Vinyl Siding Institute: www.vinylsiding.org
  Consumer Reports: www.consumerreports.org
- *Cedar*—Western Red Cedar Lumber Association: www.wrcla.org
- *Redwood*—California Redwood Association: www.calredwood.org
- *Pine, spruce, and fir* (siding made from woods that are not naturally rot-resistant. These must be painted and sealed to prevent rot and decay)
- *Plywood* (commonly used for board-and-batten siding treatments)
- *Fiber cement*—James Hardie®: www.jameshardie.com
- *Steel*
- *Aluminum*
- *Stucco*—Portland Cement Association: www.cement.org

Finding a Siding Contractor

Once you've settled on a siding material (and manufacturer, if applicable), gather the names of several local contractors who work with your product. In addition to referrals from people you know, general contractors, architects, and other building professionals may provide names of good siding contractors. Don't assume a siding installer is good just because he does a lot of work for builders, especially builders of modern cookie-cutter homes. These developers tend to favor speed and low cost over quality work.

Obtain detailed estimates from at least three contractors. Their proposals should include:

- All materials used, including underlayment and fasteners
- Installation methods, including preparation work, flashing around doors and windows, and trimwork
- Removal, containment, and disposal of old siding (if applicable)
- Liability for damage resulting from any work done
- Warranties for siding material and workmanship
- Approximate start and completion dates
- Permits: Siding installations require building permits in many areas. Find out who will be responsible for any permits and fees.

Run a background check on your top candidates (see Chapter 1), and ask for references of several past clients. By all means, check the contractors' work on past jobs. Here are some key things to look for:

Level, even courses (on any type of horizontal siding)—At corners, windows, and doors, make sure the lines of siding match up on both sides and are even across the tops of openings.

Clean joints and minimal gapping—Check all trim joints at windows, doors, and corners. Check butt joints between siding pieces and where siding meets trim. On vinyl siding, there should be a gap where siding ends meet J-channels, to allow for expansion.

Caulking—Caulking at all seams and trim joints should be continuous and neatly applied. Be aware that some caulking may be the painter's responsibility, so ask your contractor.

Current work—A job in progress lets you see the contractor's application of underlayment, fasteners, and other installation details. A clean, organized job site is a good sign.

Licenses & Insurance?

Licensure of siding contractors is common—check with your city or state regulatory office for local requirements. All siding contractors should be fully insured for general liability and workers' compensation.

☎ In the Phone Book

Siding Contractors, Stucco & Texturing.

SPRINKLER SYSTEM CONTRACTOR

For Help With:

- Design & installation of new lawn sprinkler systems
- Sprinkler system repairs & seasonal maintenance

If Greek mythology were re-written for modern times, you can bet that poor Sisyphus, instead of having to roll a boulder up an incline for eternity, would be forced to keep a lawn alive in a dry climate. Indeed, is there any other household chore that feels more like vain labor? Dragging out the hose and carefully adjusting the water pressure to sprinkle right where it's needed, you come back in an hour only to discover that the corners of the lawn are bone-dry while your driveway seems to have experienced monsoon rains.

But if the gods are merciful, they will bestow upon you an automatic sprinkler system, complete with the latest devices and an electronic control unit for watering your lawn with precision whether you're home or not. Where do you find these wise and benevolent sprinkler gods? You can start by looking in the phone book, under Sprinklers—Garden & Lawn and under Landscape Contractors. You can also learn the names of good sprinkler installers by talking to landscape professionals, like landscape architects and designers or local landscape materials suppliers and retailers.

Sprinkler companies typically specialize in lawn sprinklers and other irrigation systems, while many full-service landscape contractors install sprinklers as part of a broad range of services. In any case, your best bet is to find a company that comes with plenty of design and installation experience and also offers repair and seasonal maintenance services. If you're happy with their work on the installation, you can feel confident using them for periodic upkeep. Common maintenance tasks for sprinkler systems include adjusting sprinkler heads, troubleshooting problems, and, in cold climates, winterizing the system each year by blowing out the pipes with compressed air.

A Sprinkling of Technical Information

Automatic sprinkler systems consist of three main components: the control unit, the pipe runs, and the sprinkler heads. Most home systems are laid out it a few separate zones, or sections, designed to water a specific area of the yard. Each zone is controlled by its own valve, and all valves are linked to the control unit. The control unit opens and closes the valves automatically according to a programmed schedule. The primary reason behind the zone configuration is that a home's water supply doesn't produce enough pressure to water the entire yard at once.

The pipes, valves, and other parts used by most professionals are produced by a handful of manufacturers, and installation is pretty straightforward. Designing the system, on the other hand, is a true test of a pro's expertise. A proper design includes an efficient layout of piping and sprinkler heads (there are a few basic types of heads, each with different watering capabilities. Garden beds and landscaping plants may be watered by a drip system on a separate zone). The right amount of overlap of neighboring sprinkler heads is important—too little means inadequate coverage; too much means wasted water. Zones may be laid out in a square or triangular pattern. The latter requires more piping but generally provides better coverage.

For the record, there is still such a thing as a "manual" sprinkler system, in which you act as the control unit, turning on and off the different zones to complete each watering. Manual systems are cheaper than automatic ones, but you might decide that the savings aren't such a good deal when you're chained to a kitchen timer every watering day.

Choosing a Sprinkler Contractor

Compile a list of at least three local sprinkler companies or landscape contractors who offer many years of design and installation experience and a clean business record (see Chapter 1 for tips on running background checks). As mentioned, look for full-service operators who will likely be around for the long run to handle future repairs and maintenance of your system. For more information on hiring and working with landscape contractors, see Landscape Design & Construction, on pages 125 to 128.

Obtain design proposals and price quotes from your top three candidates. While they're at your house working up their bids, ask plenty of questions about their design ideas and product options for the proposed systems. Be sure to ask about control units to learn as much as you can about the various features available, their benefits, and what each would cost you. Prices and capabilities on control units vary widely, but keep in mind that the unit can have a significant impact on the efficiency and usability of a system.

When you've made a decision on a sprinkler installer and system, get everything in writing, including the scope of work, all equipment to be installed, and any warranties on the workmanship and the system parts.

Licenses & Insurance?
New sprinkler systems require permits in many areas, which usually means the installers must be licensed; check with your city's building department for specifics. Liability and workers' compensation insurance are essential.

☎ In the Phone Book
Sprinklers–Garden & Lawn, Landscape Contractors.

SURVEYOR

For Help With:
- Property boundary identification & marking
- Certification for home & land purchases, sales & improvements
- Reports & certificates for title insurers, mortgage lenders & flood insurers

True story: A woman in Colorado recently put her single-family home on the market after owning it for 12 years. Somewhere in the process a document turned up showing that the narrow driveway running along one side of the house (where the owner had parked for the past 12 years) was actually only half hers. The other half belonged to the next-door neighbor. A surveyor was brought in, and he confirmed that the one-car driveway was indeed split lengthwise by the property line. In the end, the house was sold, with the new owners fully aware of the importance of staying on good terms with the neighbor.

There's no doubt that experienced land surveyors (the type of surveyor used most for residential projects) have many stories like this–further evidence of why you might want to have a survey conducted before jumping into any major property investment. Land surveyors are commonly hired for things like establishing or confirming boundaries, resolving property-line disputes, and mapping the topography of undeveloped land. Here are some other reasons to have a survey done:

- Obtaining permits and/or financing for home improvements such as a fence, a garage, or an addition
- Determining whether flood insurance is required for a property
- Identifying easements (areas that must remain accessible to utilities or other municipal services) and encroachments (such as your neighbor's R.V. pad overlapping onto your property)
- Marking of lot boundaries with monuments (metal stakes or other permanent markers bearing the surveyor's registration number)
- Dividing a parcel of land for sale (or before selling any piece of land)
- Planning the location of a new house and all related public utilities

A surveyor's findings become the official word on whose property is where. But because land ownership is subject to prior designations and conditions, surveyors often research legal records and analyze historical data to determine the "true" boundaries of a parcel of land. In this way they're not unlike lawyers, who have to dig up old ghosts in the judicial archives to prevent them from showing up unexpectedly and wreaking havoc on the living. Surveyors may also appear in court as expert witnesses on cases involving the location, use, or ownership of property.

The First Step

If you need a survey done, start talking with local surveying firms that have good reputations and many years of experience with residential property issues. By consulting with several surveyors you'll learn about the various types of surveys available and hear each pro's recommendations for which type best serves your needs. It's important to work with local surveyors, because they will be the most informed about local laws and information resources. Firms with a long history in a given area also have extensive archives of previous surveys and data that can greatly facilitate their searches (which may mean a lower fee for you).

All surveyors must carry a state license. You can find surveyors in the phone book or by contacting your state or regional association of professional land surveyors. Most areas have a chapter that's affiliated with the National Society of Professional Surveyors. For personal referrals, you can talk to architects, landscape architects, and civil engineers, all of whom frequently rely on surveyors in their everyday work.

As with most skilled professional services, it's unwise to choose a surveyor based on cost alone. A surveyor's fee should be competitive, but more important factors to consider are the surveyor's reputation, experience, and education, as well as the level of customer service you receive. You should feel comfortable asking for names of former clients who had similar work done to check a firm's references.

Survey Costs

The cost of a land survey is based on many factors, including the type of survey and report required, the physical aspects of the property, and the difficulty of the records search. As a result, surveyors usually offer cost estimates for projects but almost never bid jobs with a firm price quote. An estimate can be pretty accurate if your project is routine and the surveyor is familiar with your area, but there's no guarantee that complications won't arise and end up costing you more.

The best way to lower the cost of a survey is to provide the surveyor with any documents you have related to the ownership of your land. These may include a title insurance policy or evidence of a previous survey done on the property. If you know of any existing survey monuments on your land, point them out to your surveyor (sometimes monuments are driven below the ground and must be located with a metal detector). Also, firms commonly offer discounts on current projects if they themselves have done previous work on the site. Your surveyor may request a retainer and written authorization from you before conducting a survey.

Ordering a Survey

After you've determined the services you need and have chosen a surveyor, the next step is to have a work order written up. The work order should include a description of the survey work requested, the surveyor's hourly rate, and an approximate cost estimate for the entire job. If you must have the survey completed by a certain date, make sure this is noted on the work order.

Be aware that it's your responsibility to request special services, such as specific documents or maps required by your lender or builder. Don't assume a survey will include everything you need unless you've discussed the specific details with your surveyor. Be sure to obtain an official (stamped) copy of your survey and other documents for each party who needs them (the building department, your mortgage lender, etc.), plus a copy for your own records.

FOR MORE INFORMATION...

American Congress on Surveying & Mapping: www.acsm.net
National Society of Professional Surveyors: www.nspsmo.org
American Land Title Association: www.alta.org

Licenses & Insurance?

All U.S. states license surveyors, and each state has its own set of requirements. You can confirm a surveyor's license by contacting your state's department of licensing or similar regulatory agency. Surveyors must be fully insured because their work can have expensive consequences; often surveyors are liable for damages resulting from their mistakes. Check with your state's labor department to learn about insurance requirements for surveyors in your area.

☎ In the Phone Book

Surveyors–Land.

SWIMMING POOL CONTRACTOR (& MAINTENANCE SERVICE)

For Help With:

- In-ground pool design & construction
- Scheduled pool maintenance

Who hasn't dreamt of owning a backyard pool? For some, the fantasy is all about a life of easy luxury: "Oh, Wellington (your butler, of course), Roger and I will have our cocktails out by the pool this evening." For others, it's the sweet summer sounds of kids playing: "Marco...Polo..." But now that you've put in the time daydreaming about it, you're ready to get serious. How do you find the right builder for your pool?

First, visit some showrooms to get a sense of what's available and what roughly fits your budget. Next, contact your local building department to learn about the rules and regulations governing backyard pools in your area. This will help you plan for all the extras, such as fencing and other safety features required by code. The building department may also have advice for choosing the best materials and type of pool construction for the local climate, soil conditions, etc. While you're there, find out whether pool builders and/or service technicians are required to be licensed and what permits are needed for a new pool installation.

From there, it's back to shopping, but this time your decisions should be informed by thorough research into pool materials, designs, and equipment. Pool dealers say that most buyers tend to focus on the aesthetics of their new pool and ignore the important mechanical features, such as the pump, filters, and sizing of the hydraulic system. These elements govern how easy it is to clean and maintain your pool in the long term, so they're just as important as the pool's look and design.

For each type of pool, consider the following major factors:

- Cost—Including installation, new landscaping, required safety features, and any new decking or pool surround surfaces, plus accessories like a cover or heater.
- Time—If you really want the pool to be ready for next summer, make sure you're realistic about the construction schedule.
- Maintenance & service—Ease of maintenance varies among pool types and finishes. Determine how much upkeep you're willing to take on or pay for on a weekly, monthly, and seasonal basis.

For expert tips and information, there are lots of books on planning and designing in-ground pools. Another good source is the Association of Pool and Spa Professionals (formerly–but still generally known as–the National Spa and Pool Institute). The APSP is the industry's primary organization for pool builders and offers certification programs for a variety of professional pool and spa services. Visit the APSP's website at www.theapsp.org, or call 800-323-3996 to request their free consumer literature.

Hiring a Pool Builder

Once you have an idea of the type and size of pool you want, you can start the bidding process. Seek referrals for local contractors who specialize in the type of pool you've chosen, then run background checks (see Chapter 1) and talk to references (past customers) to narrow your list down to a few top candidates. Obtain written estimates from at least three contractors. Compare the contractors on reputation and experience, warranties they offer, and their price. If a bid is considerably higher or lower than the others, find out why. Be wary of a company that appears to have underbid the project just to win the contract.

Before you sign a contract, contact your local Better Business Bureau or city or state regulatory agency to learn about local laws regarding contracts for new pools. In many areas, consumers are allowed a three-day cancellation period after signing a contract (perhaps a result of too many homeowners buying pools on impulse). Other laws may restrict the down payment a contractor is allowed to require. For example, in California, pool contractors can demand only the lesser of 2% of the total project cost or $200.

Your contract must be written and detailed. It should include all of the company's business information (name, address, and license number) and proof of insurance. Design specifications should be as specific as possible, including details such as part numbers for permanent equipment and manufacturers' complete product descriptions (e.g., 6" Sierra Buff porcelain tile, #873, installed per plan elevation). Make sure there are approximate start and completion dates, as well as a detailed payment schedule. Payments should reflect major stages of the work, giving you the authority of paying only after each stage is completed. As an added precaution, avoid making payments in cash, and be sure to get the originals or copies of all warranties (from the contractor and product manufacturers) for all parts and guaranteed services.

Hiring a Pool Maintenance Service

The first thing you'll learn about your new pool is that it needs a lot of attention, including a weekly maintenance routine during the swim season. Pool service professionals can take care of scheduled maintenance, opening and closing the pool for the season, and a full range of common repairs. Here are some basic things to consider before hiring a pool service:

- Years of experience—You want someone who knows how to treat water for the local conditions.
- Products—Discuss the chemicals they use and why.
- Process—What's included in their regular service routine (such as cleaning and backwashing the filter, testing and treating the water, and vacuuming the walls and floor of the pool)? Do these services match the recommendations of your pool's builder and equipment manufacturers?
- Contract—Get a description of all regular services in writing.
- Insurance—Make sure the company has adequate coverage for liability and workers' compensation.

Licenses & Insurance?

If licensure of pool contractors is required in your area, use only licensed professionals for any work. Considering the size of your investment and the risks of having a giant hole dug into your backyard, insurance for liability and workers' compensation is essential.

☎ In the Phone Book

Swimming Pool Contractors, Dealers & Designers; Swimming Pool Service & Repair.

TILE INSTALLER

For Help With:

- New installation of all types of tile
- Demolition of old tile surfaces
- Major tile repairs

Tile is the undisputed king of finish materials. It's great for floors, walls, ceilings, showers, countertops, backsplashes, and fireplace surrounds. It's right at home in any room of the house. It's tough, it's beautiful, and it comes in thousand of styles. Tile is indeed supreme. And yet, like Lear and George III, King Tile has one fatal weakness, and that is poor installation.

Installing tile of any type involves three distinct stages: preparing the underlying surface (substrate), laying the tile, and grouting. Properly installed, tile creates an incredibly strong and durable surface, but poor workmanship in the substrate or grouting can lead to big problems.

The Elements of Tile

The substrate is the foundation of the entire tile job. It must be stiff enough to resist flexing (a particular concern for floors and countertops), because too much movement leads to cracked tiles and grout. The substrate must also have the right materials: In all wet areas (kitchens, bathrooms, and floors), tile must be installed over cementboard, a common sheet good made from cement and other materials. Unlike drywall and plywood, cementboard won't be damaged by water that sneaks behind the tile surface, usually through cracks in the grout. Note: Some tile installations call for a thick bed of mortar instead of cementboard.

When it comes to grouting, careful work will make the installation look good but is even more critical for sealing out water. Even hairline gaps in grout let water behind the tile. In wet areas like showers, that water may never dry up, promoting mold growth and possibly rotting the wall structure. After grout has cured, it should be sealed to resist stains and discoloration. Make sure to discuss the use of sealers with your tile dealer and installer.

That's it for the technical stuff. Now let's look at the art of tilesetting. Most tile installations follow a strict grid pattern. For the job to look good, the grid lines must run square to windows, doors, trim, sinks, etc. Along the borders of a tile field, cut tiles should be of equal size at both sides, or at the top and bottom—this shows that the tiler has centered his grid properly. If a bordering element is out of whack, such as a baseboard that slopes downhill, each border tile must be custom cut to fit the gap. This is where good tilesetters really show their stuff. Bad tilers cut all the border tiles roughly the same size, filling the remaining gap with an ever-widening grout joint.

A good tile job has perfectly straight and evenly sized grout lines (in the case of non-linear installations, look for orderly patterns and consistent grout joints). The tile field should be flat across its entire surface. If the substrate wasn't flat to begin with, that's the tiler's problem and is no excuse for an imperfect job. Natural stone and handmade tiles with textured faces won't produce a perfectly even surface, but even here the general plane should appear flat, without undulations or jarring projections.

When inspecting a tiler's work, look for all of the above features. Also make sure the job was done neatly. You shouldn't see traces of splashed grout or sloppy caulk application.

Selecting & Buying Tile

Shopping for tile is fun for most people, because the range of options is seemingly endless. But if you're one of those people who prefer a set menu or a choice between A, B, and C, don't worry–a good tile dealer can quickly narrow your options to a handful of suitable types. A knowledgeable dealer will make recommendations for tile and grout based on your style preferences, budget, and intended use for the tile. If you've already chosen an installer, ask him what he thinks of your tile choices. He may offer reasons for not using certain tiles in certain applications.

It's common for homeowners to select their own tile then have their installer buy the materials. This offers certain advantages. First, tile contractors buy tile and supplies at a discount, so even if they charge you a markup, you shouldn't have to pay more than retail. Second, contractors typically assume responsibility for faulty or damaged goods they buy (this should be in your contract). And finally, why not let the pro do the purchasing, hauling, and handling of the materials?

Choosing a Tile Installer

Tiling is one of those things that almost anyone can do but very few can do well. Resist the temptation to hire someone simply out of convenience. For example, if there's a carpenter or handyman already doing other work on your house, don't let him install your tile just because he's there and is willing–unless you've seen his tile work and know it's up to snuff. A lot of people making this mistake end up either hiring a real tilesetter to redo the tile or learning to live with ugly tile.

That said, how do you find a good professional tile installer? Ask around and check references. Tile dealers who sell primarily to professionals often know of good local installers. Quality tile retailers may also give you names but not if they have their own installers. Personal referrals from other homeowners are always good, too. Narrow your list of prospective contractors to those with several years of experience as full-time tilesetters. Even more important is their experience with your type of tile and project. Specialty tiles, like marble, Saltillo floor tile, or mosaics, require specific expertise.

To obtain bids, provide the contractors with tile samples and a detailed, dimensioned drawing of the project site, or have them visit your home to see the job in person. Also discuss any demolition work or surface preparation needed. Be sure to check the work of any tiler you consider hiring. At least one of the tiler's past clients will be happy to let you in to see their tile. Or, if the tiler does a lot of commercial work, ask if there are any examples in public buildings you can check out.

Your written contract for the work should include all materials specifications and installation details. It should also include the installer's guarantees–both for the materials and the workmanship. The latter will vary based on the installer's policy and the tile application. For showers and tub enclosures, try to get a long-term guarantee against leaks (two years is not uncommon).

✏ HOME SCHOOL

If you're interested in learning more about tile installation standards for all areas of the home, contact the Tile Council of North America. Their *Handbook for Ceramic Tile Installation* features descriptions and industry-standard specifications for 94 different tile applications (the handbook is technical but surprisingly user-friendly). You can order the handbook on TCA's website: www.tileusa.com.

For general information about marble, granite, and other types of stone used for tile, visit the website of the Marble Institute of America, at www.marble-institute.com.

Licenses & Insurance?

Tile installers may carry a contractor's license (and this may be required in your area). However, licensure as a way to control tile installation standards is not common. Make sure your tile installer has liability insurance, and worker's compensation insurance if he hires employees.

☎ In the Phone Book

Tile–Ceramic–Contractors & Dealers.

TREE SERVICE (ARBORIST)

For Help With:

- Pruning for tree health, safety & appearance
- Emergency tree care
- Diagnosis of ailing trees
- Cabling & bracing to support weak limbs
- Fertilization & aeration
- Insect & disease control
- Lightning protection systems
- Recommendations for choosing & locating new trees
- Tree & stump removal
- Consulting services for tree-related disputes

Trees can be a real nuisance sometimes. Sick or neglected specimens drop heavy branches. Tree roots create sewer backups and crack foundation walls. Severe weather in any season poses a constant threat of turning our trees against us. And yet, we love and value a good, old tree as much as our home itself (maybe even more; why else would so many people risk potentially serious damage to their home before they'd cut down a nearby tree?). So when it comes to caring for a beloved tree, it pays to hire an experienced and highly qualified tree service.

Tree service professionals come in several varieties. *Tree trimmers*, or maintenance professionals, are technicians who handle pruning, feeding, and other routine tasks and should be fully trained in basic tree care. *Certified arborists* are tree experts who have acquired certification through the International Society of Arboriculture or other group such as a state arborist association. ISA certification requires at least three years of professional tree care experience and passing the Society's comprehensive exam. Be aware that, by definition, an "arborist" is any professional who cares for trees, so don't assume that the title alone means that a pro is certified.

Full-service tree care companies may have many technicians on staff and one or more certified arborists. If you seek long-term care or expert consultation, look for companies with a certified arborist on staff. Some companies specialize in only tree and/or stump removal. For this type of service, you want a company with the right experience and full insurance coverage, but you probably don't need the expertise of an arborist or a trained tree maintenance staff.

Finally, there's a tree professional known as a *consulting arborist*. This is an experienced arborist who provides information, impartial advice, and objective mediation services in tree-related cases. For example, let's say a problematic tree resides along the border between your property and the city's green space. When you complain to the city, you get a response to the tune of: "Tree? What tree? I'm looking at my computer right now, and there's no orange dot indicating a tree in that location. Must be yours." You can choose to hire a consulting arborist for help with settling the dispute. Consulting arborists are trained and certified by the American Society of Consulting Arborists. Visit their website at www.asca-consultants.org for more information and a directory for finding member arborists in your area.

Five Things to Do When Hiring a Tree Service

1. *Look for experience and reputation.* A well-established tree company offers years of experience caring for trees in the local climate and will have a long track record of client comments about its quality of service—good or bad. See Chapter 1 for tips on running a background check on prospective companies.

2. *Make sure companies have the expertise you need.* Before establishing a relationship with a company, ask about the training and qualifications of any certified arborists on staff. If you need specialized services now or in the future, you'll know whom to call.

3. *Obtain three estimates and check references.* The basic three-estimate method definitely applies here, as prices and service packages can vary widely in the tree care business. Remember, you're looking for a competitive price that offers a good value for the services, not necessarily the lowest bid in town. The Tree Care Industry Association (see For More Information…, next page) requires its accredited members to provide written estimates for all new work. From all of your top candidates, get the names of other customers in your area and call them to check references. Long-time customers can tell you how their trees have fared over the years.

4. *Confirm full insurance coverage.* Residential tree care professionals are open about their insurance, as their work is the most hazardous among all home-related trades. The great potential for damage to customers' (and their neighbors') homes, utility lines, cars, etc., necessitates extensive coverage. Good companies will give you a sheet containing all their insurance information. Take a few minutes to call their insurance companies to confirm the coverage.

5. *Get all proposed work in writing.* Obtain a signed contract before allowing work to begin. It should include:

   ☐ Description of all services to be performed
   ☐ Start and completion dates
   ☐ Party responsible for cleanup
   ☐ Total price for all work

The Perfect Scam

After a big storm you will almost certainly see a few groups of yahoos in trucks trolling the neighborhoods looking for homes with fallen trees and limbs. Under the circumstances, all it takes is a chainsaw and a low bid to convince some homeowners to hire these opportunists for tree removal or "emergency pruning." But don't do it, no matter how cheap their offer is. It's just too risky. If the crew fells a tree onto your neighbor's garage, or one of the crew gets hurt, you'll be held responsible. And most likely, your homeowner's insurance won't cover any damages.

So, door-to-door solicitation is one warning sign, especially in a crisis situation. Another indication that an "arborist" doesn't know his cork from his phloem is that he wants to use boot spikes to climb a healthy tree–this is acceptable only on trees that are being cut down. Excessive pruning and "topping" (hacking off most of the top branches) are two more ways a novice can hurt your trees.

Other inexperienced workers may fail to prune adequately. Many tree science professionals recommend that most trees should lose up to a third of their top mass during routine pruning. A contractor that does far less than this may be simply trying to find a shortcut to his paycheck.

For More Information...

The following sources offer a wealth of information on tree care and tree care professionals:

International Society of Arboriculture: www.isa-arbor.com. The ISA website includes detailed information about their arborist certification categories and standards, a locator for finding certified arborists in your area, and consumer brochures (for purchase) on a range of tree care topics.

Tree Care Industry Association: www.treecareindustry.org. The TCIA sponsors an accreditation program that audits prospective companies on customer satisfaction, business practices, employee training, safety, and insurance coverage, among other qualifications. Their website also includes consumer tree care tips and a locator for finding local contractors.

American Society of Consulting Arborists: www.asca-consultants.org. Information on the site can help you determine whether a consulting arborist is right for your needs.

Your local extension agent (usually affiliated with a major university) may offer tree information specific to your climate.

Licenses & Insurance?

Arborists and other tree care professionals are required to be licensed in some areas; check with your city or state regulatory office for local requirements. As discussed, insurance is absolutely essential. Don't hire anyone for tree work on your property unless they show proof of insurance for personal and property damage and workers' compensation insurance.

☎ In the Phone Book

Tree Service, Landscape Contractors.

UPHOLSTERER

SEE ALSO: WINDOW COVERINGS—DEALERS, DESIGNERS & INSTALLERS

For Help With:

- Recovering & repair of upholstered furniture
- Custom upholstery work

Reupholstering a favorite piece of furniture makes it literally look like new but lets you retain the comfort of an old, familiar piece, usually at a fraction of the cost of buying a new piece. Upholsterers can do wonders with many types of furniture. They can repair structural framework, replace or re-tie springs, and restore and recover old cushions or replace cushions altogether. Upholstery shops work with almost any type of textile or natural covering (leather, fur, hide, etc.), adding any trim or decorative accents you'd like.

If your plan is to have the restored furniture match your drapes, you can either work with a shop that specializes in both upholstery and window treatments or supply the same fabric and specifications to two different vendors.

By the Way, Who's Your Upholsterer?

As with most specialty trades, the best way to find a good upholsterer is through word of mouth. Talking to your friends or your friends' friends should turn up a few names. And it's always a subtly flattering question to ask a dinner-party host. Barring those sources, you can talk to local interior designers and decorators. However, keep in mind that many upholsterers who work in the decorating trade don't take jobs directly from consumers, but work only on a referral basis from interior decorators and designers. After gathering the names of recommended upholsterers, you can begin the process of assessing your needs and obtaining estimates.

The Basic Process

For most reupholstering projects, the first step is evaluating the general condition of the furniture and determining how much work it requires. You may already know that your sofa needs some new springs because of how it feels, but a pro's comprehensive opinion could uncover other problems—cracked framing members, for example, or insect damage. Call the upholsterers on your referral list and see if they'll come to your house for a free consultation. On the other hand, with standard furniture pieces requiring clearly defined repairs, it can be fine to ask for rough cost estimates over the phone. Be sure any estimate you get includes all extras, such as arm covers, throw pillows, sofa skirts, etc.

Based on the pros' recommendations and the costs for each service, you can decide which elements to restore or replace. For example, if the foam core of your cushions is still in good shape, you may decide to simply replace the soft padding that wraps around the foam. During his consultation, the upholsterer will also take measurements to use for his estimate and for calculating how much fabric you'll need. If you decide that reupholstering is too expensive, ask upholsterers about having a custom slipcover made.

Speaking of fabric (and other coverings), this is where much, if not most, of the cost of reupholstering comes in. You can either shop on your own and buy a fabric from any good textiles dealer, or you can choose a fabric through your upholsterer. Discuss your intentions early in the process, as not all upholsterers offer both options. Also find out whether your choice of fabric will affect the cost of the job—and if so, how much.

When choosing a covering, look to the professionals for advice on what types are suitable for your purposes. In general, consider the use of the furniture first. Do you need a durable, easy-to-clean material for a TV room sofa, or a fine, period-specific textile for an antique showpiece? Pay close attention to the fabric's *repeat*–the size of each duplicate motif in the pattern. The larger the repeat, the more waste there is in working with the fabric, and hence higher cost. Once your upholsterer knows the type of fabric you've chosen and its repeat, he can tell you how much fabric to buy.

Inspecting an Upholsterer's Work

When it's time to choose an upholsterer, go with the pro whose skills are the best fit for your project and budget and who offers high quality work at a fair price. Always inspect an upholsterer's work before hiring him. Here are some things to look for (with standard fabric upholstery):

- Matching of pattern at all seams and mating parts; the pattern should be centered on cushions and other elements
- Smooth, consistent padding where the covering wraps around frame parts; you shouldn't feel any wood directly beneath the fabric
- Smooth seams, with no bunching or puckering
- A fitted, tailored line along contours and corner seams
- Tightly sewn trim, welt, piping, or other decorative accents

☎ In the Phone Book

Upholsterers, Furniture Repair & Refinish.

WALLPAPER HANGER

For Help With:

- Removal of old wallpaper
- Installing new wallpaper & other wallcoverings
- Basic wall & ceiling surface repairs

An old joke says that any marriage that survives a husband and wife wallpapering together will last a lifetime. It's possible, then, that wallpaper hangers have saved many a marriage. And it explains why the profession exists.

Wallpaper hangers, or paperhangers, have been around since the 16th century, and their craft has changed little since then. Skilled paperhangers are masters at laying out an installation and pasting up the papers so their intricate patterns flow seamlessly across an entire room. They also take care of the dirty work of removing old wallpaper, preparing painted surfaces, and patching and smoothing damaged walls and ceilings in preparation for the new wallcoverings.

Professional paperhangers aren't hard to find. Many painters and painting companies who specialize in interior work also do wallpaper. If you've had a good experience previously with a painting company, ask if they have an expert paperhanger on staff or whether they can refer you to one.

Interior designers and decorators frequently subcontract with paperhangers and generally demand high quality work. Paint and wallcovering retailers often supply the names of local installers or have paperhangers on staff, although these installers may pay a commission to the store—a cost which may be passed on to you. And of course, you can't go wrong with personal referrals from friends who have hired a paperhanger and see the results of the pro's work every day.

Consider Materials First

Before hiring a paperhanger, shop around and decide what type of covering you'd like to use. Then, ask prospective installers about their experience working with your chosen material. Experienced full-time paperhangers work with many different materials, while painters who hang paper on the side may be familiar with only basic vinyl coverings. If you're using traditional wallpaper (which must be pasted with a

brush, using the right formula; it's not pre-pasted like most modern vinyl products) or specialty papers, such as embossed patterns, grasscloth, or fabric, you'll need a pro with direct experience handling that type of material. A knowledgeable installer can also steer you toward the best products to use for your specific application. Once you've hired a paperhanger, she can tell you exactly how much material to buy.

The National Guild of Professional Paperhangers

The NGPP is a great source of information on all things wallpaper. Their website at www.ngpp.org includes consumer tips for estimating, buying, and installing wallpaper, plus an extensive glossary of wallpaper terms. The NGPP sponsors a certification program for professionals who have been full-time paperhangers for at least two years. Candidates must demonstrate a minimum level of knowledge and proficiency in wallpaper installation but do not have to be guild members to obtain certification. You can find certified paperhangers in your area through the guild's website.

The NGPP recommends getting a detailed written contract for any wallpaper job. It should include:

- All materials used, including the brand and exact pattern name of wallpaper, the total quantities of paper, and any accessories and preparation materials.
- All work proposed. If the paper hanger will be removing old wallpaper or preparing surfaces to be covered, this work should be in the contract and included in the final price for the job.
- Complete description of any warranties, including the party responsible for honoring each warranty, time limits, and any limitations or exclusions.
- Special requests, such as dust containment, protecting furniture or office equipment, and cleanup plans (daily or only at end of the job).
- Total price for all work (and materials, if applicable).
- Start and completion dates.

Licenses & Insurance?

Licensure for wallpaper work is not commonly required, although your state or local government may require a contractor's or business license of some kind. Any pro you hire should be covered with liability insurance, and any employee should be covered by workers' compensation insurance.

☎ In the Phone Book

Wallpapers & Wallcoverings Hangers, Wallpaper Removing, Painting Contractors.

WATERPROOFING CONTRACTOR

(FOR BASEMENT MOISTURE PROBLEMS)
SEE: BASEMENT REMODELER

WINDOW CLEANER

For Help With:

- Cleaning:
  - ☐ Interior & exterior window surfaces
  - ☐ Skylights
  - ☐ Mirrors, chandeliers & ceiling fans
  - ☐ Gutters
- Pressure washing
- Screen repair

For everyone who won't "do windows" there's a professional out there who will. Not only that, but he might even repair your window screens, clean your gutters, remove the cobwebs from high chandeliers, and pressure wash those hard-to-reach spots under the roof peak. With an arsenal of heroic services like these, you can be sure that every window cleaner has been asked more than once to stay for dinner.

There's nothing complicated about finding a good window cleaning service. After getting personal references, and perhaps placing a call to your local Better Business Bureau, you can talk to a few cleaners, get some estimates, then choose a pro and see how it goes. Keep in mind a cleaner is someone who will spend a lot of time inside your home. Make sure you're comfortable with him and that he operates a legitimate, customer-oriented business with a good record.

Before you call prospective cleaners, take an inventory of the windows (and other items) that need cleaning. Be prepared to describe the type, number, and general sizes of the windows. This will simplify the cleaner's over-the-phone estimate, if he offers one. Many cleaners will also come to your house and give you a free estimate. Make sure to get any firm price quote in writing–the easier to settle disputes when it's time to write the check. Most cleaners charge per window, but some may bid the whole job or quote you an hourly rate along with a time estimate for the work.

As for additional services your cleaner might offer, it's prudent to start with a window job to check the quality of his work. If that goes well, you can feel more confident hiring him for other projects.

Licenses & Insurance?

Your window cleaner should carry general liability insurance, as well as workers' compensation for all employees.

☎ In the Phone Book

Window Cleaning.

WINDOW COVERINGS—DEALER, DESIGNER & INSTALLER

For Help With:

- Designing & creating custom window treatments
- Sizing & installing factory window coverings
- Bedspreads & other custom fabric creations

Pros who work with window coverings, or window treatments, range from hourly installation workers to highly trained and experienced interior designers. In between are custom shops and factories that produce coverings to your specifications. In case you haven't noticed, decorating windows can get very expensive, so it makes sense to shop around and find a service you're comfortable with.

A quick glance in the phone book gives you an idea of the abundance of window treatment specialists there are to choose from. Some offer every type of covering, while others specialize in things like custom drapery, shutters, or blinds for odd-shaped windows. You'll also notice a lot of crossover between window coverings and room decorating, as many shops offer custom bedspreads and upholstery to coordinate with your window treatments.

Arranging a free in-home or showroom consultation is a good way to learn about the services and materials offered by a shop. Because there are so many products and types of coverings available, consult with a few different shops, just to see what's out there. With blinds and other manufactured coverings, you're generally limited to choices of style, material, and color. Custom drapery, on the other hand, is open to the world of fabrics and almost any style you can dream up. If you're looking for custom work, find out whether the shop will let you provide your own fabric (and whether there's a charge for doing so) or if you must select one of their fabrics.

Depending on the type and complexity of window treatments you want, you'll choose one or more of the following services:

- Design consultation and/or design work
- Measuring of your windows
- Materials
- Fabrication of the coverings
- Installation

Unless you're buying ready-made blinds or shades in stock sizes, let the pros measure your windows. They may or may not charge for this, but either way, it's critical to the success of the job.

☎ In the Phone Book

Window Coverings, Draperies & Curtains, Blinds.

WINDOW & DOOR REPLACEMENT

For Help With:

- Window & door replacement & new installation

When you make a child's playhouse out of a cardboard box, the first thing you do is cut out a door and a few windows. Suddenly, what was a lifeless storage container is now a little dwelling with its own character. Windows and doors have the same magical effect on real houses. Truly, no other elements enhance the quality of life in a home more than windows, doors, and the air and natural light they bring in. And that's precisely why we're willing to spend so much on them.

At the low end of the spectrum, replacing a window or door can be a simple job that any carpenter or even a good handyman can handle in an afternoon. At the other end, replacing several, or all, of your home's portals can become a major remodel in itself. But no matter how extensive the project, the most important factor is the quality of the windows or doors that you choose. Proper installation is critical for a finished appearance and achieving maximum performance, but most of the expense is the product itself.

Being a Smart Shopper

Purchasing new windows and doors is a major shopping endeavor. It's all about narrowing down the choices. First, decide what type you want. With windows, for example, do you want double-hung, casement, sliding, or fixed? Then, consider style: Traditional or modern? Divided light or open pane? Next is sizing. Can you make do with stock sizes, or will some windows need to be custom ordered? And while you're having all of this fun, don't forget the biggie: materials. Wood, vinyl, or metal? Or perhaps vinyl-clad or aluminum-clad wood?

After addressing the many stylistic and structural questions, consider energy efficiency—the generic term for grouping all of a window's or door's performance specifications. But before we get to that, here's a list of the basic criteria that most people consider when shopping for windows and doors:

- Architectural styling
- Natural light
- Ventilation
- Energy efficiency
- Weatherproofing
- Soundproofing
- Security
- Ease of use
- Low maintenance
- (and, last but not least) Price

The point of all this is not to scare you into keeping your old windows; it's to assert that the key to getting what you want from replacement windows and doors is *knowing* what you want. With a little research and comparison shopping under your belt, you'll be ready to face the onslaught of sales hype (and hyper salespeople) that come with this kind of remodeling.

Also be aware that you don't always have to replace entire window or door units. Some window and glass companies specialize in replacing the glass only, leaving the old jambs and trim in place. And new doors can often be mounted right onto existing door frames. The advantages to this kind of partial replacement (as opposed to total, or "prime" replacement) are lower cost, shorter installation time, and the fact that you keep your existing woodwork.

Window Performance Ratings

Considering the glut of manufacturers, products, and features out there, how do you compare one window with the next? There's no simple answer for this, but the NFRC rating label is a good place to start. The National Fenestration Rating Council (www.nfrc.org) is a non-profit coalition that has developed a standardized testing and rating system for comparing different brands and types of windows. The official NFRC label makes it easy to identify the basic performance properties, including:

- U-factor—how well the window insulates (creates a thermal barrier between the inside and outside)
- Solar heat gain—how much solar heat is allowed to pass through the window
- Visible light transmittance
- Air leakage

Look for the NFRC label when comparing performance ratings among windows, regardless of brand, type, or style.

In addition to the NFRC, there are numerous organizations and agencies devoted to helping consumers shop for high quality, energy-efficient windows and glazed doors. Here are just a few:

U.S. Department of Energy: www.eere.energy.gov
Efficient Windows Collaborative: www.efficientwindows.org
American Architectural Manufacturers Association: www.aamanet.org
Home Energy Magazine: www.homeenergy.org

Other possible sources of information include local utilities, the local building department, design professionals, and building materials retailers.

Getting the Job Done

There are two basic approaches to window and door replacement (or new installation). One is to contract with a window and door company, who will supply all of the product and complete the installation as part of a package deal. The other is to buy the product yourself and hire a qualified carpenter for the installation. In either case, start with your own investigation of windows and doors in the general market, as discussed above. The knowledge gained will help you evaluate a company's offerings and a contractor's bid.

Window and door companies usually deal with a number of brand-name manufacturers, or they supply units directly from their own factory. If you've decided to buy from a specific manufacturer, that narrows your choice of vendor. Otherwise, see what products various companies have to offer and what kinds of guarantees are available. Any company you consider should have a long list of glowing references. Contact several former customers and ask about their experience with the company. Were they satisfied with the work, and have there been any problems since the installation? Also conduct a thorough background check on the company to make sure there is no history of complaints filed against them (see Chapter 1).

Compare companies based on their prices (as in value) for product and installation, their references and reputation, the quality of their work (hopefully you get a chance to see some jobs firsthand), their guarantees, and your overall sense of their professionalism. Window and door replacement is a competitive business, and any sizeable town will have loads of vendors to choose from. You shouldn't have to settle for a company that doesn't make you completely comfortable with your decision. As always, don't agree to anything without a detailed written contract for all materials and labor.

Now, back to the independent installer option. This can be a good approach if you're replacing only a few windows at a time or if you have a really custom job that requires advanced carpentry skills. See pages 57 to 59 for tips on finding a good carpenter. You'll want someone with plenty of window and/or door experience, as well as proven expertise with interior and exterior trimwork. Before you buy any new windows, check with the manufacturer about the warranty and what bearing the installation (and installer) may have on it.

HOME SCHOOL

A few notes about installation:

Pre-hung window and door units fit into their framed opening (called the "rough opening") with about a ½" of play all around. The installer uses tapered wood shims to secure the unit in the opening and to adjust its position to make it perfectly plumb, level, and square. Windows typically should be shimmed on all four sides, while doors are often shimmed on the sides and the top (if the rough threshold is level). Shimming helps isolate the relatively flexible jambs from the heavier framing, which can bow or twist, thus distorting the shape of the jamb and making the window or door difficult to operate.

The rough openings of all windows and entry doors must be meticulously weatherproofed to prevent water intrusion inside the wall. After the window or door unit is installed, the gaps between the jambs and rough opening are filled with insulation. If this is not done properly, all the extra money you spent on energy efficiency features goes out the window, so to speak.

Licenses & Insurance?

Window and door vendors and installers should be fully licensed (based on local requirements) and insured.

☎ In the Phone Book

Windows, Doors, Doors & Operating Devices.

WOOD FLOORING INSTALLER & REFINISHER

For Help With:

- Installing all types of new wood flooring
- Refinishing, repair & restoration of existing wood floors

Now that our swinging days of sunken living rooms and shag carpet are well behind us, wood floors are securely back in favor. This may be old news to you, but if you're in the market for new wood flooring, you might be surprised at the range of options now available. Classic hardwood strip flooring remains at the top of list, followed by a variety of engineered wood materials, wood-and-plastic laminates, hardwood parquet tiles, solid-wood planks, and even bamboo (which is actually a grass, but not like the grass passed around in those sunken living rooms in the 1960s and 70s).

If you already have solid hardwood floors, you're probably here because they need refinishing, in which case you have a different set of decisions to make. For example, if your floors are varnished (most likely with polyurethane), do you want to have them screened and re-coated, or do you want to sand them down to the bare wood and apply a new finish? Sanding a floor gives you the option of using a different type of finish than the original or staining the wood for a dramatically new look.

Installing a New Wood Floor

Start by shopping for your flooring material. The varieties listed above are just a sampling of what's out there. The best way to shop for flooring is to visit showrooms of local suppliers to see the stuff in person. At each business, ask about installation. Most large suppliers have their own installers on staff. Hardwood lumber suppliers, who cater primarily to woodworkers and trade professionals, may give you some names of local independent installers. Be sure to bring home samples of flooring you like so you can really get a sense of how they'll look in your room.

If you're shopping for traditional solid-wood flooring, one big decision is whether to use standard unfinished boards or prefinished flooring. (For the record, boards up to about 3" wide are called strips; boards 3" and wider typically are called planks.) Unfinished boards are first installed, then sanded flat and smooth, then finished—all by the same installation crew. Prefinished boards are given a high quality finish at the factory and are simply installed with no follow-up work. If you're considering prefinished flooring, you should see an example of the flooring in a real home—not just on the supplier's sample. Prefinished floors have more height variation than standard floors because they aren't sanded flat. Some types have chamfered edges to help compensate for the slight unevenness, but be aware that this changes the overall look of the flooring.

You can buy wood flooring through a full-service flooring company and get the installation as part of a package deal. Another option is to buy the material yourself and hire an independent installer. If you know exactly what you're looking for, you can even buy your flooring online and possibly save some money on the materials.

Installing wood flooring is pretty straightforward. Unless you seek specialty decorative work, like inlaid medallions or custom edgings, you're probably not looking for a craftsperson with a personal touch. What you need is a well-established flooring company or installation contractor with a good reputation for quality work, competitive prices, and decent customer service. By all means, run a background check (see Chapter 1) on all prospective companies and/or installers. Ask for references, and call several past clients to talk about their experiences with each candidate. If you are planning some specialty details or custom work, have a good look at the installer's portfolio, and check out a few examples in person. Finally, before signing up with an installer or company, make sure the entire process is outlined in a written contract (see What's Included?, next page).

Refinishing an Existing Wood Floor

As mentioned, wood floors with a polyurethane finish often can be re-coated with the same finish. However, the floor must be in good condition, and it must never have seen the likes of floor wax, oil soap, or other slippery solutions. Once a wax has been applied to a urethane finish it can't be re-coated because the new finish won't stick properly. The basic process of re-coating involves roughing up the floor with a special screen pad to give the surface some "tooth," then applying two coats of new poly.

Refinishing a wood floor, as opposed to re-coating, usually means sanding off the old finish and getting down to bare wood. Sanding brings out the original color of the flooring and flattens and smoothes the boards for a uniform surface. This process typically removes about $1/16"$ of wood from the tops of the boards. If your flooring is old and you don't know how many times it has been refinished, it's a good idea to have a professional inspect the boards to make sure they're thick enough to withstand another sanding. Some types of engineered wood flooring (which is plywood with a hardwood veneer) can be sanded, but you should have it checked out by an experienced pro before proceeding.

Most hardwood flooring installers also do refinishing. Experience is important because sanding machines are very destructive in unskilled hands. And when it comes to the finish, it takes knowledge and a little bit of art to make wood look its absolute best, especially with complicated finishes. As with hiring an installer, investigate the records of all prospective refinishers to check for customer complaints, and call several past customers to check references.

These days many flooring companies advertise "dust-free" refinishing or similar claims. Indeed, sanding a floor does create a lot of fine dust that is difficult to contain. If dust is a concern for you, compare the different contractors' dust containment systems and guarantees, and definitely ask past customers whether the contractors' claims were valid. In any case, don't take chances. Clear out everything from the work site, and cover any valuables that can be harmed by dust, even if they're far from the work site.

WHAT'S INCLUDED?

This is an important question when you're hiring a pro for any type of work on a wood floor, because the flooring itself is only part of the job. Consider the following elements when discussing the job with your contractor. If any extras are included in the estimate, make sure to get them in writing before any work starts:

- Demolition—Is there old flooring that must be removed prior to the new installation?
- Subfloor—This is the structural decking underneath the finish flooring; it may need repairs or refastening to eliminate squeaking and to ensure the flooring lies flat.
- Underlayment—Over a wood subfloor, the standard underlayment is tar paper. Over a concrete slab, additional materials may be required, depending on the type of wood flooring used.
- Baseboard and base shoe—Most wood floors are trimmed out with wood baseboard and base shoe molding. For new installation, all base moldings must be removed. For refinishing, only the base shoe is removed. Do you want to salvage the old baseboard or buy new material? Who is responsible for removing and installing the moldings?
- Trimming doors and moldings and installing thresholds to accommodate the new flooring— Floor height can be a particular concern with solid hardwood flooring, which is typically ¾" thick.
- Dust containment—All contractors should have a sound plan for minimizing dust in your home. Some actually charge extra for simple courtesies like hanging plastic barriers. Others address dust head-on with truck-mounted vacuum systems and other methods.
- Job schedule—How long will each stage of the job take? How long does the final coat of finish take to cure fully? With wood floors, you really can't make exceptions regarding drying and curing times for the finish coats; you have to stay off the floor or you'll ruin the finish.

Finish Options

Polyurethane is by far the most common finish for wood floors, but it's not the only one, nor is it necessarily the best for all applications and personal tastes. Polyurethane comes in several formulas, including oil-based, water-based, and moisture-cured varieties. Exceptionally tough and water-resistant, urethanes are the most popular of the "surface" finishes—materials that create a plastic-like seal over the top of the wood, resulting in a smooth, shiny floor like that of a basketball court. Another surface finish you might consider is spar, or marine, varnish.

The other main group of finishes, called "penetrating," includes penetrating oils and penetrating stains. These finishes soak into the wood's pores, leaving more of the natural texture of the wood exposed, rather than sealing over like a surface finish. Common varieties of penetrating formulas include tung, linseed, and Danish oils. Floors with a penetrating finish are often waxed and buffed to produce a satin sheen. Waxing is a laborious, messy job that you'd probably need to tackle once or twice a year. But in the end, you might prefer the results to the appearance and feel of a low-maintenance surface finish.

For More Information...

The National Wood Flooring Association is the industry's primary professional organization. It sponsors programs for wood flooring Installation Certification and Sand & Finish Certification. The NWFA's consumer website at www.woodfloors.org features general information on wood flooring types, finishes, applications, and care. You'll also find ideas for one-of-a-kind decorative flooring treatments.

Licenses & Insurance?

Licensure of wood flooring professionals varies by area. Your installer or refinisher should have liability insurance and workers' compensation insurance for all employees.

☎ In the Phone Book

Floor—Install, Refinish & Resurface; Hardwoods.

ZIPPER RESTORATION

For Help With:

- Teeth realignment
- Slide & tab replacement
- Emergency services for stuck fabrics

It used to be that once a zipper goes, it's gone. No matter how many times you try to align those two little leaders and carefully pull up on the slide, the rows of seemingly perfect teeth just fail to mesh. Cursing, you try again and again; you just can't understand why a zipper that worked flawlessly yesterday suddenly refuses to cooperate, as though it no longer cares to fulfill its one purpose in life.

Okay, you caught me. There's no such thing as a zipper restorer (at least we don't think so). We just needed a "Z" to complete our A to Z list. Seems like a useful service, though. If you hear of a good zipper restorer who makes house calls, please let us know.

Taking On a Big Project

When a job is big enough to require several different contractors working simultaneously or in close succession, there are two basic approaches you can take. You can 1) hire and manage all of the pros yourself and be in charge of the scheduling, materials purchases, quality control, decision making, payments, and daily supervision of all workers, or 2) hire a general contractor.

Here are some reasons to go with option 1:

- You have lots of free time you need to fill with checklists and phone calls and shopping trips.
- You enjoy calling workers at 9:00 a.m. and yelling at them for not showing up to work—every day.
- You've learned so much from this book and feel so confident in your ability to work with tradespeople that you're thinking of becoming a general contractor yourself (please see notes about construction experience, on page 192).
- You thrive on stress and aggravation.

Unless you strongly agree with at least two of the above reasons, you'd be well advised to go with option 2: Hire a general contractor. This chapter offers tips on finding a good one, as well as some other key aspects of tackling a big project.

HIRING A GENERAL CONTRACTOR

First, an explanation of basic terms: A general contractor, or GC, as they're known in the trades, is a professional who contracts with clients to oversee construction jobs from start to finish. GCs hire subcontractors, organize and supervise all workflow, purchase supplies, obtain permits, and make sure everything is completed in accordance with the job contract.

The GC is your go-to guy (or gal) for everything. If your newly installed kitchen sink drains into the dining room, you call the GC. If the painter is using flat paint where you wanted semi-gloss, you call the GC. Likewise, if you fly off the handle because you mistook the primer for the finish coat, the painter may call the GC. You get the picture.

General contractors come in all stripes and specialties. Some are strictly remodeling contractors, some stick to new construction, and some are restoration specialists. Some work for big companies and do nothing but manage crews, while others do most of their own work, often with one or two skilled helpers. A home builder is basically a general contractor who specializes in complete new-home construction.

Within the context of a contractor-run job, a subcontractor is anyone who works for the GC. Almost any professional discussed in this book's A to Z list could be a subcontractor on a project. Sometimes a general contractor will work as a sub for another GC, usually when the former is a jack-of-all-trades type who does his own work. Most, but not all, GCs offer hands-on construction experience. Many started out as carpenters, which makes sense, since carpenters typically spend more time on a job than any other trade.

On residential projects, it's common for the GC to show up every day with a small crew of skilled hands and/or laborers who are his direct employees. Their job, more or less, is to facilitate the project on the whole; they may help the electrician dig a trench or stack materials as they come in or install blocking along with the carpenter. You'll probably get to know these workers by name.

Is a GC All I Need?

By standard definition, a general contractor is a construction specialist who carries out all necessary work according to a set of plans. So who creates the plans? For that you have several options. Most homeowners choose one of the following:

Architect

For major projects such as large additions, extensive remodels, or new home construction, architects offer the most comprehensive design and engineering services. If you hire an architect you most likely also will hire a general contractor, and the two must work together to achieve your project goals. Some architects offer general contracting services or can visit a job regularly to consult with the contractor and make sure the job specs are being followed.

Design/Build Firm

These are companies or contractors who offer both design and general contracting services. Design/build teams offer you one-stop shopping for all types of projects, from bathroom remodels to new homes. Firms may have professional designers or architects on staff or may subcontract the design work. A full-service basement remodeling company is a good example of a design/build firm commonly used on residential jobs.

General Contractor

While most contractors can't call themselves designers, many are familiar with basic design concepts. By working on projects every day, contractors get a practical education on which elements and designs work and which ones don't. If you have design ideas of your own and your project plans are pretty straightforward, an experienced remodeling contractor may offer all the additional advice you need to get the job done. However, keep in mind that the building department may require detailed plan drawings before issuing permits; since contractors typically don't provide these, you may need to hire a draftsperson to draw up the plans.

THE NATURAL ORDER OF THINGS

Extensive projects (and chapters written about them) have a way of burying us in the details. With that in mind, here's a very simple list of the major steps leading up to the job start. Your project may follow the steps in a different order.

1. Planning and rough budgeting.

This starts with gathering information, brainstorming, daydreaming, shopping around for products, and thinking about designs, and ends with settling on a rough idea of what you want to do and how much you want to spend. Somewhere in this process you'll have to check in with the local building department, your homeowners' association, and any other authoritative body that might take an unyielding position on your plans.

2. Designing.

Hiring a designer (architect, interior designer, or design pro at a design/build firm) is the quickest way to make your dreams a reality—on paper, at least. After settling on a basic plan and establishing the major elements, your designer will draft a semi-final set of drawings and help you write complete job specifications (see Chapter 1, pages 20 to 25).

3. Hiring a general contractor.

If you're using a design/build firm or a full-service remodeling company, the design and contracting will come as a package. Otherwise, you'll use your design drawings and job specs to find the best contractor for your project.

4. Finalizing the design and signing the contract.

You, the contractor, and the designer will work together to refine and rework the design and specifications into a flawless plan. Following that, it's time to negotiate your contract with the contractor for all of the work to be done.

5. Breaking ground (or old drywall).

With permits in hand, contractor and crew descend upon your home and get busy like a swarm of drones pleasing the queen bee. At least that's the idea.

Interior Designer

Interior designer describes a large group of professionals whose specialties range from decorating rooms to designing floor plans. You might work with a designer to establish a new color scheme for your living room or to completely reconfigure your kitchen layout. Remodeling a bathroom or kitchen may call for the help of a certified kitchen or bath designer. Interior designers often work for remodeling companies as part of a design/build team, or they may work as independent contractors.

Because architects (or designers) and general contractors spend most of their time on different sides of the drafting table, it's in your best interest to get the two together early in the planning process. It's very common for a builder to catch a designer's mistake, and vice versa—both during planning and after work has begun. This ongoing collaboration will be most fruitful if the two pros get along, and having them meet early can possibly head off any conflict. Of course, if you use a design/build firm for your project, the designer and builder will work for the same company, and it won't be your job to make sure they get along.

Finding General Contractors

Choosing the contractor who will manage your project is likely to be the most important single decision you'll make. With one pro in charge, the GC's personality, professionalism, skill, experience, and integrity will extend to each subcontractor hired, the day-to-day operations on the project, and the overall quality of the work. So choose carefully. But where to look.... First, try your best to get personal references from friends, neighbors, coworkers, etc. Considering the many hours and days a customer spends with a GC over the course of a large project, personal referrals say a lot.

Industry professionals you trust may also provide word-of-mouth referrals for good contractors. Residential architects and designers often work directly with contractors and may recommend a GC who is a good fit for your project. Trade pros who do a lot of subcontracting know good local contractors, as do materials suppliers who cater to builders. Sometimes real estate pros and lenders are familiar with the work and reputations of local contractors.

If you don't know someone who has hired or worked with local contractors, you can check with the local chapter of the National Association of the Remodeling Industry (NARI; www.nari.org) or the National Association of Home Builders (NAHB; www.nahb.org). Both groups offer certification programs in a variety of building and remodeling categories. The local chapters can provide a list of members and certified professionals in your area–this is not the same as a recommendation, but it's a place to get some names.

Other places to find names are the phone book (under Contractors– General, Contractors–Remodel & Repair, Home Builders, and Remodeling Services) or at local home shows, where you get a chance to see what's offered by several different contractors. In this book, be sure to check out any of the following entries that apply: Architect (page 43), Basement Remodeler (page 50), Bathroom Remodeler (page 53), Interior Designer (page 118), Kitchen Remodeler (page 121).

Once you have a list of a half dozen or more names, call each contractor for a brief phone interview. This will help you trim the list down to contractors who are available and appropriate for your project. Find out:

- What types of projects they specialize in and/or do most often.
- If they are licensed and insured.
- Whether they will provide references.
- How long they have worked in the area and how long with their regular subcontractors.
- What their availability looks like; also how many jobs they typically run at any one time.

Expect the contractors to have questions of their own. The questions they ask will tell you how much interest they have in working for you. Be aware that even the best contractors aren't always prompt about returning phone calls, so you may have to be persistent. If you were referred by a former client, say so; it may move you higher up on the contractor's call list.

Interviewing General Contractors

Ideally, your phone queries have left you with three or four good candidates. The next step is setting up an appointment with each contractor to meet—at your home, preferably—and discuss the project in detail. Following the interviews, you can request formal bids from your top picks. Before calling for appointments, run a background check on each of the candidates (see Chapter 1). It's unlikely that you'll find a lot of complaints filed against a contractor, but if you do, there's no point in meeting with him.

Prepare for the interviews by gathering all relevant project documents (construction drawings, job specifications, product literature, etc.) and making a list of questions to ask the contractors. If your spouse, partner, or other household member will share the project decisions with you, make sure everyone will be at the initial interview. Don't waste the pros' time by requesting additional "get to know you" meetings.

Above all, the interviews are your chance to learn about each contractor's business, personality, expertise, and work style. They in turn will try to determine whether your project—and you—are right for them. You should expect to talk about every aspect of the project, including money. It's important for contractors to know whether your budget is realistic. If it seems low for the scope of the work, contractors will expect to be nickel-and-dimed the whole way and may want no part of it. An experienced contractor can offer valuable advice for budgeting and other matters at this early stage.

If you're soliciting work from large companies, be aware that it may be a sales representative, not the contractor, who comes to meet with you. If you're comfortable with this, fine. But you should insist on meeting the contractor before going too far toward an agreement. As charming as the sales rep may be, she's not the one you will be working with every day.

Finally, if a contractor fails to show up for the appointment, remove him from your list without another thought. Would you ever expect to get a job if you played hooky from the first interview? This may seem obvious, but you'd be surprised at how many homeowners put up with this kind of behavior from contractors.

Here are some of the points you should discuss during your interviews:

Experience

What's the contractor's background, and how long has he been involved in projects like yours? Contractors who have done a lot of work locally will know the most about local building codes.

Who will do the work and when?

How much of the work will be done by the contractor, his employees, or subcontractors? Will the work occur during standard hours (8 to 5 Monday through Friday, for example)? What about weekends and evenings? Remember, the work is going on in your home, so you'll want a schedule that fits the household's.

Subcontractors

If the contractor plans to use subs on the job, find out about each of them. Are they local? Does the contractor use them regularly? Will they provide proof of insurance? In general, the quality of the subs is critical to the success of the job, since they may be doing much of the work.

Supervision

Will the contractor be on-site to supervise the work crews every day? If not, who will be in charge? You should be assured that a supervisor, foreman, or lead carpenter who works for the GC will be on-site at all times, if not the GC himself. You may request to meet the supervisor before hiring the contractor.

Plans, designs, and designers

Get the contractor's opinion of your project plans and goals. His responses should give you an indication of his acumen and his communication skills. This is your chance to discuss ideas and test the collaborative waters: Does the contractor seem to know his stuff, and will he be open to your suggestions? If you're using an independent designer on the project, ask whether the contractor knows the designer or is familiar with her work.

Timing

How soon could work start in earnest? Once begun, will it continue without delays through completion? Discuss the proposed project schedule–does it seem realistic? If you have strict schedule requirements or intend to set a hard deadline, now is the time to discuss it.

Insurance and licenses

If the contractor doesn't arrive with proof of insurance and any required licenses, make sure to obtain all documentation before signing a contract.

Guarantees

Guarantees for workmanship and materials will vary among contractors and are important factors for comparing candidates. At this stage, you can ask about a contractor's standard guarantees, but you must get them in writing with the job contract.

Miscellaneous requests and conditions

Be sure to bring up any issues that are important to you, including contract items that shouldn't be taken for granted, such as change orders, trash disposal and job-site cleanup, bathroom use, and permits. See Chapter 2 for more ideas about contract terms to discuss.

Do you like this person?

Much of your decision will be based on your gut feeling about a contractor.

CHECKING REFERENCES & WORK

During the interview, ask contractors for the names and phone numbers of past clients whom you can call to check references. The most valuable references will be those for jobs similar to yours that were completed within the last year or so. You might also ask for the names of some of the contractor's regular subcontractors and suppliers.

See Rule #5 on page 7 (Chapter 1) for a list of questions you should ask previous clients. You should also ask specifically about the workers and subcontractors on the job and the GC's management of them. Find out whether it was easy to reach the contractor during the day. Were there any disputes or complications with the design or job specifications? Any problems with inspections or building code violations? Was the job completed on budget? Would the customer have any reservations about hiring the contractor again?

Try to talk with at least three past customers, then go see at least one completed project in person to assess the quality of the contractor's work. Inspecting a current job can tell you a lot, too: Is the job site organized and orderly? Are materials stored properly in an appropriate location? What does the contractor's trailer look like—organized or chaotic?

GETTING ACCURATE BIDS

With the third-degree interrogations over, you hopefully have at least three decent candidates to choose from. Now it's time to look at the numbers.

Estimates, Quotes & Bids

More definitions of terms: In the world of home construction and remodeling, estimates are ballpark figures, usually given by contractors, architects, and other professionals to help homeowners develop budgets or (roughly) compare competitors' pricing. Estimates typically do not state a firm price offered for specific goods or services. A bid is a contractor's legitimate and firm offer to complete a job for a specific price. When you want to know the total price a contractor will charge to fulfill your job specifications, you request a bid. A quote is essentially the same thing as a bid, but bid is the more standard term for large projects with formal price proposals.

Rules of Proper Bidding

The essential tool for getting complete and accurate bids from contractors is a detailed set of job specifications (see Chapter 2, pages 20 to 27). Using specs is the only way to ensure that all contractors are bidding on the same work and materials. It also leaves them with no excuse for omitting or altering parts of the work or substituting cheap materials.

Again, detail is critical. Look what can go wrong with a vague specification like: "New, raised-panel wood door to replace existing kitchen entry door." When assembling their bids, Contractor A might figure on a stain-grade, solid-

maple door–the most expensive type that fits your description; Contractor B may bid on a solid-wood, paint-grade pine door; while Contractor C likes to use MDF doors with a raised-panel look, so that's what he bids. If you want a traditional stain-grade door, the bids from Contractors B and C would require a change and a cost adjustment. And that's just one material spec.

All bids you receive must be in writing (they're typically done on a standard form or company letterhead), and they must include your job specs or otherwise specify all materials to be used and how they will be installed. Bids should also include fees for permits, rental equipment, temporary labor, extra utilities, and any other requirements not explicitly stated in the specs. Verbal bids, quotes over the phone, or any proposal created by someone who hasn't seen your house and analyzed the job should not be considered legitimate. Bids should be signed and dated by the contractor–but not by you. If you sign a bid, it could be used as a contractual agreement. Obtain a copy of each bid for comparing quotes and to keep for your records.

Two Types of Bids

For most large home improvements, it's recommended that you get a fixed-price bid, in which the entire job–materials, labor, overhead, and profit–are included in a single sum. Barring any changes in the work or materials, that sum is what you will pay for everything. The other type of bid is a time-and-materials bid, where the contractor quotes you a price for all specified materials and includes an hourly rate for the labor. The total cost for labor is variable, based on how much work needs to be done. Payments for both types of bids are typically made in stages.

Time-and-materials bids can be appropriate for projects in which the homeowners are doing a good chunk of the work themselves or when the project is not clearly defined at the outset. In most cases, though, a fixed-price bid is highly preferable. With a set price in the contract, making the numbers work is the contractor's responsibility, and you won't spend the entire job fretting over the labor hours spent on, say, stubborn old flooring that takes three times longer than it should to remove. An unscrupulous contractor also has more incentive to drag his feet under a time-and-materials arrangement, since you're paying for each hour.

If you do choose to go with a time-and-materials bid, it's a good idea to include a price cap, which sets a maximum amount the job can reach. However, there is no guarantee that the work will be complete when the price cap is hit. The bid should also include a detailed list of specifications for materials, appliances, and other supplies.

Another distinction among bid types is itemization. Itemized bids provide a cost breakdown of all materials, labor hours, fees, etc., allowing you to compare at a glance the different contractors' allocation of the money. Non-itemized bids sum up the works in a single dollar amount. You may also find contracts with varying degrees of itemization between these two extremes.

Some contractors itemize their bids as a regular practice, others itemize only on request, and some may not do it at all. Granted, itemizing an extensive bid proposal takes a lot of time, and the job is still speculative for the contractors. If you'd prefer to have itemized bids, ask about this during the contractor interviews. You may decide that it's not worth it to make this point a deal-breaker.

Comparing Bids

Assuming each contractor bids the job using identical (and oh-so-detailed) specifications, you should be able to compare the costs more or less at face value. Now you can consider the quoted prices in relation to how much you like or trust each candidate. For example, if your top pick's bid is the highest by a reasonable margin (say 5%, perhaps as much as 10%), he still might offer the best value for your project. But beware of applying this logic to the opposite scenario. In other words, you shouldn't choose your least favorite candidate simply because his bid is somewhat lower than the rest.

Be careful with really low bids. Contractors may bid low for a variety of reasons: carelessness in creating the bid; attempting to undercut competition just to win the job; or misunderstanding something significant about the job specs or project scope. In any case (and especially when the low bid was intentional), the contractor will try to make up the difference with poor quality work or cheap materials. If you get a low bid from an experienced contractor with a good reputation, chances are something was missed or misinterpreted, so you should inquire about it.

A note about pricing of materials and supplies: Contractors buy many job items—building materials, cabinets, fixtures, etc.—at a discount through their suppliers and typically charge you, the customer, a price at or slightly below retail. Fair enough, since they're going to the trouble of purchasing and hauling the goods, and they assume responsibility for faulty or flawed product. This is also a way for pros to increase their profit slightly without charging you more. If you suspect a contractor's pricing is too high, you can compare it to prices at a few local home improvement megastores and/or lumberyards.

Finally, you can always get help when comparing bids. If you're working with an architect or designer, have her analyze them and render an opinion. Other building professionals or homeowners with remodeling experience may offer help as well. (Also see: Higher Price Consciousness, on page 14.) In the end, of course, the decision is yours. But if you've taken care to meet with each contractor and thoroughly discuss the project, and now you've seen the bids, you'll probably have a strong feeling about which one is best for the job.

SPECIAL CONSIDERATIONS FOR BIG JOBS

You've read the first three chapters of this book, right? Which means you've had plenty to think about in preparing for the big project. Well, here are a few more things to throw into the mix (just in case you were beginning to think this is easy). Don't worry; it's mostly just clarification of stuff you've seen before.

Payment Schedules & Final Payments

As mentioned in the discussion of contracts in Chapter 2, big jobs usually call for a well-defined payment plan. Staggered payments are an effective way to keep contractors on schedule, and they give you considerable leverage for enforcing contract requirements.

There's really no standard method for establishing payment stages. Your contractor will probably explain his normal procedure, and you can negotiate for modifications to that plan, if desired. Generally, payments follow the percentage of work that has been done: After 20% of the job is complete, a 20% payment is made; at the 40% progress mark, another 20% is paid out, etc.

Since it can be difficult to define progress in terms of percentages, payments can be arranged to follow key inspections, such as foundation, framing, electrical, and mechanical inspections. You can also tie payments to tangible stages of the work, like "drywall taped and finished." Never make payments based on a time schedule, such as weekly or monthly payments, because the contractor gets paid regardless of how much work is done.

The most important aspects of any payment plan are the down payment and the final payment. Down payments for large jobs usually range between 5% to 10% of the total job cost. As mentioned earlier, if one of your contractor candidates asks for much more up front than the others, take it as a warning sign. The final payment is a specified sum that's held back until the work is done–completely, absolutely done, so there's not a single piece of trim left off or a smudge on the wall that needs touch-up paint.

Consider the final payment as a retainer, a security deposit, that motivates your contractor to tie up those loose ends that remain after most of the workers are gone. Final payment amounts are typically 10% to 20% of the total job cost but should never be less than 10%. Some contracts also stipulate an automatic waiting period, of perhaps two to four weeks, prior to final payment. This gives the owners a chance to live in the new space and test out the equipment before setting the contractor free.

And speaking of loose ends.... After the dust has cleared and the paint has dried, it's time to do a thorough walk-through and make note of any unfinished details. This is called the punch list. It's an informal checklist of all items you expect the contractor to take care of before you will make the final payment (if you've hired one, your architect can help create the punch list).

Who Should Buy Supplies?

This is a question that comes up on many sizable remodels. There's no quick answer that applies to all jobs, but here are a few things to consider: When it comes to building materials, including lumber, plumbing supplies, wiring, insulation, drywall, and even flooring, it's usually best to let the contractor buy. He knows what he needs, and he knows where to get it. He can also get a good price for it, which may or may not be passed on to you.

For special items, like cabinets, decorative light fixtures, and appliances, you can let the contractor buy them using your shopping list, or you can supply them yourself. If you shop around, you may be able to beat the contractor's prices (his bid prices, that is) and save some money by doing the legwork. Keep in mind that if the contractor does the purchasing, he's the one who has to make returns for common problems like missing parts, scratched paint, and broken glass.

Details covering who is buying what should be spelled out in the job contract. Homeowner-supplied goods are often funded by a "purchase allowance," a specified amount set aside to use for buying the goods. The allowance is part of the total job cost, and this comes with a potential catch: If the allowance is not big enough for what you want to buy, you've automatically increased the price of the job. So just make sure the allowance can support your shopping habits.

Keep a Job File

The simplest task in your whole project could save you from the biggest headaches. All you have to do is stash away every bit of paperwork related to the job into an accordion file. Having a paper trail could prove invaluable in resolving a dispute. Be sure to include:

- Contract, plans, and specifications
- Change orders
- Building permits
- Invoices, bills, and receipts
- Cancelled checks
- Lien releases
- All written correspondence with anyone involved in the project
- Notes about things discussed with your contractor and important events and dates
- Photographs taken regularly of the job in progress
- Manufacturers' warranties and all written guarantees from your contractor

A Few Thoughts on Budgeting

First and foremost, don't go into an expensive home improvement project without a carefully planned budget. Without a budget, you'll have no reference for how much you're spending or, more importantly, how much each expenditure is adding to the total cost. Neglecting to budget is the surest way to spend more than you can afford.

Contractors and consumers alike point to project cost overruns as one of the leading causes of disputes (and stress). That's why industry professionals always recommend budgeting an extra amount to cover unexpected costs or to pay for useful upgrades. How much? Most advise to build in a buffer of 10% to 25% of the total job cost. However, making a contingency fund work for you requires following some rules:

1. Keep it to yourself. If you tell your architect or contractor about the extra money, it's as good as gone. Lots of building professionals love to spend other people's money.
2. Don't consider the money as part of the official budget. A contingency fund is there as a cushion to help you absorb cost overruns without having a heart attack. If you spend it right away on an extravagant upgrade, it won't be there when you need it.

For More Information...

Here are some good resources for help with the many aspects of a large remodel or building project:

National Association of the Remodeling Industry: www.nari.org.

National Association of Home Builders: www.nahb.org.

National Kitchen & Bath Association: www.nkba.org.

"DETAIL IS CRITICAL"

Appendices

ON THE FOLLOWING PAGES, you'll find two sample contracts that will closely resemble the agreements and forms you should see from the various pros you work with. Get familiar with them so you'll know what to look for when working with pros in real-life settings. If you're not comfortable with the type of contract he or she uses—or run into someone who doesn't have a standard contract—you could use these. Just photocopy them and fill them out appropriately.

The actual wording of contracts may vary widely, depending on the requirements of your state, but the basic features should be present on any contract.

CONTRACT FOR SIMPLE HOME REPAIRS

_____, Homeowner, desires to contract with,

_____, Contractor, to perform certain work on property located at:

_____

1. Job Description

The work to be performed under this agreement consists of the following:

_____

_____

_____

_____

_____

2. Payment Terms

In exchange for the specified work, Homeowner agrees to pay Contractor as follows

(choose one and check the appropriate boxes):

❏ $_____, payable upon completion of the specified work by ❏ cash ❏ check.

❏ $_____, payable one half at the beginning of the specified work and

        one half at the completion of the specified work by ❏ cash ❏ check.

❏ $_____ per hour for each hour of work performed, up to a maximum of $_____,

payable at the following times and in the following manner:_____

_____

_____

_____

3. Time of Performance

The work specified in this contract shall (check the boxes and provide dates):

❏ begin on _____

❏ be completed on _____

Time is of the essence.

4. Independent Contract Status

It is agreed that Contractor shall perform the specified work as an independent contract. Contractor

(check the appropriate boxes and provide description, if necessary):

❏ maintains his or her own independent business.

❏ shall use his or her own tools and equipment except: _____

_____

_____

_____

_____

_____

❏ shall perform the work specified in Clause 1 independent of Homeowner's supervision,

being responsible only for satisfactory completion of the work.

5. License Status Number

Contractor shall comply with all state and local licensing and registration requirements for type of activity

involved in the specified work.

(Check one box and provide description)

❏ Contractor's state license or registration is for the following type of work and carries the following number:

_____

_____

_____

_____

_____

❏ Contractor's local license or registration is for the following type of work and carries the following number:

_____

_____

_____

_____

_____

❏ Contractor is not required to have a license or registration for the specified work, for the following reasons:

_____

_____

_____

6. Liability Waiver

If contractor is injured in the course of performing the specific work, Homeowner shall be exempt from liability for those injuries to the fullest extent allowed by law.

7. Permits and Approvals

(Check one for each pair)

❏ Contractor   ❏ Homeowner

shall be responsible for determining which permits are necessary and for obtaining the permits.

❏ Contractor   ❏ Homeowner

shall pay for all state and local permits necessary for performing the specific work.

❏ Contractor   ❏ Homeowner

shall be responsible for obtaining approval from the local homeowners' association, if required.

8. Additional Agreements and Amendments

Homeowner and Contractor additionally agree that: _____

_____

_____

_____

_____

_____

_____

_____

_____

_____

All agreements between Homeowner and Contractor related to the specified work are incorporated in this contract. Any modification to the contract shall be in writing.

Homeowner: _____ Dated: _____
Contractor: _____ Dated: _____

DISCLAIMER: THIS FORM IS INTENDED TO PROVIDE EXAMPLES OF THE KINDS OF TERMS THAT, AT A MINIMUM, SHOULD BE INCLUDED IN SUCH A CONTRACT. IT IS NOT INTENDED TO SERVE AS A SUBSTITUTE FOR THE ADVICE OF AN ATTORNEY-AT-LAW. BEFORE ENTERING INTO A CONTRACT INVOLVING GIVING SOMETHING OF VALUE TO ANOTHER FOR GOODS, SERVICES OR MATERIALS, BE CERTAIN THAT YOU HAVE A CLEAR UNDERSTANDING OF ALL OF THE TERMS IN THE CONTRACT AND WHAT REMEDIES ARE AVAILABLE UPON DEFAULT OF ONE OF THE PARTIES. AN ATTORNEY-AT-LAW CAN HELP YOU WITH ANY QUESTIONS YOU MAY HAVE ABOUT THE PROPOSED CONTRACT.

CONTRACT FOR HOME REPAIRS OR REMODELING

_____, Homeowner, desires to contract with,

_____, Contractor, to perform certain work on property located at:

_____

_____

1.   Job Description

The work to be performed under this agreement consists of the following:

_____

_____

_____

_____

2.   Payment Terms

In exchange for the specified work, homeowner agrees to pay Contractor as follows

(choose one and check the appropriate boxes):

a. $_____, payable all labor and materials, in installments by   ❏ cash   ❏ check, as follows:

_____

_____

_____

b. $_____, payable in installments for labor by   ❏ cash   ❏ check, as follows:

_____

_____

_____

Homeowner shall pay for material upon their delivery to the worksite, or as follows:

_____

_____

_____

_____

c. $_____$ per hour for each hour of work performed, up to a maximum of $\$_____$,
plus cost of materials to be billed by Contractor as follows: _____

_____

_____

_____

d. $\$_____$, including labor and materials for the first phase of the specified
work; $\$_____$ payable by ❑ cash   ❑ check at the beginning of the specified
work; and $\$_____$ payable by ❑ cash   ❑ check at completion of the first phrase
of the specific work. Terms for additional phases of the specific work shall be agreed upon by Contractor and
homeowner prior to the beginning of each additional phase and added to this contract as a written amendment.

3.   Time of Performance
The work specified in Clause 1 shall be (check the boxes and provide dates):

❑ started on or about _____

❑ completed on or about _____

❑ started and completed as follows: _____
Time is of the essence.

4.   Independent Contract Status
It is agreed that Contractor shall perform the specified work as an independent contract. Contractor (check the
appropriate boxes and provide description, if necessary):

❑ maintains his or her own independent business.

❑ shall use his or her own tools and equipment except:

_____

_____

❑ shall perform the work independent of Homeowner's supervision, being responsible only for satisfactory
completion of the work.

❑ Contractor may use subcontractors, but shall be solely responsible for supervising their work and for the
quality of the work they produce.

5. License Status and Number

Contractor shall comply with all state and local licensing and registration requirements for type of work involved (check one box and provide description):

❏ Contractor's state license or registration is for the following type of work and carries the following number:

_____

_____

❏ Contractor's local license or registration is for the following type of work and carries the following number:

_____

_____

❏ Contractor is not required to have a license or registration for the specified work, for the following reasons:

_____

_____

6. Liability Waiver

If contractor is injured in the course of performing the specific work, Homeowner shall be exempt from liability for those injuries to the fullest extent allowed by law.

7. Permits and Approvals
(Check the appropriate boxes)

❏ Contractor   ❏ Homeowner shall be responsible for determining which permits are necessary and for obtaining the permits.

❏ Contractor   ❏ Homeowner shall pay for all state and local permits necessary for performing the specific work.

❏ Contractor   ❏ Homeowner shall be responsible for obtaining approval from the local homeowner's association, if required.

8. Liens and Waivers of Liens

To protect Homeowner against liens being filed by Contractor, subcontractors, and providers of materials, Contractor agrees that (check one box and provide description, if necessary):

❏ Final payment to Contractor under Clause 2 shall be withheld by Homeowner until Contractor presents Homeowner with lien waivers, lien releases, or acknowledgment of full payment from each subcontractor and materials provider.

❏ All checks to Contractor shall also be made out jointly to all subcontractors and materials suppliers.

❏ Contractor shall not:

a. Use a subcontractor without first obtaining a lien waiver or release and delivering a copy to Homeowner; or

b. Use any materials without obtaining an "acknowledgement of full payment" from the materials supplier and delivering a copy to Homeowner.

❏ Homeowner and Contractor agree that Homeowner shall be protected against liens in the following manner:

_____

_____

_____

9. Materials

a. All materials shall be new, in compliance with all applicable laws and codes, and shall be covered by a manufacturer's warranty if appropriate, except as follows:

_____

_____

_____

_____

_____

_____

The materials shall consist of (check one box and provide description, if necessary):

❏ the materials described in Clause 1.

❏ the materials described in the Schedule of Materials attached to this contract.

❏ the following items:

_____

_____

_____

_____

_____

The materials shall be purchased by (check one box):

❏ Contractor, to be reimbursed as specified in Clause 2.

❏ Homeowner.

10. What Constitutes Completion

The work specified in Clause 1 shall be considered completed upon approval by Homeowner, provided that Homeowner's approval shall not be unreasonably withheld. Except for the "retainage amount" of 10% of the contract price, substantial performance of the specified work in a workmanlike manner shall be considered sufficient grounds for Contractor to require final payment by Homeowner, except as provided in Clause 8 (Liens and Waiver of Liens).

11. Limited Warranties

Contractor will complete the specified work in a substantial and workmanlike manner according to standard practices prevalent in Contractor's trade. Contractor warrants that (check one or more boxes and provide descriptions, if necessary):

❑ the specified work will comply with all applicable building codes and regulations.

❑ the labor and materials provided as part of the specified work will be free from defects for

_____

from the date of completion.

❑ Additional warranties offered by the Contractor are as follows:

_____
_____
_____
_____
_____
_____

12. Dispute Resolution

If any dispute arises under the terms of this agreement, the parties agree to select a mutually agreeable neutral third party to help them mediate it. If the mediation is deemed unsuccessful, the parties agree that (check one box):

❑ the dispute shall be decided by the applicable small claims court if the amount in dispute is within the court's jurisdiction, and otherwise by binding arbitration under the rules issued by the American Arbitration Association. The decision of the arbitrator shall be final.

❑ the dispute shall be directly submitted to binding arbitration under the rules issued by the American Arbitration Association. The decision of the arbitrator shall be final.

❑ the dispute shall be settled according to the laws of the state that apply to this agreement.

Any costs and fees (other than attorney fees) associated with mediation and arbitration shall be shared equally by the parties. Attorney fees associated with arbitration or litigation shall be paid as follows (check one box):

❑ Each party shall pay his or her own attorney fees.

❑ The reasonable attorney fees of the prevailing party shall be paid by the other party.

13. Late Performance

If performance of the specified work is late, Contractor agrees that (check one box and provide description, if necessary):

❏ Homeowner shall be damaged in the amount of $_____ per _____ and that Contractor shall be liable for such sums, which may be credited against any sums owed to Contractor by Homeowner.

❏ A dispute over any damages or loss claimed by Homeowner for the delay in performance of the specified work shall be resolved as provided in Clause 12 of this agreement.

14. Change Order (Mid-Performance Amendments)

The Contractor and Homeowner recognize that:

a.   Contractor's original cost and time estimates may prove too low due to unforeseen events, or to factors unknown to the Contractor when the contract was made;

b.   Homeowner may desire a mid-job change in the specifications that would add time and cost to the specified work and possibly inconvenience the Contractor; or

c.   Other provisions of the contract may be difficult to carry out because of unforeseen events, such as a materials shortage or a labor strike.

If these or other events beyond the control of the parties require reasonable adjustments to this contract, the parties shall make a good faith attempt to agree on all necessary particulars. Such agreements shall be put in writing, signed by the parties and added to this contract. Failure to reach agreement shall be deemed a dispute to be resolved as agreed in Clause 12.

15. Indemnification (Hold Harmless) Clause

Contractor agrees to (check appropriate boxes and provide description, if necessary):

❏ Hold harmless and indemnify Homeowner for all damages, costs, and attorney fees that arise out of harm caused to Contractor, subcontractors, and other third parties, known and unknown, by Contractor's performance of the specified work, except as follows:

_____

_____

_____

_____

_____

_____

❏ Obtain adequate business liability insurance that will cover Job and any injuries to subcontractors or employees.

16. Surety Bond

Prior to beginning job, Contractor shall be required to obtain a surety bond covering Contractor's obligations under this contract, in the amount of $_____.

17. Site Maintenance

Contractor agrees to be bound by the following conditions when performing the specified work (check the appropriate boxes and provide descriptions):

❏ Contractor shall perform the specified work between the following hours:

_____
_____
_____
_____
_____

❏ At the end of each day's work, Contractor's equipment shall be stored in the following location:

_____
_____
_____
_____
_____

❏ At the end of each day's work, Contractor agreement to clean all debris from the work area and leave all appliances and facilities in good working order except as follows:

_____
_____
_____
_____
_____

❏ Contractor agrees that disruptively loud activities shall be performed only at the following times:

_____
_____
_____
_____
_____

❏ Contractor agrees to confine all work-related activity, materials, and products, including dust and debris, to the following areas:

_____
_____
_____
_____

❏ Contractor agrees that:

_____

_____

_____

_____

_____

18. Additional Agreements and Amendments

a. Homeowner and Contractor additionally agree that:

_____

_____

_____

_____

b. All agreements between Homeowner and Contractor related to the specified work are incorporated in this contract. Any modification to the contract shall be in writing.

Homeowner: _____   Dated:_____

Contractor: _____   Dated:_____

DISCLAIMER: THIS FORM IS INTENDED TO PROVIDE EXAMPLES OF THE KINDS OF TERMS THAT, AT A MINIMUM, SHOULD BE INCLUDED IN SUCH A CONTRACT. IT IS NOT INTENDED TO SERVE AS A SUBSTITUTE FOR THE ADVICE OF AN ATTORNEY-AT-LAW. BEFORE ENTERING INTO A CONTRACT INVOLVING GIVING SOMETHING OF VALUE TO ANOTHER FOR GOODS, SERVICES OR MATERIALS, BE CERTAIN THAT YOU HAVE A CLEAR UNDERSTANDING OF ALL OF THE TERMS IN THE CONTRACT AND WHAT REMEDIES ARE AVAILABLE UPON DEFAULT OF ONE OF THE PARTIES. AN ATTORNEY-AT-LAW CAN HELP YOU WITH ANY QUESTIONS YOU MAY HAVE ABOUT THE PROPOSED CONTRACT.

Index

Associations

Also by

PHILIP SCHMIDT

ISBN: 1-58923-287-9

ISBN: 1-58923-285-2

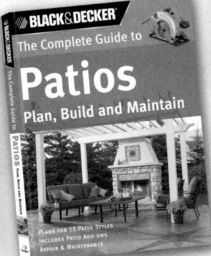

ISBN: 1-58923-305-0

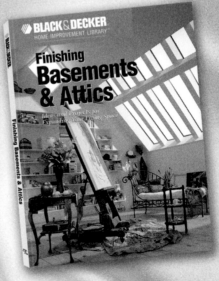

ISBN: 0-86573-583-2

CREATIVE PUBLISHING INTERNATIONAL

18705 LAKE DRIVE EAST
CHANHASSEN, MN 55317

WWW.CREATIVEPUB.COM

Also from

CREATIVE PUBLISHING INTERNATIONAL

Projects You Really Can Do Yourself

The course catalog for our popular new 101 book series is growing fast. We're pleased to offer four additional texts that are aimed specifically at the beginning do-it-yourselfer. Each beautifully photographed book features at least 25 well-selected projects in the subjects you'll need to study the most. *Outdoor Fix-it 101* covers the basic maintenance of a home's exterior shell—its siding, foundation and roof—as well as maintenance and repair of driveways, walkways, fences and other essential outdoor structures. *Flooring 101* will teach you how to maintain every type of floor and fix those pesky flooring problems yourself. And for the first-time homeowner, *Wiring 101* and *Plumbing 101* are the ultimate in handy reference books, put together the 101 way. Enroll today.

ISBN: 1-58923-300-X

ISBN: 1-58923-263-1

ISBN: 1-58923-278-5

ISBN: 1-58923-246-4

CREATIVE PUBLISHING INTERNATIONAL

**18705 LAKE DRIVE EAST
CHANHASSEN, MN 55317**

WWW.CREATIVEPUB.COM